BUILDING
A CHAIN OF CUSTOMERS

BUILDING A CHAIN OF CUSTOMERS

*Linking Business Functions
to Create
the World Class Company*

Richard J. Schonberger

THE FREE PRESS
A Division of Macmillan, Inc.
NEW YORK

Collier Macmillan Publishers
LONDON

The Free Press
A Division of Macmillan, Inc.
866 Third Avenue, New York, N.Y. 10022

Collier Macmillan Canada, Inc.

Printed in the United States of America

printing number
3 4 5 6 7 8 9 10

Library of Congress Cataloging-in-Publication Data

Schonberger, Richard.
    Building a chain of customers : linking business functions to
create the world class company / Richard J. Schonberger.
        p.   cm.
    ISBN 0-02-927991-7
    1. Organizational effectiveness.   2. Industrial management.
I. Title.
HD58.9.S36   1990
658.8—dc20   89-77552
                                                        CIP

Contents

Preface

EARTHQUAKES and aftershocks that shattered the complacency of the world's manufacturing companies in the 1980s are now causing tremors in all businesses. It's a good thing, too—for the owners, the employees, and the customers.

It all started with quality. One by one, the Western world's leading manufacturers had to line up for their lessons in how to get their quality up to tough new world standards. They, in turn, pushed those lessons onto their suppliers.

Later, those manufacturers found happy havens for quality improvement in their offices. Quality became a strong unifying theme across the functions, from marketing to design to production to the work force to outside suppliers—and all the support offices as well.

Just as quality started to take root, other unifying seeds for improvement made their appearance. I refer to dozens of simple but potent new (or unused) concepts and techniques for curing chronic problems. The cures include taking out waste and delay, slashing overhead expenses, simplifying designs and methods so as to stave off the high costs of automation, fixing the costing and control system, and *accelerating the pace* of quality improvement.

A number of the new techniques, such as those that cut delay, have been honed to a fine edge in highly competitive fast foods and serve-yourself retailing. When the same simple, commonsense practices work wonders in industries ranging from textiles to tractors and from TV's to tacos, we begin to see the possibilities. But organizations have their own ways of seeing to it that possibilities remain just that: possibilities.

CONFRONTING THE ORGANIZATION

In large companies, the four main functional groups—design, marketing, accounting/finance, and operations—have scarcely been able to talk to one another. Further, those at the top, middle, and bottom of the organization have had different concerns and agendas. We need a great cannon that will level the high walls that compartmentalize the business. Donald Petersen, CEO of Ford Motor Company, calls it "chimney breaking."

Is there a way to break the chimneys and link the organization? There is. It's not a cannon, but rather a superordinate goal: *serving the customer*. Those sound like puff words, unless you hold the enlightened view: that *everyone* has a customer—at the next process. Linkages from process to process form a chain ending at the final paying customer.

Serving the customer—next in the chain of customers—becomes *the* overriding goal. It cuts up and down and across the organization. It also provides universal tools and concepts, plus a common language— one that shouts down divisive specialized jargons.

STRATEGIES AND CUSTOMERS

Most employed people haven't been able to think that way. They come to believe their company is unique—and probably everybody else's company is, too. Then, the thinking goes, the management task is to analyze its *own* problems, mold its *own* strategies, and devise its *own* unique success formula.

The viewpoint is wrong. All firms and each work unit within the firm need to adopt about the same strategy: to serve the customer with ever-better quality, lower cost, quicker response, and greater flexibility.

Once those goals were thought to be in conflict. *Trade-offs*, we called them. (Henceforth, we shall call it the *T-word*—not to be uttered in earnest, civilized conversation.) The world's best are now persuaded that those goals are not in conflict. Rather they are mutually supportive— if the right concepts and techniques are in use.

That brings us to the next persuasion: In the name of serving the customer, firms in any industry should use about the same new concepts and techniques—the same management tool kit. One example is work cells: clusters of operations (people and equipment) arranged by the way the work flows. Work cells are correct for machining metal parts, for processing claims in insurance companies, for developing a new information system, and for investigating crimes. Another example is kanban, the signal system that keeps waiting lines short. Kanban is important in store checkout lanes, in design projects, and in factories.

There's much more in the new tool kit, and most of it is counter to common practice. Therefore, there will be no progress without extensive schooling—not a one-time course, but never-ending learning and development of human potential. That is, commitment to continual improvement in serving the customer requires total, continuous learning. The budget for providing operating people with continuous learning goes from nearly zero to several percent of the payroll. It is a small price to pay for the certain large, competitive benefits.

Oh, one thing more: As Charlie Bingham, executive vice president of Weyerhaeuser's Forest Products Group, put it (to his executive team), for the total improvement effort to succeed, "we must be convinced that there is a *hellish* opportunity for *quantum* improvements!"

1

⚮

The Great Awakening: Earthquakes in the Business Functions

WE HAVE LEARNED more about the right way to run a business*
in the 1980s than in the preceding half century. In a nutshell,
we've learned this: that world-class performance is *dedicated to serving
the customer.*

By that I don't mean tender loving care, service with a smile, all
returns accepted—no questions asked, ten-year warranties, consumer
telephone hotlines, and customer satisfaction polls. While all those
are good practices, they generally apply to just the *final* customer.

How much good can it do to try to make it right for the final customer
when much of the organization that provides the goods or services is
delay- and error-prone and self-serving? That is the sad truth about
business and industry. It has taken a series of earthquakes, tremors,
and aftershocks to wake us up. The wide awake now see the final
customer as just the end point in a chain of customers. Everybody
has a customer—at the next process (where your work goes next).
Making the connections along the chain is our common task.

I'll not dwell on the consequences of staying asleep. That is, we

---

A Chain of Customers is intended for any kind of organization, whether in the
profit or public sector. The short words, *business, company,* and *firm,* are used for
the sake of concise language.

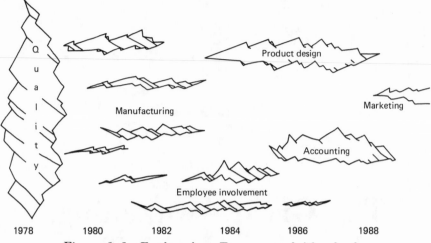

Figure 1–1. Earthquakes, Tremors, and Aftershocks

won't go into the recent history of lost jobs, pay cuts, shut-down plants, bankruptcies, and whole industries migrating across oceans. Those might sound like quakes and tremors, but let's not repeat well-known tales of woe.

Instead, it is time to look at the bright side. I'll label as earthquakes momentous new ideas that are reshaping the way we think about and run business enterprise. The quakes and tremors are toppling and rending asunder old concepts and practices that resulted in poor performance and failure.

Figure 1–1 indicates the major and secondary shocks and, roughly, when they occurred. I'm not including quakes that affected just a single country (such as Japan's head start in quality) or a single company (such as the ability of McDonald's to provide a uniform product in spick-and-span restaurants all over the world). Rather, Figure 1–1 suggests when the shocks woke up whole industries around the world.

QUALITY: FIRST AND GREATEST QUAKE

In the late 1970s a few Western companies that were suddenly faced with withering competition from the Far East saw through the fog. They cleared away the excuses (unlevel playing fields and so forth) and looked at clear measurable evidence: both the defects and yields in Western semiconductor products were far below world standards.

It was the same for cars and power tools, air conditioners and steel, TV's and dozens of other electronic products.

Most of the great Western manufacturers eventually got around to estimating their costs of bad quality. Even in proud companies like IBM, Kodak, Philips, and Rolls Royce, bad quality was costing over 10 percent of sales. Defect rates themselves weren't that high, but the costs of rework, returns, warranties, lost customers, rescheduling, and so on, were.

Briefly, what happened was that hundreds—no, thousands—of companies were frightened enough to take the quality pledge. Literally, CEOs and presidents issued quality declarations and put them into corporate mission statements. Top executives who earn in excess of a million dollars a year sat through courses in statistical process control. A few followed the Texas Instruments model: Top exec trains next-level execs, who train their subordinate managers, who train theirs—and so on down to machine operator, assembler, office clerk, and stockkeeper.

What superlative shall I use in describing the outcome? Awesome comes to mind. *I* certainly am awed. Who could have believed that, for many items, defect and nonconformity rates could fall from percentages to negligible in companies all over the globe. Yet they did in just a few years. Here are just four examples:

- At Kodak's copier division the defect rate had averaged around 50,000 parts per million (PPM) in 1985. That means 50,000 bad ones (bad components, bad welds, bad-fitting assemblies) out of each million. Less than a year later, defects were down near the world benchmark of 950 PPM. At the same time the number of internal quality inspectors dropped from twenty-five to zero, because the assemblers, well-schooled in statistical process control (SPC), had assumed responsibility for quality.[1]
- TRW's steering and suspension system division has been reorganizing its four factories into work cells and teams that take over the job of quality. In 1987 one work cell shipped 500,000 pieces with only two rejected by the customer. Larry Kipp, plant manager, says it hurt the technicians' pride that those two got out of the plant. Kipp observes that "This is the most exciting thing I've done in my twenty years" in manufacturing.[2]
- The U.S. Internal Revenue Service trained 10,000 managers in quality management (Juran approach). Organization of quality teams throughout the agency followed. One result: In 1986, out of 1.2

million tax accounts received, weekly processing errors averaged 30,000 to 40,000. In 1987 the error rate was down to 3,000 to 4,000, while volume increased to 1.5 million per week.[3]

- Last rites had been said for Big Steel in the United States, the causes of its impending death being high costs and bad quality. For example, in 1983 the Ford Motor Company was rejecting as much as 8 percent of steel from domestic plants. By 1988 the reject rate was down to 0.7 percent, on a par with the Japanese.[4]

Those examples come from a bulging file folder of similar ones from other companies and industries. The dramatic quality improvement stories do not come from just the wealthy industrialized nations. Managers and operators know about and use SPC in good companies in Mexico, Thailand, Brazil, and the countries that surround them. And why not? It's easy to learn, training materials are available in every language, and educated managers all over the globe are looking for low-cost solutions that work.

The quality turn-arounds are no longer limited to the major companies that have training budgets. Big industry has been inviting people from key supplier companies to training courses in quality concepts. Now, with public and private training in SPC widely available, that is becoming unnecessary.

QUAKES AND TREMORS THROUGHOUT MANUFACTURING

The quality earthquake softened everything up for tremors to come in all else. The second big quake, which began in manufacturing, was called just-in-time (JIT) production. Some saw it as inventory reduction (many still do). Those in the know see it as quick response to the customer, plus another jolt for quality improvement.

Quick Response in the Chain of Customers

The payoff for the JIT leaders has been much like the quality payoff: five-, ten-, and twentyfold reductions in waste—in JIT's case, waste of time waiting for work to start at each step in the chain.

Long queues all over the world signify why improvements of that magnitude should be possible. Human waiting-line problems are obvious. Delays in offices are much worse, except that what waits is a document buried in an in-basket, not a impatient person standing in line. In manufacturing, piles of parts sit idle between every stage of production; often the quantities are so large that they serve their sentence in plant stockrooms. They are waiting to be summoned into action on a work bench or a machine. Sometimes they wait for months.

Documents and parts forced to wait can't, in a huff, take their business elsewhere. The final customer can! Thus, quick response and the JIT techniques are keys to competitive gain in any business.

For example, supermarkets in some highly competitive cities have turned to promoting shortest checkout lines, not just lowest prices or freshest produce. Quick response has spawned several whole new industries, such as overnight mail and facsimile copying. Some say that the rapid spread of one-hour photo film processors is the cause of the plunge in sales of instant cameras.

Some of the best examples of achieving quick response are in manufacturing, where just-in-time concepts have penetrated deepest. Consider, for example, CalComp, Inc. (a self-contained subsidiary of the Lockheed Corporation), which produces graphics peripherals for the computer industry. In 1982 a rival, Hewlett-Packard, came out with a cheaper and faster model of plotter. That sent CalComp reeling. Profits nose-dived, and unsold machines piled up.

Today CalComp has fully recovered—a fast-reacting, tough competitor. For example, throughput time* to build an average plotter was cut from a high of nine weeks to about five working days—through all stages of manufacture. Prices on its 5800 series electrostatic plotter were slashed 38 percent, which doubled sales volume within six months. Market share climbed as well.

A tenfold reduction in flow time sounds like a classic JIT story. At CalComp basic quality improvement plays an equal role. All operators use quality techniques collectively known as statistical process control. SPC requires them to record all process problems on visual control charts and tally boards.

---

*Just-in-time and time-based competition have generated great interest in what I've just called *throughput time*. Alternate terms are *flow time*, *lead time* (traditional in production control), and *cycle time* (used often today, especially in electronics). In an effort to avoid confusion, Robert Hall, editor of *Target* magazine, has issued a plea to call it lead time—as I've been doing for several years. Since I haven't had much luck getting others to use that term, I'm giving up and using all of them interchangeably in this book.

Operations Support

Tightly tied to the slashing of delays and defects in operations are sharp reductions in operations support: scheduling, material handling, stockkeeping, counting, checking, inspecting, accounting, trouble-shooting, expediting, entering data, and setting up for new models. These types of support, once thought to be necessary aids and controls, are now seen as non-value-adding waste. So find a way to get rid of them. They are costly, they are havens of delay, and their existence blocks operations from taking full responsibility for results.

When work zips through all the processes lickety-split, the apparatus for tracking the work flow and accounting for it falls by the wayside. In CalComp's case, computer use for monitoring production was cut by 76 percent. When operations takes over responsibility for quality, the number of inspectors plunges. Sometimes, as was cited earlier for Kodak copiers, the number of inspectors goes to zero.

The list goes on. But one of the conditions for making these deep cuts in operations support is employee involvement, which has had its own earthquake.

EMPLOYEE INVOLVEMENT AND PROCESS OWNERSHIP

The term *employee involvement* (EI) doesn't tell us much. Employee involvement in *what?* The EI earthquake could not occur until we had an answer. And the answer is: *involvement in everything that is important to the customer—the one at the next process as well as the final one.* Tops on the customer's list are low costs, high quality, and flexible, quick response—without fail!

It is an ambitious list—in fact an impossible one without EI. You can hire large numbers of inspectors to assure quality, but what do you get? You get high costs—for inspection and for redoing or throwing out the rejects. You get delay, which might include waiting for inspectors to arrive and then inspect, waiting for rejects to be fixed, waiting for transportation, and waiting for a suitable lot size from which to take a sample. What you probably will *not* get is world-class quality, because inspection itself admits errors and often is intermittent, not continuous control.

Ownership

Employee involvement can offer (1) continuous control of factors shown to cause bad quality and (2) continual improvement in correcting the

---

Stress and Frustration

Some say that the demanding environment of employee involvement is stressful to the employee.[5] Maybe so. On the other hand, the opportunity to *finally* see something done about chronic frustrations in the workplace—and to be involved in the changes— surely *relieves* a good deal of stress.

---

causes. The foundation of EI is for all employees to record everything that goes wrong, to join others in finding ways to fix chronic problems, and to continuously monitor and control what is not yet fixed.

In machine-intensive operations, the equipment itself contains many of the problems: the bad quality, the delays, and the failures. EI offers a potent solution: Machine operators take over preventive maintenance, simple repairs, area housekeeping, machine setup, control charting, machine history, process instructions, and sometimes control of spare parts, tools, and manuals. They also participate in machine selection and installation, machine modifications, and area layout (floor plans).

The descriptive term is *ownership:* In the world-class company employees assume ownership of the processes. Operating-level people come to feel they own the machines, tools, area, instructions, quality, controls, and all else in their sphere; no longer are supervisors, professionals, technicians, engineers, advisers, and others from staff support departments the owners by default.

Of course, so profound a change does not happen overnight. It takes years and is in small steps. In the process, the former owners become teachers, helpers, team partners on improvement projects, and monitors of the overall effort.

Suggestions: World-Class Numbers

What kinds of results may we expect when all employees become involved owners? Since Japanese companies are the leaders in employee involvement, we must look to the world-class companies in Japan for an answer. The numbers are mind-boggling. According to one report, the number of suggestions per employee per year in selected firms are as follows: Nissan, 19; Canon, 50; Hitachi, 81; Citizen Watch,

Tanashi, 201. There are reports of numbers much higher even than that.[6]

Those are in contrast to the number *zero* for most employees in most companies throughout the world. Formal suggestion programs usually have brought in only a trickle of suggestions made by only a small percentage of the work force.

Measuring EI based on a suggestion count can, of course, become a numbers game. A company with excellent EI could have a low count simply because the counting is not formalized, or because only suggestions of a certain significance are counted. Still, it is clear that world-class standards of employee involvement are exceedingly high.

Focused Teams, Cells, and Flow Lines

Individual employee ownership of a process is a good start. *Team ownership* of a segment of the chain of customers is even better. When there is team ownership, team problem-solving and team suggestions should follow. A correctly organized team, which owns a segment in the chain of customers, is called a *cell* or a *flow line:* people and their equipment arranged by the way the product flows or the service is provided.

In common usage, the word *team* can refer to about any collection of people. For our customer-serving purposes, team refers to a group of people connected by work flow, because, by definition, that comprises a *chain of customers*.

Consider the way people and their facilities are usually grouped: by common function. In offices, we may find order-entry people and terminals in the far corner, purchasing in the next room, invoicing downstairs, and so on. In factories, molding machines are all together in their little world, lathes have their own area elsewhere, and everything else is grouped similarly. Strive for teams and teamwork, and what happens? At best, you get *gangs*—and ganglike behaviors. The customer is part of another gang, and they are the enemy! Or, if not the enemy, they are, at least, not part of your team.

Putting it differently, cells and flow lines are *natural* teams, which are *focused* on a narrow family of subproducts, services, or customers. What remains is to cross-train team members, assign them ownership of their segment of the total product, and then give them time for data analysis, problem diagnosis, brainstorming, and special projects. Those are the ingredients of the continual improvement effort.

Much of the improvement is in the direction of making things simpler. But teams of operators and clerks can only do so much. Total simplification and improvement requires total involvement. The rest of the business must be drawn in.

MAJOR AFTERSHOCKS: DESIGN, ACCOUNTING, MARKETING

Bringing in the other main parts of the business—design, accounting, and marketing—starts with seeing the possibilities. After that comes creativity to shake out and replace old practices that won't do in the new age.

Possibilities of making an impact are greatest in design and development: Design it right and avoid problems heaped upon problems later in the chain of customers. In accounting, the big impacts are in providing information to guide and stimulate rapid, continual improvement. In marketing, the opportunities lie in an expanded view: Not just sales revenue, but locking into tight alliances with customers who prefer to deal with firms that are on a course of continual improvement.

The shakeout in these three business areas hit design and development first—and hardest—followed by accounting and then marketing. The changes to date are summarized below in that order.

Design—Out of Isolation

The best efforts of product designers are below par when they are kept isolated from the rest of the enterprise. That is precisely what had happened to the design function (except in small firms). They were unconnected, a breed apart.

The potent formula for correction has three main thrusts: extended design teams, design simplification, and designing for loss minimization.

Design teams. The extended design team attacks the core problem of isolation. Delco-Remy, the multiplant electrical components arm of General Motors, fixed the problem by reorganizing into four business units: power systems, control systems, batteries, and heavy duty systems. The purpose was *not* the usual one of creating profit centers and profit-mindedness. According to Doug Barron, who heads one of Delco's newly created product and process development groups, "The driving reason . . . was to get the product and manufacturing guys physically located in proximity to each other."[7] Another result of business units is that market research people get close to their immediate customers, who happen to be the product designers.

The design team extends further. It includes purchasing, because much of what is designed is bought. It includes quality assurance, because all designed goods and services are fraught with quality issues. It includes counterparts in supplier and customer companies. The idea is for their designers to work with yours—the simultaneous design concept.

Design simplification. Getting designers latticed into the chain of customers is a good start. Design practices and customs also need an overhaul—toward designing for simple, error-free operations. That means easy-to-produce goods and easy-to-provide services. Conventional design had no such concerns. Designs tended to require too many steps, too much coordination across too many far-flung departments, and too many supplier companies.

Design approaches that have emerged to cope with those problems have various names: design for assembly, design for manufacturability, design for serviceability, design for delivery, design for service. They focus on such things as standardization; modularity; and minimizing the number of parts, number of operations, and need for new resources. Numerous new books, consulting practices, and training programs offer guidance on those themes—and leading companies have quickly absorbed the guidance and put it into practice.

The new design approaches require a strong follow-through: a set of new measures of design performance. One example is number of customer returns in the first six months. The thinking is that good

---

Neat Products, Neat Processes

William Wiggenhorn, director of training and education at Motorola, says that designers think their job is "to design the neatest product available." To that, Wiggenhorn says, "No it isn't. Your job is to design a neat product that meets the customer specs [and] that somebody else can make." To get that message to sink in, Motorola sent nine thousand engineers through a course in design for manufacturability.[8]

design has much to do with results in the field. If designers are not measured on such outcomes, they'll not be much aware of or concerned about them.

Setting forth customer-oriented design guidelines and performance measures amounts to *managing* the design function. The design problem was one of management neglect, not bad design.

Loss minimization. Good design is something that works, right? This is the common viewpoint. The uncommon world-class viewpoint goes a step further. Good design is one that minimizes all losses—to the maker, the customer, and even to the greater society. Social losses are important, because they have their ways of coming back to haunt the maker.

Since losses occur at all stages in the life cycle of a product or service, it makes sense to nip those losses in the bud. Design and development is the bud.

One of the basics of loss minimization is *robust design.* It is a design that works not just in the laboratory but in the field, and not just under ideal conditions but under physical or social stress. Assuring robustness requires experimentation: Test each design alternative under a range of conditions. For a product, the conditions might be low, medium, and high humidity. For a service, they could be low, medium, and high customer arrival rate—with a few outraged customers thrown in. The "Taguchi methods" (discussed in Chapters 4 and 10) provide today's designer with streamlined experimental methods.

Accounting, Control of Performance, and Costing

While loss minimization is new to design, it is old hat in accounting. But what do you do if the cost accounting system says your efforts are causing costs to rise when you *know* that costs are falling? Answer: You continue on the *right* course—and fix the accounting system.

Cost accounting's modern name is *management accounting.* Its purpose is to serve management, not give orders or stifle progress. In view of the earthquakes in our beliefs about what constitutes progress, management accounting measures have to change too. And they are changing—drastically, in one company after another.

Control. In the area of *control*, a new basic belief is emerging (or reemerging). It is that the best way of controlling cost and bad performance is by controlling *causes.* That belief arises for two reasons:

One is the availability of many strong new approaches for simplification and for control of quality, delay, waste, and cost. The other is the *utter failure* of historical accounting data—narrowly focused on cost variances and resource utilization—to stimulate improvement.

Costing. Management accounting's other job is to find out what things cost. The traditional system can't do this accurately because direct costs have shrunk while hard-to-allocate overhead costs have skyrocketed. No small part of that explosive growth is in the apparatus for keeping track of all the costs.

When focused teams take charge of their own resources, quality, and problem-solving, overhead as a percentage of total cost plunges. Another result is sharp reductions in delays, wastes, customer returns, storages, and other hard-to-cost negative events—which are responsible for much of the cost transactions and costing apparatus. These changes in operations open up new opportunities for simpler and more accurate costing of products and services.

Accurate costs are important, but not for the accountants or auditors. Their legal obligations are easily fulfilled by aggregated costs based on historical averages. Rather, accurate product and service costs are vital for good pricing, bidding, and product-line decisions.

Bad decisions on those sensitive issues can destroy a company. In fact, there is mounting evidence that industry has been undercosting and underpricing low-volume products and doing the opposite with high-volume ones. The same kind of evidence suggests that big industry has been sending profitable (but overcosted) products off-shore and retaining unprofitable (undercosted) products!

In leading companies, the management accounting changes generally lag behind the leaps forward in quality, design, purchasing, changing roles of people, and so forth. In other words, activists are not waiting for the accounting and control system to be fixed first. But there is no point in waiting long to fix accounting too.

The Marketing Challenge

There is no point in waiting to strengthen the marketing function either. Marketing's weapons for bringing in business greatly expand and change when the rest of the firm becomes customer-minded. A goal is loyal customers, sometimes fostered by exclusive long-term contracts, so that the company's costly capacity aims at filling real customer demands rather than just keeping busy.

That kind of customer commitment is only possible if the firm is on the path of continual improvement: quality improving, costs and prices contained or falling, and response time and flexibility good and getting better. Under those conditions, selling is a piece of cake—and marketing's promotional focus shifts.

Ads, bids, catalogs, and personal selling efforts trumpet the firm's competencies and capabilities. To make this happen, promotion and sales staffs need full awareness of the firm's continual improvement practices. They must learn how the company improves quality, cuts delays and waste, responds to changes in model mix or sales volume, and synchronizes and coordinates with customers.

A logical starting point is to fuse marketing people into tight alliances with operations, design and development, and financial people. In other words, it is time to reconnect the functions for the good health of both the firm and its customers.

RECOMBINING THE FUNCTIONS

The Great Shakeup that has spread through the business functions one by one has a striking effect on the whole. All functions begin to see several common purposes and tasks, namely:

1. To serve the customer: the grand goal
2. To localize the grand goal, a new mindset for each individual and small group: that everyone has a customer—the next process
3. To fuse combative organizational units into a well-connected business team, a parallel new mind-set for every department, office, or shop: that each has a customer—the next department, office, or shop
4. Continual, rapid improvement as the single-minded, grand operating goal

A special word to people in very small firms: You already are okay on points 1, 2, and 3. In other words, small businesses don't have combative organizational units and next processes out of sight in another room or another building. Rather, the president will meet customers and take orders—and when things get busy, pitch in filling orders. The sales manager may help with hiring or fetch late materials. Line employees routinely do any and all line jobs. Everybody knows who the final customers are. Your people may be poorly trained and lacking

---

Everyone Customer-Minded

According to one headhunter (executive employment agency), "The rules have changed. People skills, marketing skills, and customer-relations skills are now critical for manufacturing executives," because they spend a "great deal of time" in the external world outside manufacturing—particularly with customers.

"Operations VPs now help start or close a deal, assure an edgy customer that the product will be delivered on time, and often handle product complaints."[9]

---

in the skills of process control and continual improvement, but at least you're well connected.

Too bad the connective spirit is so easily lost when the business grows. A long-term plan for regaining it must include moving people around. In the lower ranks, that means cross-training and job rotation. In the professional areas, it calls for multiyear career-change assignments. The goal is for people's perspective to grow with experience, not narrow.

OBSTACLES: FUNCTIONS AND FACTIONS

As presented so far, it all sounds too pat, too easy to be true. If it were so easy, you might ask, why aren't the results evident to all of us? Why doesn't everyone know about ideas so earth-shaking?

As it turns out, the path to world-class is straight enough, but many companies that get on the path stray off it too easily. As a result, they are leaping forward in some areas, quality perhaps, and not gaining much in others.

Companies get sidetracked by their own *functions and factions*. The functions problem refers to maintaining a functional work life well away from the customer: chefs staying in the kitchen and avoiding contact with patrons, buyers shut in the purchasing department and not visiting users or supplier companies, managers hiding out in their offices and not out looking for ways to help press shop supervisors who do not want to see a press pulled out and moved into a cell, and so forth.

The factions problem pertains to a fixation on *their way* to become excellent. Factions advocates tend to be well informed, progressive, modern, willing to change, and motivated toward rapid improvement. But they hold to a narrow agenda on what to do or how to do it. We have seen that the world-class company has a broad customer-serving agenda based on the full range of knowledge breakthroughs.

Functions and factions problems become serious when they preserve or cause growth of a staff empire. An example is building a large staff to promote quality or just in time. Quality and JIT are essential, but led by people in operations; staff efforts should be minimal—mainly providing training materials.

Another example is growing a large computer staff and facilities to process work-flow transactions. Computers are efficient transaction processors, but many companies have shortened flow times to where tracking the flow by transactions is no longer useful.

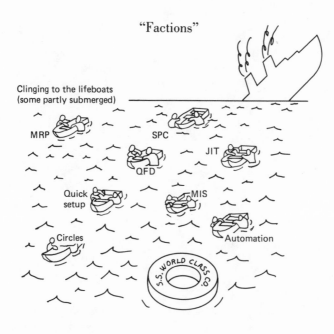

The challenges are clear:

- *Factions.* The only factions to allow are those that unite resources in the common cause of continual improvement. That means ever-simpler ways of providing higher quality and quicker, more flexible response at less cost.

- *Functions*. The functions must be broken up and reconnected in a focused way in order to recapture the pitch-in, serve-the-customer way of life.

In the following chapters the themes introduced here are treated more fully. As you make your way through the remainder of the book, keep this in mind: The marketing message doesn't belong just to the marketing people; we *all* must assume part of the job of presenting our products, services, talents, and capacity to the customer. Likewise, the design chapter is not just for the designers, accounting materials are not just for the accountants, and so on. We are all in this together.

2

❧

Universal Strategy: The Shattering of Strategic Business Thought

THE THEME of this chapter may be stated right off: It appears that world-class (WC) business strategies may be reduced to a single set, applicable in all businesses. The common thread in those common strategies is that they *shore up the chain of customers*. Several examples follow:

- *New products.* The WC strategy is to make sure the product or service is *good,* even if that means delay in getting it to market
- *Quality.* WC strategy is continual, rapid improvement—not just "competitive" quality
- *"Stand behind" your product or service.* WC strategy calls for a growing reputation for excellence and shrinking reliance on warranties (standing *in front,* more than *behind*)
- *Response time.* WC strategy is for continual, rapid reduction in response time, not just quicker than the competition
- *Line of products or services.* WC strategy is to do what you are, or can be, good at—not a strategy such as leaping from widget production to selling insurance or from refrigerators to high-margin, high-tech hardware or software
- *Pricing.* WC strategy is to meet and beat market prices via continual, rapid cost reduction—not pricing by percentage markups

- *Pay.* WC strategy is pay by knowledge—not by prevailing wages, not by job classification, not by seniority
- *Labor.* WC strategy is to upgrade, upgrade, upgrade people's skills—not to control, control, control
- *Organization.* WC strategy is focus, focus, focus, top to bottom throughout the firm—not grouping similar resources together
- *Sourcing.* WC strategy is long-term stable relationships with suppliers and with customers—for mutual gain—not a mindless search for the lowest bid

Is there *any* business or public agency that should not adopt these (and similar) world-class strategies? Before you answer, bear in mind that we are talking about strategies for building and sustaining a dynasty. Lesser strategies are for less-than-world-class ambitions, such as just getting by or "take your money and run."

The skeptic might say that the world-class strategies are high-sounding and noble but not realistic. The reality, the skeptic says, is that everything is a T-word. But is it?

THE MYTH OF TRADE-OFFS

We win, the customer loses. That is a discouraging point of view if there ever was one. Yet it is ingrained, a shaper of strategies in companies large and small. The dreaded T-word resides in the backs of our minds, ready to inject itself between provider and receiver, all through the chain of customers.

Quality Payoff

Of all the harm caused by the T-viewpoint, probably the worst is that related to quality. Quality, we said, has its price; and at some point quality costs too much.

Design Trade-offs

The word *trade-off* has legitimate uses in the product design arena; for example, trading speed for payload. But when business strategy makers and goal setters use the T-word, they are copping out. It becomes the justification for low expectations and performance.

That view was a casualty of the Great Quality Earthquake. In its place is the belief that quality pays for itself many times over. It avoids costs of rework, scrap, various forms of insurance (including backup stock), and warranty claims; prevents losses of customers; leads to repeat business; and enlarges the customer base.

Most important, good quality management includes transferring responsibility from inspectors to operators. That wipes out inspection as a category of cost. It is also far more effective: Operators can stop discrepancies at the source; inspectors, on the other hand, catch quality problems only here and there, and usually after too much bad quality already has passed onward.

As Tom Peters has put it, Quality has always made companies rich.

Quick-Response Payoff

Another T-belief to be refuted is that quicker response costs more. That view holds that the way to get speedy response is to build inventory or add people, which raises cost.

Just-in-time, a superior way to get quick response, has opposite results. In pursuit of short waiting lines, JIT slashes delays of all kinds and cuts the need for staff whose work revolves around delay management. In everybody's JIT tool kit are methods for quick setup, short flow distances, preventive maintenance of equipment, and materials and tools in precise locations right at the point of use. These are simple and cheap to implement and clearly have large and continuing cost-cutting effects.

Quick response also has been thought to conflict with quality. But working faster and taking quality-threatening shortcuts are *not* quick-response techniques. On the other hand, slowing or stopping the line to get the quality right *is* a basic of quick response/JIT. Slowdowns

---

Fast-Moving Bank

The marketing strategy of a certain bank was to develop and promote quick-response capabilities:

> The bank learned that its 24-hour time to process car loans was twice as quick as the competition. Instead of resting on its laurels, the bank changed all its procedures to speed up on all kinds of banking; for example, it pushed loan approvals down to a low level.
>
> The natural next step was to market itself as "the fast-moving bank." One ad said, "Time is money. People shouldn't hold up banks, and banks shouldn't hold up people either."[1]

The bankers, we are told, were clever in turning a tactical advantage into a strategy. We're told further that, by being first with the strategy, "the bank also blocked competitors from copying the concept."

Yes, the bankers were clever. No, they did not freeze out the competition. Other banks would be foolish not to copy the strategy. They may be too late to be "the fast-moving bank," which is the authors' point. They are not too late to gain all the other advantages of quick response: lower costs, simpler systems, better quality—and keeping some of their customers from defecting to "the fast-moving bank."

---

or stoppages are opportunities to permanently fix chronic causes: Make machines run right, improve designs, iron out problems with materials and tools, and eliminate rework and returns. The joint results are quicker response, better quality, *and* lower cost.

One thing more. Quick response requires quick-change artistry: flexible people, cross-trained to do a variety of kinds of work, and flexible, quick-change equipment and procedures. So, we add to the list once more: The joint results are quicker response, better quality, lower cost, and *greater flexibility*.

Other No-Trade Strategies

The T-concept also warps our thinking about pricing and pay:

- Price cutting is thought to increase market share but decrease earnings. True enough when it's price cutting alone. On the other hand, employing world-class strategies for quality, quick response, employee involvement, sourcing, and so forth drives costs down even as prices are cut. Lower prices, in turn, increase sales which pushes costs down even faster via economies of scale.
- Low wages equal high profits—so the common thinking goes. The outgrowth of that thinking is an unfortunate but entrenched job-and-pay strategy: Define and classify jobs so narrowly that most are worthy of low wages. Today's enlightened view is that employees are a valuable asset to be continually trained and broadened through job switching; the result is an employee-driven improvement engine—worth higher increments of pay.

We could go on with other examples of unsound strategies based on wrong-headed T-viewpoints (and bad decision rules at the operating level as well). But it is time to see if anything can be salvaged from conventional thinking.

Rank, Don't Trade

The T-concept gave rise to searches for optima, such as just the right amount of pay and optimum level of quality. World-class strategies require chucking the notion. The right strategy has no optimum, only continual improvement—in all things. All those things add up to a weighty agenda, which needs to be prioritized. Say that it becomes clear that a certain company unit's quality is superior but training and employee development are awful. The unit keeps quality on its continual-improvement list but pushes training and employee development to a higher priority on the list.

The point is that all the strategies for continual improvement stay on the list of objectives year after year. (The view that "successful strategy self-destructs"[2] is dead wrong.) Periodically, the company unit reexamines and reranks its strategies. Reranking is based on customer needs, new knowledge or technology, and competitive opportunities.

That part of strategy making is nothing new. That is, sound strategies have always considered needs, knowledge, and competition. What is new is the stability and consistency of strategies—and the discovery of a superordinate one: continual, rapid improvement.

Improvements across the Board

If you still believe the T-word has its place in business, it may be because you haven't yet seen continual improvement in action. The sad truth is that most of us have spent most of our working lives in organizations in which improvement in one area was offset by decline in another. We have seen it over and over with our own eyes: companies that are plagued by clear opposites at every turn. It is still true—*of weak or not-yet-strong companies.*

Not so of strong companies—companies that get on the world-class bandwagon. They are remarkably transformed, gaining the upper hand over T-obstacles. They improve continually in cost, quality, response time, and flexibility simultaneously. They do it simply because they have learned how. They have kept abreast of the knowledge explosion that has triggered the earthquakes in management of business enterprise.

INDISTINCT AND DISTINCTIVE COMPETENCY

If these points are valid—if all firms should pursue about the same customer-serving strategies—how can any firm gain the upper hand? A couple of answers come to mind. First, the world-class strategies are general and demanding. The best companies will implement the strategies well, the worst will fail even to try. In other words, there is plenty of room for competitive gain in understanding, accepting, and acting out the strategies.

Second, company-to-company distinctions lead in different directions. Those leading in favorable directions have been called *distinctive competencies.* Good term. Distinctive competencies include products and services that are popular and patent- or copyright-protected; location in good markets; talents and equipment that fit well with current demands (what Alan Frohman calls "distinctive technical competency");[3] and others. These are like the photogenic side of the face. You present it whenever the lens aims in your direction.

Early in the chapter we saw that there is even a WC strategy on distinctive competency: "Do what you are, or can be, good at." The commonfolk way of putting it is "stick to your knitting."

While stick to your knitting is an old saw (lately popularized for business consumption by Peters and Waterman)[4] and the term distinctive competency has been around for a few decades, they must be brought down to size for our purposes. Those phrases have been used by some companies to justify a strategy of, say, sticking with cost leadership—and allowing another firm distinctive competency in, perhaps, quick response. Bad strategy—a formula for decline.

It seems certain that plenty of companies will continue to follow that formula—and decline. We may call them Tier 2 companies, which contrast with Tier 1 companies as follows:

- Tier 1 companies evolve to a single-minded strategy of continual improvement and customer-responsive leadership.
- Tier 2 companies cling to a precarious strategy of just exploiting a current strength.

BENCHMARKS, GOALS, AND CONTINUAL IMPROVEMENT

If we've settled the issue of what knitting to stick with, we may turn to the issue of prioritizing the world-class strategies. Good priorities require good information, which can come from the customers, the competitive environment, other external sources, and internal sources.

For example, customer and competitive analysis might reveal that your firm is losing sales because of late delivery problems. But don't just look at your own industry. Finding out what's going on in other industries could reveal a new way to gain a competitive edge; for example, a financial institution using just-in-time manufacturing methods to achieve same-day loan approval when the rest of the industry is stuck at a week.

Competitive Analysis and Competitive Benchmarking

A survey revealed that only one third of automotive industry suppliers do competitive analysis. In other words, most of the industry has a bad case of complacency and lacks vital strategic information.

The automotive suppliers are not alone: I've found that *most* companies don't do competitive analysis. A result is misguided goal-setting and prioritizing. Commonly, companies resort to changing goals on a round-robin basis. What's more, the goals tend *not* to address the interests of customers. Instead, senior executives sit and fret about internal goals, such as raising direct labor productivity or increasing sales of a certain product line; the customer doesn't care about either. Ignoring the customer is a sure path downward.

Increasingly, companies are coming to the same realization: that they have been leaving the customer—and the competition—out of strategy setting. An approach pioneered by Xerox Corporation, called *competitive benchmarking*, has helped some firms correct that weakness. The idea is to put numbers on best performances: average time to respond to a complaint, number of suppliers, defect rate, and so forth. The narrow approach to benchmarking is looking at the best in the industry; the broader, and better, approach is looking at the best in any industry.

Knowledge Carriers

It has been rare to look outside one's own industry for answers and success strategies. Today, with all the ferment going on throughout the business world, it is risky not to. Trouble is, it isn't easy to keep up even with your own industry. How can a firm also keep abreast of outside trends and new ideas?

One way is to hire from outside. I'm not thinking of seeking to fill all vacancies with outside managers and professionals. Some of the world's strongest companies have held to an opposite policy of trying to promote from within. In contrast, weak companies cannot hold their talent. They constantly are forced to bring in "new blood." While they have a steady infusion of new ideas (good), they have no stability and cannot set plans into motion and stay on course (bad).

We've all admired companies that have made promote-from-within part of their culture and success formula. In the last few years I have been an adviser and trainer in a few of the well-known ones. Sadly, I go away thinking, "These people don't know what's going on!" These companies have some people who are outward-looking, but not enough of them to overcome organizational inertia.

I am not suggesting an abrupt change in hiring in those firms. A modest policy change will do: Make sure that a certain small proportion of vacancies are filled with outsiders.

To those who say, "We've done fine with internal promotion in the past," the response is this: The knowledge explosion of the 1980s—which shows no signs of abatement for the 1990s—is the reason your policy has to change.

Strong companies like 3M, Philips, and Marriott have policies that mostly favor internal promotion but call for careful selection from the outside as well. Their leading competitors do likewise. In other words, they do a certain amount of people trading, which benefits each company.

Assuming the firm has good access to competitive and external benchmark data (via "knowledge carriers" and other methods), the next issue is, What should it do with the information?

Benchmarks as Milestones

Let's put the question another way: If the central commitment is to continual, rapid improvement, what is the role of competitive benchmarks? The answer is that the world-class company considers competitive benchmarks as:

good for arousing people to the competitive challenge,
good as a milestone target,

but . . .

fluid, because world standards are on a fast incline, and too modest as a company goal.

In other words, equaling the world's best on any benchmark is like having your sports team run off enough points to gain a tie. A quick cheer, and you press on, hoping for another score before the game ends. But unlike team sports, in business you don't just want a 4 to 3 win. You want a slaughter—14 to 3!

Or should 14 to 0—total annihilation—be your goal? Not necessarily. Your main goal is to be the customers' first choice—and to let competitors fight for scraps.

Allegiance

What we are talking about is a company goal—in this case winning customers' *first allegiance*. This is *not* the same as a goal of being first in sales. That's too easy: Just slash the price, spend madly on advertising, and operate around the clock. Allegiance is harder to achieve and to measure than sales, but it is more rewarding and enduring—and more profitable.

Strategies as Goals

Time to straighten out some confusion. This section began with discussion of strategies and then shifted to goals. What's the connection?

Since I am making the point that strategies should be similar in all companies, it sounds as if company goals should be about the same from firm to firm, too. That raises the question: Can a goal be a strategy?

Yes. Continual, rapid improvement in cost, quality, quick response, and flexibility are "golden goals"—like a set of golden rules for companies: *Provide to the customer as you would have the customer provide to you.* They are also strategies for achieving central company goals, including growth, security, profit, and the golden goals themselves: A successful quick-response strategy meets the goals of cutting cost and improving quality; a successful flexibility strategy helps achieve quick-response goals; and so forth.

Executives have always had trouble translating broad company goals in a way that fits with group and personal goals all the way down to the individual. If the individual's goal is to find another job, or a work team's goal is to keep the pace slow, there is sure to be a conflict.

The conflict can go the other way. These days, it is not unusual to find pockets of enthusiastic advocates of the total improvement point of view at low levels in the organization. The audience for a public seminar that I conducted in Chicago was three-fourths managers and professionals and one-fourth operators. In a question session one of the operators stated that he and his group were believers, but "how can we get our managers committed?" Those operators have remade their goals, but the company's managers, all the way to top executives, may still cling to old ones.

That's too bad—but not necessarily a disaster. In 1987 Caterpillar, the heavy equipment manufacturer, established its "big-four" company

---

Golden Goals

AT&T's corporate goal of 1988 was *quality*. Its 1989 goal was *service*. This practice, an annual corporate goal, may seem to conflict with the idea of continual improvement across the board. But when the annual goals are quality and service, there's no harm done. They are "golden goals" that carry along and draw upon other worthy customer-serving goals, such as having a flexible, cross-trained work force.

goals: consolidate, automate, simplify, and integrate. The last goal, integrate, can be taken to mean about the same thing as focus: break up functional departments and regroup resources by type of product. There is an unfortunate tendency, however, to use "integrate" to mean *computer*-integrate: Get everything onto computers that talk to other computers.

Computer-integration cannot be a world-class goal. Anything a computer does is in the same class as what a hammer does. Computers and hammers are tools.

If *computer*-integration is stated as a corporate goal, will the company suffer? Caterpillar didn't. The reason, I think, is that the company's new *strategies* are generally world-class, regardless of the wording of the company goals. Cat's fine set of strategies go by the name, "plant with a future (PWAF)." PWAF calls for revamping every plant, mostly according to world-class principles, including moving nearly every machine into product-focused cells. Pierre Guerindon, executive vice president in charge of PWAF, says his group has avoided technology for its own sake—such as unproven computer-integration of all the business functions.[5]

Senior executives seem unable to resist goal-setting—they've always done it. Maybe the practice will die out when it becomes clear that WC strategies can do double duty as company goals too. If this happens, companies may require fewer executives—and will want remaining executives to act as facilitators who clear away obstacles.

Rapid Improvement

One goal that does make sense—for all levels in the organization—is continual improvement in serving the customer (next process). The *amount* of improvement per time period is stated only in general terms: *rapid*.

Executive involvement. In the old days, if a senior executive perceived late deliveries as a serious competitive problem, it would have been edict time: Improve on-time deliveries by some number, like 15 percent. Bad edict. It deals with effects, not causes.

Today's savvy executive treats the problem as follows (not necessarily in this order): (1) See that everyone in the firm gets the facts about the competitive problem; that is, get comparative data (competitive performance versus your own) up on wall charts, played over company video channels, discussed in group meetings. (2) Get out and talk with lower-level managers, order clerks, buyers, operators, and others; talk not about late orders but about causes—things like order batching and lack of product focus in the organization. (3) Stimulate formation of project teams to deal with causes and give high visibility to project team results.

This approach may be unsettling to executives and managers who are used to asking for a "10 percent reduction" or "25 new customers." It is far more important to be clear about the many items on the improvement agenda than to be quantitative about the amount of improvement expected.

Who prioritizes? Okay, then should executives at least prioritize the improvement items?—"For this period, our first priority is reducing time to respond to complaints; let's all pull together. . . ."

Yes and no.

In the world-class company everyone, from window washer to senior

---

Great Leaps

In 1979 John Young, Hewlett-Packard's president and CEO, perceived quality as the competitive battleground of the 1980s. He set a quantum-jump, company-wide goal: a tenfold improvement in quality within ten years. The company has responded magnificently. Walter Craig, corporate quality director, reflects that, "if John had asked for only an improvement of 30 percent or so, nothing probably would have been done for years."[6]

But did the goal cause the improvement? Seems unlikely. H-P is highly decentralized and loaded with talented, aware, competitive people. They were keenly aware of the Western quality gap with Japan, and they learned the new concepts and techniques of total quality and related improvements. Then they plunged ahead.

It may have worked about the same way at AT&T's Network Switching Division. Al Basey, division president, once believed in fixed targets. He changed his thinking some years ago when he asked an engineering manager to set a cost reduction goal for the next year. The manager preferred a goal of "as much cost reduction as possible." The result: ten times more cost reduction than Mr. Basey had expected.[7]

executive, becomes an expert in the concepts and methods of customer-serving improvement. But, at least in big companies, how much can upper-level executives know about such things as customer complaints and their causes? Customers are everywhere in chains that run through the company, and the highest-priority problems of one may be entirely different from what's bugging another.

Senior executives (in large companies), don't lord over priority setting. It is part of the job of everybody in your organization to stay abreast of the changing concerns of the next process and to correct problems fast. So get yourself and all your people educated. Then get involved along with them.

Making Wrongs Right

Continual, rapid improvement is not just a hoped-for result. It requires "screwing your head on differently." I have witnessed some good examples. Two or three times I've been told, by a grinning team of change implementers, something like, "Everything we did, we did wrong!" They were cheerfully doing it over again—better.

That is the right attitude. It is right for several reasons: For one thing, their "wrongs" were not costly, because continual improvement is a stream of small things (though we still welcome the occasional great event). Also, when a small change is labeled "wrong," it may actually be an improvement—but not as good as it can be. Say that a packer is moved right next to the person doing order picking—so they become a close-knit team of two. The task force responsible for the move may say, "Oh, we did it wrong. It would be much better to move the picker to the packer, nearer to the point where the order goes out." So the task force changes what it just did—without a trace of shame.

We may state it as a three-part code of improvement:

1. In the world-class company, there are no mistakes—only learning experiences.
2. What we are doing today will look silly (but not like a mistake) before long.
3. We quickly improve whatever looks silly.

Do Nothing You Can't Change

This code of improvement should not be used as license to screw up. Painting yourself into a corner is evidence of thoughtlessness. Thus, another aspect of continual improvement is to take actions that allow easy changes later. As David Schlotterbeck, vice president at CalComp, puts it: "Never do anything that's permanent."[8]

Since bricks and mortar are, by nature, quite permanent, the emphasis shifts to what's inside the bricks. There is much that can be done to make physical changes easier; for example:

- Nokia Oy, in Finland, has outfitted the ceiling of a plant producing personal computers with row upon row of utility hookups—electric power, air, and so forth. Anything can be moved anywhere.
- In today's version of the open office, partitions are easily movable— and contain plug-in power and communications wiring (sometimes even area temperature controls). Mars (the candy-bar company) is a firm believer in *very* open offices: Plants in boxes on rollers are the main partitions in Mars's factory offices in Holland—where "office garden" is their name for open office.
- The production manager of a Hewlett-Packard plant told a group of visitors to look at the equipment: "Much of [it] is on casters."[9] The factory equipment could be moved nearly as fast as the PCs and phones in a modular open office.

THE BASICS AS STRATEGY

Never-ending rounds of incremental improvement rely heavily on a good set of tools. It is like the reliance, in team sports, on basics such as passing and blocking.

Trumped-Up Strategy

The team-sports analogy is useful to show that the basics are more than just tools. Ask a coach about how to win, and you are likely to hear any of the usual answers: "Put a lot of points on the board." "Control the ball." "Keep the puck away from the other guys." Some will even make the lofty claim—to sportswriters, ever in need of copy— that this is the game plan or strategy.

Who wants to hear the coach say, "Our strategy is to shoot, pass, and block better than the other guy." But isn't that a more accurate answer? Those are the basics.

Company executives have invested so much in strategic planning and strategic consultancy that they hate to think it might be time and money ill spent. They take consolation in any shred of evidence of strategic brilliance. The evidence has been anything but comforting of late. Rather, according to Hamel and Prahalad, "We have seen [in Western companies] a pattern of competitive attack and retrenchment that was remarkably similar across industries"—a strategy they call "the process of surrender."[10]

Still, we are advised to keep the faith—those doing the surrendering merely have defective strategies. The strategic wisdom, we are to believe, has shifted to the Far East. As evidence, just look back on the highly successful strategies of, for example, Canon and Komatsu in manufacturing and Dai-Ichi Kangyo Bank and Sumitomo Bank in banking—strategies that exploit technical opportunities, competitors' weaknesses, and customers' needs.

Successful companies do indeed exploit those things—just as successful sports teams do. But the brilliance has little to do with what is usually thought of as executive-level strategic planning. Rather it is executive-level knowledge, skill, leadership, and full involvement in *the basics*.

If you have a strong team, you look for someone else to knock off. Thus, Honda marched up the scale in motorcycles and in cars, and along the way made a "brilliant" strategic shift into power mowers. It would have been no less brilliant if Honda had chosen air conditioners or plumbing fixtures instead of power mowers as the next target. When you have a great team, you can take on almost anybody, and usually win. What makes a great team is the basics. Then almost anything the coach chooses to do makes the coach look like a shrewd strategist.

More on the Basics

In business, *world-class* basics are things like calling on customers, doing competitive analysis, developing supplier partnerships, recording every disturbance, continually solving problems, and continuously learning. If these sound a lot like what I've also called strategies, that's the intent.

There's another way of looking at it. The firm that takes care of the here-and-now in those ways finds that long-term results, profit and growth, take care of themselves. If that sounds contrary to the view of profit and growth as short-term concerns, that too is the intent.

Small companies, including their executives, tend to be up to their ears in what many would call the basics. But we must understand that smaller firms tend to be poorly managed, and more fail than

---

Marketing the Basics

The essence of traditional strategy in marketing is the selection of growth markets, the rejection of dead-end markets, and the conception of clever segmentation schemes.

Yet these concerns ignore the most important . . . issues: the achievement of superior quality, the attainment of enough corporate flexibility to permit lightning-fast market creation as soon as the slightest opportunity is sensed, and the constant improvement of every product and procedure that involves the customer.

—Tom Peters[11]

---

prosper. The real need is for the small firm to find out about and quickly adopt the *right* basics—those that build capability and reputation in the eyes of the customer.

In large companies, senior people tend to see the basics—right or wrong ones—as the purview of "the troops." So our message to those executives is: Elevate the world-class basics to strategic status. It's the surest path to sustained success.

MORE WORLD-CLASS STRATEGIES

We'll end this chapter the way it started: with a few more examples of world-class strategies that connect up and prop up the chain of customers:

- *Backward integration.* WC strategy, in dealing with undependable suppliers, is *supplier development*—not backward integration into unfamiliar businesses
- *Growth.* WC strategy is controlled growth—not sales at the cost of customer esteem
- *Job classification/training.* In companies with many job classifications, the WC strategy is to evolve to very few; continuous learning enables employees to be multiskilled and the firm to reduce job classifications

- *Automation.* The WC company has no strategy for automation, any more than it has a strategy for a wrench or a typewriter
- *Technology.* WC strategy is to learn about and use worthy technologies—but with a preference for simpler technologies that do not strain the company's capabilities
- *Profits.* WC strategy is to let profits be the effect of continual, rapid improvements—not the driver

We could go on with more examples of the world-class way of thinking about strategies, but there's no point. Rather it is time to draw a summary conclusion: that in the world-class company, strategy is a dull subject. It is not worth much time, because strategies are, or should be preordained.

The art of progress is to preserve order amid change and to preserve change amid order. —Alfred North Whitehead

3

∞

The "Customer-In" Organization

THE CUSTOMER is *in* the world-class organization, not outside of it. The reasons are sound: If left on the outside, the customer gets treated with indifference (at best), and offers the same in return. That spells temporary relationships: Customers are poised to fly, like a nervous flock of geese in a grain field.

The "customer-in" organization bonds supplier to customer in a multitude of ways. Since every customer is also a supplier to another customer, a chain of customers, each well connected to the next, is the goal.

PRODUCT AND CUSTOMER FOCUS

A chain of customers is the result of *aligning resources by the way the products (goods or services) flow.* It is an idea whose time has come. While there are a few narrow terms associated with it—namely, cells, flow lines, and group technology—the broad term is *focus*; that is, focus on the product and the customer, not the function.

Though its time has come, product/customer-focused organizations still are far from being commonplace. Grouping by functions is entrenched.

Terminology: Chain of What?

A few years ago, some firms began devising tactics for *supply-chain management*—a worthy new term, because supply chain captures the essential idea of a long-linked partnership. *Customer chain* (or chain of customers) captures the same thing—and has two extra virtues: (1) It reaches forward toward the source of demand and revenue. (2) It sounds like a broad undertaking, whereas some might assume "supply chain" to be just a logistics concept.

Focus on Human Nature

Why? Could it be that focus is counter to human nature? Sometimes it seems so. People tend to cluster with others who do the same thing. One object may be to vent frustrations on a common target: their common set of customers. Thus, teachers get together in the faculty lounge, sometimes to scorn students. Artists gather in coffee houses partly to ridicule those who buy their art. Some nurses on break belittle their patients. Paper shufflers at the water cooler defend their "red tape" and may vilify others who can't fill forms properly.

If that's human nature, it certainly is not in anyone's best interest. Organizing people by common job type brings out the worst in employee and employer, while product/customer focus is in the best interests of both. Thus, we need to combat mean-spiritedness that would break the linkages in the chain of customers.

The good side of human nature includes feelings of pleasure at serving well and fulfillment from being party to an improvement. Those feelings are fed by and support the chain-of-customer organization. Sports teams offer good examples: The passer may just aim at a spot, knowing a teammate will be there at the right time. A score may come at the end of many accurate passes, just as delivery to a final customer does in business.

An internal team-focus on perfection in the work flow does not happen by itself. It takes bold, action-oriented leaders to break up the functions, move internal resources to form flow lines, and tie the tail ends of the internal organization to outside customers and suppliers.

The management system needs overhaul as well. Management systems deal with policies, procedures, resources, and controls, but the standard system is anything but product-flow focused. The revised system *is*, across the board: In process design, first emphasis is on reliable, delay-free product flows—ahead of emphasis on design of individual jobs or machines. The accountability system converts itself to customer-oriented measures, and the control system is largely visual and immediate. The information system keeps the troops informed about successes and challenges, and showered with rewards for each action that helps win customers' esteem and loyalty.

Process Focus = Tragicomedy

Oh, yes, we're completely focused, says the spokesperson for XYZ Insurance: The underwriters are all together on first floor, administration is on second, and processing is in the annex; we are "process focused."

Even though one can find scholarly references to the notion of process focus, it is a crazy idea—a contradiction in terms. Grouping by common processes is antifocus, and when we see the effects of it, it looks like tragicomedy: Processing a normal order involves interminable delays and mazelike, crisscrossing flow pattern traversing thousands of feet.

Aetna Life and Casualty Company was inspired to reorganize into customer-focused service teams, partly to deal with the "black hole" effect. Policy applications and other transactions simply got lost. It was taking an average of ten days to process an item that required only thirty minutes of actual processing time. Now, twenty-four branch offices have merged underwriting and processing into service teams, which process items in three or four days.[1]

Aetna is slowly untangling some of the bad effects of its past organization by function. For example, people on the mixed teams are becoming familiar with the expertise of teammates. This has given rise to a new transitional job, associate underwriter, which opens the door for go-getters in processing (applications, coding, etc.) to further their careers. Some are able to advance all the way from associate to full underwriter.

Product or Customer Focus?

Focus is uncomplicated when my product goes to only one customer. In that case, I am both customer-focused and product-focused.

Things often get more complicated than that. There may be a choice as to whether to focus by product or by customer. In Aetna's case,

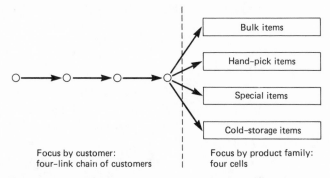

Figure 3–1. Mixed Focus: by Customer and by Product

each of the newly formed teams is focused on a set of customers. A team is *not* at the same time product-focused; it handles medical, casualty, home, and other kinds of insurance for its fixed set of insurance agents.

They are following what ought to be an axiom of focus: Look for customer focus first, product focus second. Customer focus gets first priority, because linkage with a customer opens up special opportunities for process improvement—joint action to solve problems that might destroy the supplier-customer relationship.

Figure 3–1 represents a wholesale warehousing operation. It starts out customer-focused: four clerks in a flow line processing all orders the same way through four steps.

The fifth step is order-filling, which requires dozens of stock pickers, packers, and loaders in a warehouse holding thousands of items. An option is to arrange those people into one or more long bucket-brigade-like product-focused chains to pick, pack, and load. The other is to organize by product family. For quick, low-cost, high-quality response, the best choice, shown in Figure 3–1, seems to be the latter: one cell (team, equipment, and stocks) for bulk items, another for hand-pick stock, another for special items (e.g., drugs or diamonds), and another for cold stores.

HIGH-LEVEL FOCUS

For all the volumes written about organization, little of it, until recently, dealt directly with product or customer focus. Companies paid no attention to focus either. Still, careful inspection of the solid and dashed lines connecting little boxes on existing company organization charts can reveal a few gross clues about the company's degree of focus.

Focus at the Enterprise Level

Do the boxes show a company owning a chain of donut restaurants, a racetrack, several manufacturing companies, and an oil pipeline? If so, the company looks to be badly out of focus at the *enterprise level*. Conglomerates are out of fashion these days—and, the customer hopes, forever. In recent years, many a large, unfocused corporation has sold off ill-fitting pieces in order to get focused. The thinking is, Either we do it, or a corporate raider will do it for us and walk off with megabucks.

Once the enterprise gets focused, its job is to offer capital and overall guidance. Parent companies often think they should exact *control* as well. Not much. In the world-class company, control is in the trenches and much of it is visual.

Table 3–1 shows the enterprise (as a whole) as the topmost of six levels where there can be organizational focus. Each lower level offers opportunities for focus to a finer degree; the world-class company extends focus all the way down. Each level is explained briefly below.

Focused Business Units

In medium and large companies, next below the enterprise level is *focused business units*. As the term is commonly used, a business unit *is* focused, because each has its own compact line of products, resources, and collection of customers.

The business-unit concept has been around for years. Boeing used it for the 747, which got its own separate division and massive greenfield factory. The concept received a shot in the arm when IBM set up a separate business unit for the PC. It was a rousing success, and in the 1980s, hundreds of companies followed the IBM lead and started

Table 3–1. *Product/Customer Focus—Six Levels*

Focused enterprise ⎫
Focused business units ⎬ High-level focus
Focused plants ⎭
Focused plants-within-a-plant—Focus within the plant
Flow lines and cells ⎫ Focus for people and machines
Focused support teams ⎭

creating their own business units. Westinghouse Electric, for example, has moved corporate staffs for planning, communications, marketing, manufacturing, and human resources out of corporate headquarters and downward into business units.

Stephen Coley, of McKinsey and Company, believes that corporate staffs were valuable in the 1950s, because large companies needed ways to attract expertise. Today, he contends, "that expertise is readily available throughout the economy—and it is cheaper" than paying for it in the form of large corporate staffs.[2]

In other words, the pull of focus is augmented by the push of more economical sources of expertise.

Focused Plants

A business unit might have multiple buildings or geographical locations—*plants*, we'll call them. If so, we look for the best way to focus at the plant level; for example, plant A for brand name products or services, plant B for the commodity line, and plant C for customized items.

In focusing at the plant level, the tough issues center around the degree of vertical integration in each plant. Should each pizza outlet make its own dough or each motel do its own laundry? Should each focused electronic assembly plant—one for CD players, one for audio cassette players, and one for stereos—stuff its own printed circuit boards? The alternative is for the business unit—pizza chain, motel chain, or electronics division—to set up or contract with a focused plant that just mixes dough, launders, or stuffs boards.

These questions have no fixed answers. We can, however, develop some helpful commonsense guidelines:

1. Avoid backward (or forward) integration into territory that requires investment in wholly different kinds of technology and human talent.
2. Keep plants fairly small. Large plants have too many people and layers of management, which are harmful to communications and to generating a sense of one team; they also have too much space to arrange for efficient operations.
3. Keep the number of different technologies, operations, and (in manufacturing) parts small. When those numbers are large, senior managers lose touch and can no longer practice hands-on management effectively.

4. Where items 1, 2, and 3 are not a problem, consider integrating backward (or forward), if it can be done economically. By economical, I mean (to continue with our example) not much more costly than getting dough mixing, laundry, or board stuffing done outside. Doing it yourself *can be* worth a bit higher cost because: (1) it lengthens the chain of customers under one roof, (2) it closes the door on blaming someone else for poor performance, and (3) it provides people with a fuller understanding of more of the business.

Sometimes small simple versions of big machines can be found, which can make backward integration—a pizza outlet mixing its own dough, for example—*less* costly than buying from a high-volume, focused, dough-mixing plant.

FOCUS WITHIN THE PLANT

Focus generates high energy, especially when applied low in the organization. The focused *plant* may be too big for jobholders to feel the energy. Therefore, large plants—large in area or number of people—need to be subdivided. The subdivisions, called *plants-within-a-plant*, must be product- or customer-focused. Greatest needs for this treatment are in manufacturing, transportation, insurance, utilities, and government agencies—sectors in which hundreds of employees under one roof are not unusual.

One of the first Western manufacturers to turn itself around via focused-plant and plant-within-a-plant strategies was Copeland Corporation, a producer of compressors for refrigeration units. Copeland had built two focused factories and had another one on the drawing board in 1980. The company's higher-volume products were moved to those plants from the "mother" factory in Sidney, Ohio.

That left the big Sidney plant with thirteen lower-volume products. Sidney had suffered two strikes in the previous four years, and had high inventories, poor delivery performance, and questionable quality. The 600,000 square-foot plant itself was old and sprawling, having grown by piecemeal additions over the years. What to do? Close the plant?

The plant stayed open—but reorganized into two product-focused plants within a plant. One is for manufacture of machine-intensive compressors, the other for labor-intensive (lots of welding and brazing) compressors. The company snaked a wall through the building to separate the two, and each side got its own resources right down to separate

---

Ideas from the Board

Copeland's CEO and president, Matthew Diggs, Jr., and senior vice president for operations, Dean Ruwe, were savvy men of action who launched the focus strategies. The idea person was Professor Wickam Skinner, who was serving on Copeland's board of directors. Skinner is author of a seminal 1974 article, "The Focused Factory."[3]

Lucky for Copeland that Dr. Skinner was on the board. Unlucky for most companies that they *don't* have idea people on their boards.

---

plant managers, parking lots, and labor bargaining units. They share a cafeteria but eat at different times. Purchasing is about the only common support function.

Results include reductions of 30 percent in indirect labor cost, 10 to 15 percent in direct labor cost, and 50 percent in inventories and lead times; big quality improvements; and virtual elimination of past-due orders.

Focused plants-in-a-plant can apply to support services as well as operations. Monsanto Electronic, a producer of semiconductor wafers, focused its order processing. First, all its production ordering and scheduling people moved into one office location. Next, marketing's customer support people moved into the same building and office area. These steps, plus related changes, cut average order-processing time from about a week to twenty-four hours or less, depending on what time the order comes in from sales reps all over the world.

Companies that have subdivided their big plants are not yet finished getting focused. Subdivided units still will be quite large. (The two focused plants within Copeland's Sidney plant average 300,000 square feet and a few hundred employees.) Thus, focus continues at still another level.

FOCUS FOR PEOPLE AND MACHINES

Medium and small plants skip the plant-within-a-plant step. Their journey toward focus goes directly from the focused-plant level down to the job, the jobholder, and the machine. Organization of *cells and*

From Layout to Organization

If you want a floor-plan expert, you call for an industrial engineer. The IEs call it plant and office *layout*.

For decades IE students have been taught two basic ways of laying out facilities: by function and by product flow. The flow layout, so say the books, is for high-volume operations; the functional layout is for low volumes.

Wrong! Product-flow layout is *always* better.

The hot topic in today's layout studies is *cellular* layout: For low volumes, use ingenuity to find similar product flows; then design cells around the product flow paths.

But designing cells takes more than just the IE's layout expertise. Since it rearranges *people* according to work flows, cell design really is organizing or reorganizing resources—both human and physical.

---

flow lines brings focus to that level. The floor plan—the design of people and processes in space—is the issue.

A bad floor plan is one that places people at a distance from where their work goes next. In human services, the client is the "work." Do most clients have to go from room to room (and waiting line to waiting line) to receive treatment, to get a license, or to register a complaint? If so, it's a bad floor plan.

Visual Control and Coordination

Whether the work flow consists of documents, burgers, widgets, or human clients, the aim of reorganization is to shorten the time and distance to the next process. When distances are long, things get in the way, and the chance for simple, visual, direct control and coordination is lost.

Ray Flygare is a manufacturing manager at Imprimis's large disk memory plant. A believer in the visual factory, Flygare told a work team, "Nothing should be higher than my shoulders [Ray is about 5' 7" tall] or lower than the top of my boots [Ray competes as a professional rodeo cowboy on weekends and wears cowboy boots in the plant]." A few days later he returned to the area to find everything moved up to boot height and below shoulder height. The changes cut stooping, make cleaning easier, foster sight-line visibility, improve the lighting, and reinforce the easy visual-flow concepts that grew out of Imprimis's world-class manufacturing efforts.[4]

Michel Greif, a lecturer and consultant in France, has done pioneering research among firms in several countries on "the visual organization." Greif notes that visual control is linked with *space* factors: people sharing a common territory, and space itself becoming a medium of communication. Further, states Greif, visual control is like a new language. It is not a language *in* the group, like talking. Rather it is a language that *federates* the group—makes people communicate even if they don't want to.[5]

Snarled Work Flows

People who do not want to communicate with their customer at the next process are safe in the conventional organization. It does not position people next to prior and following processes to form a chain; instead they are grouped with others who do the same thing: the functional organization.

Among its flaws, a functional organization snarls work flows. Say that a small apparel company has four people cutting fabric; across the hall four people at sewing machines sew sleeves, collars, back panels, and other main components; upstairs, four more sewers produce finished shirts. With just those three functional departments and four people in each, there are sixty-four different flow paths.

When seams come apart or are not straight, where is the problem? Did one of the cutters cut short or long or crooked? Or was it one of the sewers in components, or in finishing? We have sixty-four flow paths to check. In the language of quality control, it is a problem of machine-to-machine and operator-to-operator sources of variability—in this case, far too many sources to check or control.

Time to unsnarl the flow paths.

The unsnarling (breaking up the functional organization) can be done in small never-ending steps. A cell of just a single pair, a maker (provider) and a user positioned side by side, yields all the benefits—for that pair. Create another maker-user pair elsewhere in the business. Add another and another. Add a third link to one of the chains. Add a fourth. And so on. At some point cells dominate, and only a few specialized processes remain to be converted.

Building these unsnarled flow paths is something like converting common roadways to freeways. There are numerous routes on and off an ordinary road. Close off some cross streets, and it's a limited-access highway. Upgrade some more, and it's a freeway with on and off ramps few and far between. Freeways are controlled and boring. Just what the business world needs.

Stars, Starlets, and Extras

Wait, you are thinking. Everything can't be on a freeway, nor even at cross streets intersecting an expressway. In business terms, most plants have too many products to be on unsnarled pathways.

True. But plants (except those that are terribly unfocused) do *not* have too many *product families*. First task is to unsnarl the products—group them into families that follow about the same flow path and use about the same resources.

In most plants the Pareto principle applies: A small number of products produces most of the revenue, or, at the component level, draws on most of the resources. Each may have enough volume to justify its own resources arranged into a cell or flow line (its own freeway). They are the *stars* of the product line, and like stars in a more glamorous profession, they get their own resources. Furthermore, they get taken care of *first*. In other words, a time-phased plan for focusing at the local level should start with major products—the stars—then progress downward to lesser products.

Table 3–2 summarizes the treatment we accord our stars, along with that for starlets and extras. Starlets have intermediate volume and must share reserved resources, whereas extras (like custom orders) wait in line for their resources.

Wang, the office systems company, has reorganized its contract administration into stars and extras (no starlets). In six regional offices Wang has set up what it calls "fast-track lanes," which process most

Table 3–2. *Naming the Players in a Focus Strategy*

1. *Stars*. Dominant revenue-earning (or resource-using) products. They get their own resources (as movie stars get their own dressing room, fan club, etc.); we pamper them—and serve them first.
2. *Starlets*. Intermediate revenue-earners. They share reserved resources with other starlets and get served after the stars.
3. *Extras*. Low revenue-earners. They wait in line for resources of uncertain quantity and availability—and are served last.

contracts. An initial screening station sorts out the few contracts that require special processing; they are the "extras," which spend time sitting in places like an attorney's in-basket. The stars go right into fast-track processing, which has reduced their flow time from two weeks to four days and eliminated batching, flow-tracking paperwork, and other overhead costs. Wang's contract backlogs have been cut 80 percent.

Grouping into stars, starlets, and extras can be done at the end-product level or any lower component level in the product structure. We see this in the following discussions, which offer more specifics on cells and flow lines.

Cells—in Manufacturing

While few companies have thought of cells as ways of unsnarling flow paths, many have seen enough good in cells to flip-flop their organization in that direction. Harley-Davidson, the motorcycle company, is an excellent example. Harley's phenomenal comeback story is well known, and cells are a part of it.

In 1980 in Harley's engine and transmission plant, several hundred machines were grouped by function—milling machines here, hobbing machines there. Machine operators were grouped the same way, each out of earshot and sight of where the work went next. Five years later nearly all had been moved into cells, one to produce shafts, another to cut gears. The large heat-treat ovens were about the only specialized process not merged into cells.

Cells were formed gradually, starting with the stars—in this case higher-usage shafts, gears, and other components. A few cells are dedicated to making just one part—a "superstar"—as needed by the engine assembly line in the same building. Most cells alternate among a family of similar parts—starlets. Irregularly used parts—extras— tend to be produced on numerically controlled machines instead of in cells.

Harley's transformation has been repeated in countless other factories around the world, with variations. One variation is in remanufacturing (overhauling goods returned from the field), in which there's no telling what will be wrong until the unit is opened up. Thus, in a remanufacturing cell a typical job is routed to some but not all of the cell's repair stations. Companies that have organized cellular plants for remanufacturing include Copeland in the U.S. and Lucas Industries in the U.K.

Cells are easiest to arrange when machines are not too large (are

---

Crucible of Cellular Thought

Who thought of cells first? The point could be debated, because several European countries, including the Soviet Union, had outbursts of conceptual thinking about cells—and some practical application in manufacturing—twenty and thirty years ago.

A notable flurry occurred in Great Britain. Leading thinkers, a loosely federated research group mostly associated with U.K. universities, traded and extended each other's ideas over the decade between about 1965 and 1975. They include Professors John L. Burbidge and G. A. B. Edwards, consultant Joseph Gombinski, along with works managers Gordon Ransom and Charles Allen. Allen was manager of a Ferranti plant (defense contracting) in Edinburgh that was fully converted to cells between 1968 and 1971.[6]

It didn't help that the term used in the old days was *group technology* cells—not a term whose meaning is apparent or likely to grab the attention of a company chief executive.

---

small enough to move) and when there are multiple machines of each type; then multiple cells can be formed, and output rates of each machine more easily balanced.

Integrated circut (IC) assembly and testing is a case in point: lots of each type of machine (saw, die attach, etc.), not too large to be moved. In the last few years, a number of electronics companies have "cellularized" their IC assembly and test plants. Apparel is another good example, because it's easy to move sewing machines into cells; in fact, they could be moved into new cell configurations several times a week as orders change. Of the thousands of small and large apparel houses around the world, only a few have discovered the power of cells and teams, as well as elimination of the bundle (large-lot) system. I worked with one company that has begun organizing cells for low-volume specialty garments (professional athletic uniforms), which cuts flow times from the usual two weeks to less than a shift.

Jim Knapton explains the old and new approach as applied to volume production at Jantzen, the large maker of sportswear: In the old way, bundles of "cut pieces to make 24 shirts or 36 swimsuits" went to "skill centers where operators work piece rates doing one particular repetitive job." Concern for quality is scant: "One in ten garments needs repair, and one in thirty is regarded as irreparable!"

Knapton contrasts that way with the cellular method, which is as correct today as it was "at the turn of the century. The first two pieces of a garment were sewn together by an operator, who then handed it on to the next person, [which] continued until the garment was complete." In the cellular method, "floor layouts become flexible and organized into product centers (modules). Flow rates are balanced by employing multi-skilled labor, and work is pulled through rather than pushed." Cycle times fall "by factors of ten."[7]

Perhaps by the year 2000 cellular factories will be as dominant as functional ones were a decade ago. It may take longer than that in offices (paperwork factories). Or maybe not. Office facilities are easier to move about than machines in factories.

Cells—in Offices

The small but quickly growing cell movement in office work got its start in offices that support manufacturing. Typically, it happens as follows: The plant succeeds in driving its flow time down from weeks to days, which makes the office delays and problems stand out, demanding to be attended to next.

A. Ahlstrom Corporation, a large manufacturer of specialty industrial products in Finland, is a case in point. Some of its plants are becoming world-class, which turns attention to world-class order processing. Problems in order processing included long and uncertain lead times, wasted effort (such as extra copying), rework, mistakes and delays, poor process-to-process communications, and a tendency for orders to pile up at some points in the flow. Ms. Auli Koivunen, project manager, along with consultant Matti Pöyhönen, arrived at a plan to reorganize the office into three independent, self-sufficient cells. One is for domestic sales, the second for other European and American sales, and the third for Middle and Far East sales.

Figure 3–2 shows the old and new layouts. As the flow lines show, the old required ten operations over long distances. The new one—see flow lines for the second cell—requires only five operations, which are contained in a compact area. Typical flow distance has been reduced about tenfold, order-entry lead time has fallen from one week to one day, and variation in lead time has dropped from up to six weeks to up to one week. In the cells, work roles were broadened; for example, tasks of sales secretaries and correspondents were integrated.

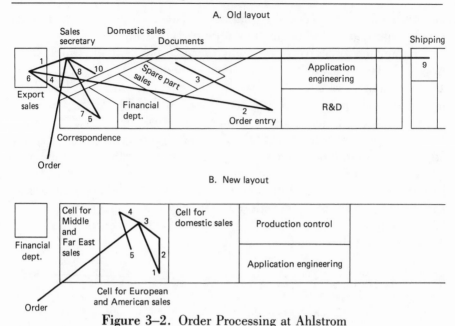

Figure 3–2. Order Processing at Ahlstrom

Cell members have jointly written action rules for all different situations, and together with sales have adopted a "right the first time" way of operating. Specification sheets used by sales contain technical data needed by manufacturing; the new rule is that sales must put all essential data on the form, or the order does not move on to production.

As a simple visual control, all papers on one order are kept in a special hanging file. Customer name, work order number, and delivery time are easily seen in the top corner of the file. The file rack is centrally located for easy access by each cell member.

A North American company with results similar to Ahlstrom's is Nashua Corporation (one of the first Western companies to embrace W. Edwards Deming's teachings on quality) in New Hampshire. With the aid of consultant Tom Billesbach, Nashua cut its order-entry lead time from eight days to one hour, with a 40 percent reduction in space and 70 percent falloff in customer claims.

Flow Lines

Link two or three cells and you have a flow line—many maker-user pairs joined together into a grand chain of customers. Continual improvement is extending the flow line and compressing its distance and space—and adding another when demand grows enough.

Flow lines can extend lengthwise or as spurs off the main line. Northern Telecom's plant in London, Ontario, is a good example. The plant is a focused, high-volume producer of telephone sets—several million per year. It is a profitable, growing business, and one of the rare ones of that type that has not migrated to the Far East.

In the center of the plant are four focused "departments"; each assembles, tests, and packages telephone sets. Northern's star product is a single model, the Harmony, offered in multiple colors. Harmony has its own department, consisting of two side-by-side serpentine flow lines. Each of the other three departments has a single flow line that is focused on small families of "starlet" products.

The flow lines have been added to gradually, becoming separate departments when the printed circuit board assembly function was broken up and reassigned to the four areas. Each of the four now has its own automatic-insert and flow-solder equipment and touch-up station.

While the assembly area is focused, several feeder processes, which make components for the four product-focused departments, are traditional. The feeder areas include sheet metal, injection molding, cordage, and wire. Little has been done about these unfocused departments so far, but they present a clear course of action for continual improvement.

For example, sheet metal and injection molding each house several dozen machines for making the many metal and plastic parts that go into a telephone set. Some presses are small enough that they can be moved to points of use on the focused flow lines. On the other hand, bigger machines can be dedicated to just one part (for example a plastic hand set) without moving to the line; as a dedicated machine, it would never incur setup costs and problems, although its distance from the line would necessitate costly material movement.

The small, relocated press becomes a captive of the assembly line—part of the team; it is dedicated to just one part number and runs at a stop-and-go pace that matches the speed of the production line. That would be a speed much slower than the press's rated capacity, but never mind. There is over-capacity in Northern Telecom's press departments anyway. Better to run machines slowly than sell them for a paltry sum on the used-equipment market.

As processes are moved from functional departments to the flow lines, the lines may grow spurs. Some spurs can be whole cells. Presently, for example, a single cell with both metal- and plastic-forming machines produces modular jacks for all four focused lines. Ideally, each of the four would have its own dedicated cell for jacks, located as a spur at the point of use on the flow line. Forming three more identical cells perhaps does not make economic sense; still, adding spurs to each line is progress, and the continually improving company seeks ways to bring it about, such as finding a smaller, simpler, cheaper method of making modular jacks.

As has been mentioned, cells are becoming common in the integrated circuit industry. (Analog Devices, Inc., has vastly improved all its key performance indicators through use of cells and related techniques in IC assembly and test)[8]; but one company, International Rectifier, has gone beyond cells. The company's innovative plant in Temecula, California, has the three basic IC processes—wafer fabrication, IC assembly, and IC test—on one floor. Most other firms send wafers around the world for later processing in different plants, with lead times stretching out to one or more months. International Rectifier completes the whole process (for its special type of "power" chips) in one week. While other firms resist breaking up the processes (diffusion, alignment, etch, etc.) in wafer fab, Rectifier completely did so, creating a long flow that does *not* require recycling as more chemical layers are added to the silicon base.

Another of the world's notable examples of flow lines is in a plant

Figure 3–3. Flow Lines and Cells in a Prefabricated Home Factory

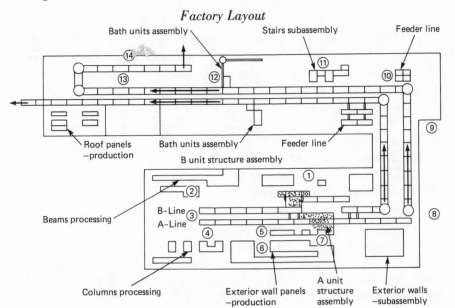

producing prefabricated houses in Japan: the Musahi factory of Sekisui
Chemical Company. Figure 3–3 shows the layout, consisting of two
parallel main assembly lines fed by about ten subassembly cells, each
located at the point of use. Ten different models of Western-style
houses are produced every thirty minutes; they come off the lines
complete with furniture and cooking appliances. The houses have steel
frames coated with zinc, and fireproof wood and plastic inside.

Lead time from customer order to completion at the site is forty
days, but production lead time (first to last operation) is just one
day. The plant uses 60,000 different part numbers but keeps just
one to two days' inventory on hand. At the end of assembly, an orange
card (kanban) goes to each supplier, who resupplies within half a
day.[9]

The world's boat and aircraft manufacturers should diligently study
Figure 3–3, then get to work.

Shapes

Cells should be U-shaped, and flow lines serpentine—as Figure 3–3
shows for houses and Figure 3–4 shows in general—unless there is
some special reason to run them straight.

Figure 3–4. Shapes for Cells and Flow Lines

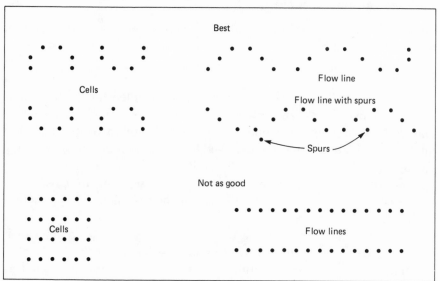

In a serpentine flow line with several loops and spurs, the number of people becomes, too large for its members to think of themselves as a *single* team. Rather, we view the long line as a linkage of several small teams that fall into arcs between natural break points in the line.

Advantages of the U shape include:

1. *Staffing flexibility and balance.* The U shape enables one person to tend several work stations—adjacent or across the U—without much walking. That opens up options for balancing work among the people: When demand grows, add more labor until every station has an operator.
2. *Rework.* When the chain bends around itself, it is easy to return bad work to an earlier station for rework without much fuss or travel distance.
3. *Handling.* From a center position within the U, a handler (human, vehicle, crane, or robot) can deliver materials and handle tools.
4. *Passage.* Long straight lines interfere with cross travel. It is annoying when shelving in a supermarket is too long. People protest when a superhighway cuts a neighborhood in half. It is the same with flow lines.
5. *Teamwork.* A semicircle even *looks like* a team.

The fifth benefit, teamwork, perhaps is the most important. It is an issue that bears further discussion.

Focused Support Teams

Teamwork has a good start when U-shaped cells are organized in operations and others are formed in staff support offices. Next issue is to bridge the gap—usually by moving the support person or team to operations.

In medical and dental clinics, staff support people who handle scheduling, patient records, and billing are close to the action. It's seamless enough that patients sometimes can't tell the support people from the medical or dental professionals. And I'm not complaining. From my vantage point as a client, I take my hat off to any service provider that doesn't send me all over the place for service. In most other business sectors, support people are on another floor or in another building.

In the manufacturing sector that is changing. A few years ago it was unheard of for manufacturing or process engineers to be located within or next to plant operations. Now in some companies, such as IBM, Hewlett-Packard, and Eli Lilly, that is the norm.

Focused Physicians

Eight beds are arranged around a central axis like spokes in a wheel. A surgeon stands at the head of each bed, on which only the eye of the patient is visible. After each doctor finishes his portion of the task, the wheel makes one-eighth of a turn. The next surgeon verifies that his predecessor performed properly and then does his own part of the operation. The eight doctors talk to each other through tiny microphones and headsets. Soft music plays in the background.

So it goes in Dr. Svyatoslav Fyodorov's high-quality "see-without-glasses" eye-care clinics, which are expanding outside the Soviet Union. Perestroika turned Fyodorov loose to become his country's—and one of the world's—boldest health-care entrepreneurs.[10]

On the other side of the entrepreneurial coin, the typical new patient-centered health-care business retains a basic flaw: organization by physicians' specialties, not by patient needs. While this gives the doctors a peer group, contends Regina Herzlinger, "it also sets up a barrier for the many patients with cross-specialty needs, like those with back problems or chronic pain." Further, she says, in such cases it "undermines assignment of responsibility for results—because no one person is accountable."[11]

Another trend is to move some testing and calibrating out of the labs and onto the floor. The same goes for large central toolrooms, stockrooms, and maintenance departments: Split them up and relocate each smaller element; for example, dedicate a small toolroom to a plant within the plant, or fully disburse tools to operators and machines in the cells and flow lines.

Physio Control, an Eli Lilly subsidiary producing and marketing defibrillators, reorganized all its assembly and testing into eleven product-focused cells. Later, key staff support functions were split up and reassigned to the work cells. Those reassigned now are members of "response teams," each consisting of a buyer, process engineer, sustaining engineer, test engineer, and quality engineer. Since there aren't enough of those professionals to go around, some serve on more than one response team. Response team members "live" in or near to the work cells they serve. The group leader of the cell is also the leader of the response team.

At Physio, by the way, the groupings are not called "cells" or flow lines; they are TEAM-BUILT lines. Physio always capitalizes the words, emphasizing the effect on the *people*, rather than the new work flows and space arrangements.

TEAMWORK DILEMMAS

Cells and flow lines are still the exception in the world of work. Most people and equipment remain clustered by common function. Most firms are thus denied the advantages of real teamwork.

Teams, Circles, and Gangs

What are all those companies doing, then, when they hire consultants for "team-building"? It is a fashionable thing to do.

Bring people from a function together to team up in a common cause, and what sort of cause will it be? Since their customers are not part of the group, they are not likely to focus on customer concerns. Instead of discussing their delays, errors, stoppages, capacity limitations, and inflexibility of response, the group will air their common gripes: cafeteria food, breaks, recreation programs, personality of the boss, and the like. Such aggravations are real, and companies are right to provide forums for them to be expressed. But is this teamwork? Hardly. Customers at the next process are a rival gang. So are suppliers. So, probably, are the support staffs.

The Western world's first attempts to make quality circles work suffered precisely this problem: The circles had the wrong membership. A few did excellent work anyway. I suspect that the effective ones were in bottleneck areas, where customer problems with quality and delay are painful and immediately felt by everyone. But most circles were disappointments, and many bit the dust. Quality circles and their close cousins (including small-group improvement activities) will reemerge and serve us well *after* organizations have been refocused down to the level of cell and flow line.

Work Gangs

I used *gang* in a negative sense, but the word also has another, nonnegative, usage: the *work gang*. Work gangs are formed to dig, pick fruit, stuff envelopes, gather refuse from roadways, dip candy, sort materials going down conveyors, and perform gang assembly. The weakness is that the members of work gangs are together in space but act as isolates—with no team mission. Often there is a better way.

I recall a plant producing plastic bags designed to hold liquid medical solutions. About twelve individuals in a crew lining both sides of a belt conveyor grabbed bags from the belt and inserted tips, seals, stoppers, and tubes. They tossed completed bags back on the belt, which conveyed them to two inspection stations. Inspectors kicked aside the rejects and toted up losses by type of error. Someone else kept track of hourly and daily crew productivity.

In this mode of assembly, inspectors and productivity counters are the assembly gangs' enemy, even though they may sit just a few feet away from the assemblers. Assemblers squabble among themselves, too; someone is always the target of blame when error rates go up or productivity down.

Does this sound world-class?

There is an easy solution: multiple flow lines. Bags coming out of the bag-forming machine go onto, say, four parallel narrow-width belt conveyors. The big gang of twelve becomes four small teams of three. In each team, the first person checks the bag and installs tips, the second checks tip installation and installs seals and stoppers, and the third inserts tubes and does the final quality check. (This example is illustrative and not intended to be technically accurate.)

All are *required* to hit the button to stop the bag-forming machine if bad bags are coming out and to stop their conveyor segment for a team problem, such as defective tips or other components. Assemblers tally every incident on a large check sheet. Teams complete a fixed number of units per shift, then stop and hold data-analysis and problem-solving meetings.

Quality checkers and the count person are gone. Productivity per person—good bags produced—goes up, up, up as the teams solve little problems. Output per shift is dependable, as is quality. Marketing, of course, is unaccustomed to the idea of dependable output from production; they will want to give thought to what that means.

Crews

One group format that *does* pass the teamwork test is the *crew:* for example, construction, logging, and ships' crews; also cowboys. For a crew, training and timing are vital; otherwise buildings, trees, ships, and livestock—and sometime lives—are lost. A crew is an ideal situation for team-oriented continual improvement: every mishap recorded on a check sheet, brainstorming meetings, and so on. Some lumber companies are just beginning to implement team-based improvement in their logging operations; other industries have not even made a beginning.

Unitary Processors

In some businesses it makes sense to load many jobs into a single work station—a *unitary processor,* we'll call it (a one-machine or one-person cell). Are team benefits lost in such cases? Before taking up that question, we'll look at a few examples and benefits.

One-stop shopping. One example is "full-service banking"; Go to a single teller and make a deposit, receive traveler's checks, pay on your credit card, or get a cash advance. Some banks have done a similar thing in their loan department: One account manager at a personal computer handles all industrial accounts; another has all retail accounts; still another is responsible for public service companies.

The benefits of unitary processors are clear: quick, one-stop service to the customer.

There are many other examples: Cashiers at supermarkets weigh, add, make change, sack groceries, and accept returns. Numerically controlled (NC) machines and their operators can do many different machining steps with a single setup, producing a complete part. Westinghouse Electric's Controls Division has set up what they call "villages," in which a single operator does assembly, wiring, testing, packaging, inventory, minor maintenance, and housekeeping (see Figure 3–5).

Another type of unitary processor is used in long-cycle assembly work, such as assembly of mainframe computers and mass spectrometers. Companies such as Amdahl, Control Data, and Varian equip each of several subassembly benches with all the tools and parts necessary to produce a certain subassembly; there are lots more benches than there are assemblers, and assemblers go from bench to bench, making a subassembly as customer orders require.

Clinics, hospitals, and other human services organizations are equipped the same way: "Just step over here, madam," says the nurse or clerk, leading the client to a special kind of unitary processor (e.g., an X-ray machine).

While the unitary processor seems to be "flying solo," not a member of a team, there is a positive way to look at it. In each case, the

Figure 3–5. Village Operator—Westinghouse Controls Division

processor (whether a person, an assembly bench, or a machine) delivers a rather complete service or component to a customer quickly on demand. The processor is connected and very responsive to the customer's needs. This is teaming up with the customer in an excellent way. As was pointed out earlier, a customer focus is usually better than a product focus (where you can't have both).

Overdoing it. I don't mean to belabor the obvious. This discussion has a point: There is a tendency to push the unitary-processor idea too far.

Unitary processors in supermarkets are effective. But the grocery store that draws the raves in Lincoln, Nebraska (my former hometown) is Ideal Foods. At Ideal, a senior employee (often one of the managers) in the produce area has a smile and a good word to say as he weighs and marks your sack of tomatoes or oranges; a checker adds the bill and takes your money; and a young man bags and carries your purchases to your car. The team of produce man, checkers, and baggers is not a nice clean flow line, but it is a teamlike group who could improve performance by using the usual team problem-solving methods.

In manufacturing, NC machines have excellent overall track records as unitary processors, but they command a high price. Sometimes a cell of already-paid-for conventional machines can do almost as well.

In her book *In the Age of the Smart Machine*, Shoshana Zuboff tells of disturbing human effects in the unitary mode. A large insurance company put claims processing people at video display terminals, each partitioned off from the next.

> Exiled from the interpersonal world of office machines, each clerk became isolated and solitary [except that two of the employees] beckoned me over to their desks . . . ; they pointed out a small rupture in the orderly high-tech appearance of their work space: the metal seam in the partition that separated their desks had been pried open. . . .
> Why? The small opening now made it possible to peek through and see if the other worker was at her seat. . . . Through that aperture, questions could be asked, advice could be given, and dinner menus could be planned.[12]

Enriching the Assembly Line

There are other versions of unitary processing in industry. For example, a new plant for assembly of personal computers in Scandinavia incorporates many world-class concepts, but not team assembly. Instead, the assembly floor consists of about twenty-five workstations, which are unitary processors, each fully equipped for complete assembly and testing; the assembler even takes the tested PC to a nearby area and packages it.

That assembly method is likely to be cost-efficient and to yield good quality. Its main rationale, though, is humanistic: the pride and satisfaction the employee feels in completing the whole product and having the technical skills to do so.

IBM and Hewlett-Packard used to design jobs that way. In fact, in the 1950s, IBM pioneered the idea of job enlargement, following founder Thomas Watson's strong belief in giving people meaningful work. Today IBM, Hewlett-Packard, and many others are going back to the progressive "assembly-line" mode, but enriched with world-class concepts: job rotation to ease boredom and broaden everyone's skills, data collection duties, line-stop authority, brainstorming meetings, responsibility for quality and preventive maintenance, continual training, and the social attractions of working in a team instead of in individual "cages."

Is this the same thing as another old idea, job enrichment? It is not. Both job enlargement and job enrichment are concepts of *job design:* Enlargement means adding more tasks to a job; enrichment means adding more meaningful and fulfilling tasks and responsibilities.

Bull Pens and Cages

Looking out over a vast room in XYZ Insurance Company, I see 200 upper bodies sticking up over 200 desks. I overhear one of the clerks using the unflattering term they have for their place of toil: the *bull pen*. I'm reminded of a strikingly similar scene in a metal-forming plant, only it was machine operators running an acre of presses.

In each case all those people receive piles of work from a material handler, who got it from a holding room of some sort. The handlers come back now and then to pick up completed work and take it into another holding area. Somebody tallies output and error rates for every operator.

Recently I saw another scene, not quite the same. It was 200 heads poking up over assembly benches alongside a belt conveyor. The conveyor receives work from the stockroom, carries it to an assembler, and delivers completed assemblies back to the other stockroom. No material handlers. Aha! Progress!

Or is it? As far as each operator is concerned, the customer is a stockroom. So is the supplier. No one among the mass of people packed together has a clear work-flow connection with anybody else.

I've heard a term for this: *caged*. Operators are not in physical cages, but they may as well be, for all the connection they have to other processes.

If that is our concept of work and jobs, why not go all the way with it? Set up the operation in a prison—with real cages. Run conveyors along the corridors. Cut holes in the bars, and run batches of work in and completed units out. That way, there is *complete control* of the individual—at low-cost prison wages to boot!

But this chapter is not about designing job A, job B, and job C. It is about organizing chains of human and physical resources. We are saying, Find ways to get people into teams and out of jobs. The chain-of-customers way of organizing has job enrichment (through cross-training and job-switching), socialization, team-based improvement, and efficiency, too!

Fuzzy Cells

In the strict (or narrow) sense, a cell or flow line calls for progressive flow: from first work station to second to third . . . to last around the U or serpentine flow path. In many kinds of work, especially services, the flow path is not that uniform and predictable; it's fuzzy.

Aid Association for Lutherans (AAL), an insurance provider, reorganized itself into focused plants-within-a-plant, and then into what we may call *fuzzy cells*. A writer described moving day: "At precisely 12 noon, the entire insurance staff—nearly 500 clerks, technicians, and managers—piled their personal belongings on office chairs and said good-bye to fellow employees. Pushing the chairs along crowded corridors, crisscrossing and colliding at intersections, all 500 made their way to newly assigned work areas."[13]

Employees had been grouped into three "bull pens"—for health insurance, life insurance, and support services. Now, at the plants-in-a-plant level, the five hundred are in five groups, each serving insurance agents in one of five regions. Each group consists of three teams (focused cells) of 20 to 30 people: a team for new policy issues, another for claims, and a third for services. An agent in the field will always deal with the same team for, say, a new policy. Under the new "one-team processing" method, policies are issued in five days, whereas it had previously taken twenty.

In planning these moves, AAL analysts identified 167 different tasks and made sure each group includes people with expertise in all the tasks. Within the teams, work gets done via lots of informal consultation with team members, rather than by a regular document flow pattern; hence, the term "fuzzy cell."

All employees are being cross-trained to handle a greater number of the 167 different tasks. Each employee thus becomes less team-dependent and more like a unitary processor, which may cut processing time still more. Faster service is good; loss of a team sense isn't.

In such cases, a good deal of thought should go into finding ways to preserve or build teamwork. For example, look for ways to simplify and standardize forms; if forms are filled out right, they can be processed in a more standard, less jumbled flow pattern. At AAL a promising approach might be to examine the 167 tasks. Repeating clusters of tasks are the stars, deserving special treatment: Organize them into real cells with more of a fixed flow path—each cell still focused on a small number of agents in an AAL region. It is hard to be improvement-minded if the chain of customers is fuzzy.

To restate the point, if there are too many places where your work might go next, teamwork possibilities are lost. Such a situation calls for cleaning up the muddle to get a clearer chain of customers.

BLURRED MATRIX

Well-organized people shine in the world of work; it's always been that way. Now here we are in Chapter 3 advocating complete disruption of present organization structures. Is it disruption in the direction of disorder? The luminaries of the business world—those who got where they are by dint of their organizing expertise—will want to know.

The answer, I'm sure, is that we have order of another, stronger, more beneficial kind. When people are isolated (*caged* off from next and prior processes), it may look orderly on an organization chart or in a photograph. The reality of the functional organization—isolated people and departments—is that the bonds tying people to the organization and its mission are weak. In Table 3–3, this mode of organization is labeled as the first (primitive) dimension in the organization of work and people.

Bonds

The second dimension is the customer/product-focused team. Focus—right down to cells, flow lines, and support teams—ties people together for reasons that are clearly important to everyone; those reasons include livelihood, job security, and self-satisfaction.

What about social bonds? Are they stronger among people doing the same thing side by side in a "bull pen"? It may seem so. On the other hand, people get very friendly and open with their barber, hairdresser, or bartender. Why shouldn't social needs be satisfied just as readily in a focused team as in a functional group?

Table 3–3. *Three Dimensions in the Organization of Work and People*

1. *First dimension.* Operators as isolates ("caged"); no connection with prior or next process
2. *Second dimension.* Operators in customer/product-focused teams (cells, flow lines), closely linked by the way the work flows
3. *Third dimension.* Small customer/product-focused operator teams, each with its own technical support team, all having a common focus on process control and improvement; no functional departments; little hierarchy; collapse of line-staff walls

Third Dimension

The third dimension is an extension of the second: focused operator teams, each having its own technical support team. Physio Control is organized this way. Such an extended team has the expertise to be able to zero in on process control and continual process improvement. An effect of teaming up technical experts with operators is evaporation of functional departments and collapse of walls between staff and line (thinkers and doers).

Control Data's Computer Systems Division has taken giant steps toward the third dimension, steps best viewed as a continuation of plans to get fully focused. A few years ago, most of the division's plants were specialized by process: wiring here, circuit boards there, and so on. Now nearly all plants are product-focused. The largest plant, in Arden Hills, Minnesota, is further split into three mostly self-contained factories within the factory: Arbitron terminals in one, Ticketron terminals in another, and the new 3800 model of mainframe computer in the third.

Focus carries down still further. Each of the three "factories" has its own printed circuit assembly. Arden Hills made use of equipment saved from a plant that Control Data had closed down, but some additional equipment had to be acquired.

For the 3800, all stages of production link up to form a grand flow line, which consists of several small cells, each with its own small team. The cells are arranged around the floor so that the output end of a feeder cell is close to the input end of a user cell; "linked cells" is the division's term.

Ticketron, a second plant-in-the-plant, has enough people and production volume to be divided into two mirror-image teams, each with the same equipment. This is preferable to a single large, unwieldy team.

Line-staff walls have been torn down in stages. Each focused area got its own continuation engineers; they handle continuing product development—and have CAD (computer-aided design) workstations right out on the plant floor. Each also has its own process engineers, material control, maintenance, and other direct support. Later, accounting and training were broken up, so that each focused area got its own dedicated accountant and trainer (the training office was abolished). A few systems analysts and programmers have been moved as well. Task force member Mary West states that "the personnel department has not been split up—yet."[14]

Teams of operators and support people, all wearing the same smock, may be seen here and there at small conference tables right on the plant floor. They stop and hold a quick meeting on any issue, as it arises.

Organizational levels were chopped from four to two, and plants were completely re-laid out based on the work of an "I team" ("imagineers"). Nearly everyone's job description was rewritten with all rewrites containing language aimed at ensuring that new walls don't build up around the focused plants; in other words, make it easy for people to move to where they are needed.

There is the feeling among the management team that they are breaking new ground—that they may be the first to wipe out the functional organization and most of the hierarchy. People are excited, and the early results seem to justify their feelings: throughput times cut five- to tenfold, yields way up, and product cost down 36 percent in one year.

Charts

Those of us with a low tolerance for disorder and ambiguity are never quite comfortable with ideas about organization that can't be drawn. We wonder what the organization chart looks like for the focused world-class company. Among the novel options that have cropped up in recent books are concentric circles and upside-down triangles.

Some people see no need for novelty. Just dust off the old matrix form. When drawn, the matrix organization is a grid with rows representing product families and columns functional departments. Work centers, which fill in the grid, thus have allegiance to both a product family and a function.

If we tried to draw an organization chart for, say, Control Data's Computer Systems Division, a matrix would be about the best we could do. Or, take a small business, such as OPCON, a Renton, Washington, producer of optical control devices and one of the world's leaders in reorganizing into cells and adapting to the other conceptual earthquakes of the eighties. Same thing. Their organization chart might look something like a matrix. But in neither case does a matrix come close to describing the companies' pitch-in way of operating.

When a company has things right, job titles and positions on charts do not mean much. Each team member will have one or more areas of special expertise, but all members interact on each special issue;

and each gradually acquires some expertise in several other areas. Think of it as a blurred matrix.

Traditional organization charts have clear, uncluttered lines, but the lines keep getting redrawn. Companies are forever reorganizing. The major reorganizations are what I have called "the seven-year itch": If centralization lasts as long as seven years, nobody can stand it any more. Time to decentralize. After seven years of that, it's back to centralization again.

The instability and turmoil of continual minor and major reorganizations is not healthy. Rigid organizations are bad as well. The world-class organization stays fluid but with a constant focus on customers and products. Some form of blurred matrix seems to do just that.

TOTAL-QUALITY ORGANIZATION

We have been examining some of the issues and dilemmas of bringing the organization into focus. Our goal is to build a total-quality organization—one that is great to work for, invest in, buy from or sell to, and have in our community. Getting the organization right does not in itself create a TQ organization, but it is one of the essentials. We take up more of them in later chapters.

4

❧

Total Quality: Toward Delighting the Customer

"THREE'S A CROWD!" A third customer pushing a cart of groceries just got in line for checkout at Lucky Market. The cashier didn't notice, so the helpful customer yelled out the slogan. At that point the cashier looks up, and, with a combined half-smile and look of mock annoyance, repeats the cry over the intercom: "Three's a crowd!" The nearest Lucky employee, who has been stocking shelves, quickly comes forward to open another checkout lane.

Lucky Market is a California-based supermarket chain. The company's competitive ploy is to assert to shoppers that there will be no long waits in checkout lanes. Banners proclaim that a Lucky employee will come on the run to open another cash register whenever a third customer lines up.

THINKING ABOUT QUALITY

Most business people think about quality in narrow, outdated terms. They would tend to put Lucky Market's policy on customer waiting lines in some category other than quality. It's time to expand our thinking. Waiting time (or lack of it) must be included, because, if there is a single dominant measure of quality, especially quality of service, that is probably it.

In all the world, Americans are the most demanding of quick service—

no long lines. Among American businesses, those in California are especially innovative in finding ways to serve their restless, impatient, demanding, sometimes quirky clientele—with quicker response, innovations, glitzy promotions, and gaudy fashions that tend to migrate elsewhere.

Since they can attract and delight customers, glitz and pizzazz must be included in today's definition of quality—along with more sober notions of quality, such as acceleration of an automobile or heady aroma in a fine brandy. But the performance—be it dazzle, aroma, or speed—must be repeatable, or its appeal to customers fades.

Thus, *quality is what attracts, delights, and holds our loyalty.* If we may accept that as a working definition of quality, what, then is *total* quality?

TOTAL QUALITY

From the discussion so far, it may be clear that this chapter is not aimed at the quality professional—unless you hold the enlightened view: That *all* jobholders must be quality experts. This way of thinking partly captures the *breadth* of the total-quality (TQ) viewpoint. There is more.

Total quality includes quality of goods, of services, of time, of place (high-quality buildings, plants, offices), of equipment and tools, of processes, of people, of environment and safety, of information, and of measurements. For each of these, we judge total quality in two ways. One is the average (or typical) level of quality; the other is variability around that average.

The older, narrower view excluded or barely touched on most of

---

Quality Trio

At Amdahl, the mainframe computer maker, a distinctive logo is stuck on letterheads, forms, reports, and most anywhere else where there is a bit of room. The logo is a triangle with three capital letter *Q*'s filling the three inside corners. The *Q*'s stand for quality of *people*, quality of *process*, and quality of *product*.

the above dimensions of quality. Our limited concepts centered around quality *of goods*. Moreover, goods producers checked their average quality levels but rarely looked at variability of quality. Quality *of services* was to hard to pin down, poorly defined, and thought to be manageable more by art than by principles.

The TQ view applies equally to goods and services, but the spotlight is more on *processes* than the goods or services themselves. It is more on improvement—better averages with less variability—than fixed notions of goodness. And in the new view listening to the final customer and the one *at the next process* is basic to everyone's job. When the quality of the processes—run by people listening to their customers—improves, the goods and services do too.

Warranties and claims about quality won't do. A claim not backed up by performance cannot retain customers very long. Customers can see through the mask.

Thus, the following get pushed into the background: fixed goals of good quality, fixation on quality of end products, service quality as a fuzzy art, and quality as a separable profession.

Into the foreground comes a new set:

- Continual and rapid improvement as the only necessary goal
- Focus on quality of processes—all the resources (human and physical) that comprise processes
- Response to the final and next-process customer
- Quality as everyone's job

This does not mean firing the quality department. Nor should we start throwing out product quality specifications and searches for defectives. As we usher in TQ, old concepts are just used less, not abandoned.

NATURALISTIC QUALITY

Total quality is more than just techniques. It also has a naturalistic component: the natural positive effects on quality that come from processing one item and immediately checking it or trying it at the next link in the chain of customers. If anything is wrong, stop, search out the cause, and fix it; only then may processing restart.

Big Business strayed badly from the naturalistic way. Instead it adopted large process and transport lots and long waiting times, which make it impossible to inspect or try out the item right away at the next process. Moreover, operators weren't trusted to do the checking. It had to be done by independent inspectors, which is too costly to do at every process and for every piece. To hold down costs, inspection was done only at a few selected points and by sampling out of large lots.

Slashing lot sizes and reducing delays has two quick and powerful effects:

1. Costs of scrap, rework, and the long trail of corrective actions plunge. Explanation: When a process malfunctions, the errors keep occurring until finally discovered at a later process. So keep the number of units between processes small (or zero), and the costs of correction will be small (or near to zero) as well.

2. Chances of finding causes are greatly improved. Explanation: When discovery of a mishap is delayed, the trail of evidence of causes grows cold, and the number of combinations of causes quickly becomes astronomical. (From Western Electric's 1956 quality control manual: "It is an axiom in quality control that the time to identify assignable causes is while those causes are active [and] delay may mean that the cause of trouble is harder to identify, and in many cases cannot be identified at all."[1] So keep interprocess delay short (or zero), and the cause of a problem *is likely to be clear and obvious to the operator.*

K2, maker of premium snow skis, began to implement just-in-time production in fall 1987. By the following summer, rework in finishing had plunged from over 50 percent of skis to less than half a percent. Flow time to get through the finishing department fell from three weeks to one shift. A few small steps toward implementing statistical process control had been taken, but it was clear that the quantum rework reduction was almost totally the result of cutting stock and delay, thereby finding out about problems fast at every process.

Dorman-Smith Ltd., a manufacturer of switchgear in Preston, England, had a similar result when it set up a U-shaped cell. (The Dorman-Smith story is featured in a BBC videotape for implementing JIT the *right* way—with extensive employee involvement from day one.) The cell had no defects in its first five months of operation.

Naturalistic quality examples abound in electronics. One is at National Cash Register (NCR)'s printer plant in Ithaca, New York. Its JIT effort (which cut lead time for forecast orders from sixty to six days), plus a strong supplier quality program, resulted in cutting its quality assurance staff from eighty to four people.[2]

Another wrinkle on naturalistic quality occurred at Caterpillar's huge new diesel engine factory in Mossville, Illinois. One of the plant's improvements was to closely synchronize deliveries of purchased castings for engine blocks with usage rates. Cat's inventory of castings fell to two days' worth in 1988—from two month's worth in 1981. The castings aren't protectively painted any more, states one Cat manager, because they are used before they can rust!

Many companies that have reduced delays and queues for other reasons have been pleasantly surprised by the big quality bonus. They shouldn't be. It *always* occurs. It's a natural and predictable effect.

THE QUALITY PROGRESSION

The broad TQ viewpoint (with a strong dose of naturalistic quality) sharply contrasts with recent narrow beliefs and practices. The TQ outlook is startling in both its scope and the suddenness of its appearance. Prior to, say, 1980, much of what is in this chapter wasn't even in our thoughts, much less on paper or in practice. Now it's open season and happy hunting for a still broader, more relevant quality concept.

The emphasis on processes, instead of end products, is not so new. Books on quality always advised controlling processes in order to prevent bad products and services. But companies didn't follow the advice. Now all the good ones are mending their ways. The best are moving their entire organizations in the direction of TQ. John Battey, director of quality assurance at Steelcase, Inc., calls the old quality concept (focus on product quality) "little q"; his company's total quality commitment is called "big-Q" quality.[3]

The TQ World

TQ is a world movement. Regardless of country or industry, the laggards are at risk; conversely, the leaders acquire insulation against failure. A good promoter can still sell junk, but it's tougher when another firm down the street, across the country, or beyond the sea sells quality at the same price.

The jobholders of the world have a nose for quality, too—a quality organization in which to work. Attractions include better safety conditions, job security, and chances for monetary gain. The poor-quality organization fails on each of these counts—and more. What is so demoralizing as a job designed to allow shoddiness and to block one's ideas for improvement? What is so sterile as one that obstructs contact with and chance to serve the customer. The antidote is continual improvement and employee involvement, which are TQ's backbone; they can become a force for sustaining the TQ effort, even if champions depart and leaders fumble.

A vital role of the organization's managers is to lead the effort to create this stem-to-stern sustaining force. Their ultimate success is when all jobholders become champions and leaders of the TQ effort in their own arena.

Quality Concepts: Negative to Positive

After years of stagnancy, our concept of quality is now in a state of rapid change and expansion. Indeed, in many companies the first step was to reverse a mind-set. Quality had been a negative concept. Now it is postive, forward-looking, and a rallying issue for the entire work force.

In the transition period, the old mind-set sticks out. I recall what one middle manager, in a large company's fiber box division, told me. Our TQ emphasis "isn't coming from the division level," he said, but from plant-level people, who are "nervous about going it alone" without senior management's backing. Everybody had heard the company's chief operating officer say, "We don't want to pay to be a quality producer." His preference was to just make a "commodity" product.

The box industry is notorious for making boxes that jam up in automated cartoning equipment—which plant people were painfully aware of. Instead of the COO's attitude, "What can we do to get by?" plant-level people wanted to ask, "What can we do to please the customer?" Then, "How can we please the customer even more?" and "How can we please more customers?" Keeping the customer off our backs is out; bringing the customer into our circle is in.

There is a yawning gap between getting by and bringing the customer into our circle. The following discussion, backed up by a summary in Table 4–1, probes the gap. We'll touch on the negative approach, then see how the quality concept has progressed through four positive stages. The four are *correction, prevention, cost-based quality*, and *serving the chain of customers*. We shall see why strong organizations rely on

Table 4–1. The Quality Progression

"Sell Your Duds"	I — *Corrective*	II — *Preventive*	III — *Cost-Based*	IV — *Serving the Chain of Customers*

Caveat emptor	Identify bad ones (based on specs) & "make it right"	Process certification
		Process capability
		Process control
		Auditing (PPM)
			Fail-safing
			Robust design
			Taguchi loss function
			Control of changes
			Quality system audit
				Multiple dimensions of quality:
				  Conformance to specs
				  Performance
				  Quick response
				  Quick-change expertise
				  Features
				  Reliability
				  Durability
				  Serviceability
				  Aesthetics
				  Perceived quality
				  Humanity
				  Value
				Extended design team:
				  Customer-marketing-design-supplier-operations support-EI teams
				Quality function deployment
				Reduce variation

all four positive concepts of quality in their never-ending quest to become stronger still.

BUYERS BEWARE!

First, the negative concept. There are, of course, plenty of companies whose quality concept is *caveat emptor*—let the buyer beware. In other words, "sell your duds." If the customer complains, push your product or service on another sucker. In manufacturing, if your lot has too many duds and is sent back, slip 'em in on the next shipment.

I. CORRECTION

That appalling viewpoint—and behavior—is to be scorned, and sometimes criminally prosecuted. Good businesses have always followed a more positive approach. Most common is the effort to "make it right"— the *corrective* approach. Policies for making it right require defining "rightness." That is, start with specifications—"specs," for short— about the goodness or performance of the product or service. When it isn't right, do it over, or scrap the bad ones and offer a replacement.

Seeing Better with "Specs"

A spec is a specified or generally understood level of acceptable quality. On that basis, good companies accept returns. Some do so grudgingly, others bend over backwards. Nordstrom, a widely admired U.S. department store group, takes almost any returns— "no questions asked."

While its basis for returns is loose and relaxed, a top-notch store such as Nordstrom will employ explicit specifications of quality with its suppliers. What's important is that a spec be clear and true. That means: relevant and up-to-date, no ambiguities, reflects customer's real or perceived needs or wants, and customer and provider interpret it the same way. Among department stores, Marks & Spencer in the U.K. is noted for its quality specs—and for tough adherence to them.   (*continued*)

In some cases, "clear and true" points to a spec involving physical measurement, in numbers—which reduces but does not eliminate judgment (different people will even read a thermometer differently). In other cases, nonnumeric specs will do; e.g., judging a table setting in a posh restaurant or blemishes on a finished surface. These kinds of specs, relying on vision, touch, smell, hearing, or taste, require more judgment. Still, a sensory spec is not a second-class spec. In some cases it is just what the customer cares about.

There is a body of lore on how to use specs. Basically, it boils down to sampling versus checking every product or service unit. Off-spec cases are then fixed or thrown out.

II. PREVENTION

The tough world market that many companies have been rudely thrust into has forced the best to progress from correction to *prevention*. The idea is to prevent problems in the process so that outputs of the process are good.

Process Certification

A basic approach is *process certification*. Before a process can be certified, it has to be specified. That means *process specs*, which are different from product specs. Process specs are traditional in hazardous work, such as in handling explosives; also, well-run, fast-food companies like McDonald's carefully specify everything about the process. Process spec sheets may go on for many pages, including sketches, photos, and flow diagrams.

Recently, companies in many other industries have found it prudent to specify and certify processes. Process specs may include operator skills, training, and tests for mastery; environmental requirements (dust, static, fumes, and the like); equipment settings; safety requirements; and workplace organization and arrangement.

If this sounds like plain old industrial engineering, it isn't. The world-class approach is for an interdisciplinary team to specify the process; while an IE could be on the team, the important thing is to include one or more operators. A similar team periodically certifies compliance with the specs.

"Seepy Kapability"

Compliance with specs is not a yes-or-no question. It is a matter of degree. A highly variable process may fail to comply most of the time (e.g., too much or too little flour, so white sauce is too thick or too thin).

The manufacturing sector is quickly learning—and applying—a technique for measuring how capable a process is in complying with specs. The technique's name is the *process capability study*. It yields a "seepy kapability index," an indicator of how much bad product seeps out of the process because of chronic error or too much process variation.

Seepy kapability is my own term. The real term is C_{p_k}, pronounced "see-pee-kay," but we needn't put up with mathematical symbols, especially double subscripted ones, in the everyday world of running and controlling processes.

Typically, the process capability study is a check on the physical parts of a process, not the human ones. We want to see if the machine and tooling, including timers, temperature controls, and so forth, are capable of meeting one or more key product specs (thickness of white sauce, breakage strength of glass). It is supposed to be a "hands-off" test, which means natural variability, without a human operator's meddling attempts to control.

Calculating the seepy kapability index is straightforward:

1. Take samples of the process to find its average and standard deviation.
2. See if the average is right between upper and lower spec limits (as it should be). Distance of the average from the nearest spec limit goes into the numerator.
3. Put 6 times the standard deviation of the process into the denominator.
4. Divide. If the answer is less than 1, it means the process is not very capable—too much seepage.

Say that the viscosity of white sauce must be between 110 and 130 centipoises. Based on samples from batches of white sauce, the average is 118, and standard deviation is 2. So 118 minus 110 gives us the numerator, 8; 6 times 2 is the denominator, 12. The index, then, is 8 divided by 12, or 0.67.

That's bad. Need to fix the average (numerator) or the variability (denominator). Getting the average centered between the specs might require a slight change in the recipe: more or less flour, more or less heat. To dampen the variability, maybe just attach a mechanism that shakes the flour sifter so the amount going into the cooker stays closer to what the recipe calls for.

If the shaker on the flour sifter cuts the denominator to 8, the seepy capability index becomes 1.0. Not very good. Industry has gravitated toward 1.33 as a minimum target index; in our example to get that, cut the denominator (reduce variation) to 6.

If the process is quite capable (you *know* it is, or you've done a study to prove it), you may want to monitor it—using a process-control chart.

Process Control and SPC

The classic preventive approach is process control charting, which requires plotting quality samples on charts. When plotted points drift from norms, stop and find the cause: variations in materials, procedures, or temperature, for example. Finally, fix the cause.

Process control charting dates back to the 1920s but had few users until forty years later. Today control charts have a supporting cast of characters: Pareto analysis, fishbone charting, histograms, run diagrams, pre-control charting, check sheets, and scatter diagrams. The full set of techniques is called statistical process control (SPC).

SPC is weak in the hands of quality-assurance staff people. It is powerful when all employees learn about it and put it to use in their own jobs. Companies like Kodak, IBM, and Ford have gone a long way toward doing just that. Figure 4–1 illustrates the idea: process control data owned by line operations and on display in the operating area for all to watch and react to. The photo comes from Kodak Park's sensitizing facility. The chart tracks chemicals prepared "right the first time."[4]

Besides SPC techniques, which are simple to learn and use, process control includes advanced statistical methods. The set called *design of experiments* has been around for a long time (I studied them in a two-week concentrated course over twenty years ago). Today, a short-cut version, generally called the Taguchi methods, after their Japanese proponent, has come into wide use in big industry. Short-cut or not, it still takes two weeks of concentrated study to learn the Taguchi methods. A computer is required.

Note that prevention aims at the process, not the product. Still, it is good practice to audit the results now and then.

Reprinted courtesy of Eastman Kodak Company.

Figure 4–1. Operator-Centered SPC

Taguchi Methods

Genichi Taguchi has devised a short-cut method of testing combinations of design options and operating conditions. The method is especially important in the manufacture of complex products, because the number of combinations to be tested can be in the thousands. The approach cuts testing time and cost and helps get a better design to the customer sooner.

Taguchi's books and articles became widely available in the mid-1980s.[5]

Auditing (PPM)

Audits—occasional quality inspections—show that prevention works. It works better than anybody might have predicted back in the 1970s when top firms were just getting their feet wet in prevention. For example, consider dimensional defects in metal cutting (diameter, length, etc.), soldering defects in printed circuit board manufacturing, and data-entry errors in clerical processes like order entry. It is now common for industry to report results like 50 to 500 defects per million units—industry's term is "parts per million" (PPM). In the 1970s it was more like 50,000 PPM.

In summary, prevention features *process certification, process capability, process control,* and *auditing* as an overall check. While the process emphasis is necessary, it isn't always enough. Cost-based quality brings more forces to bear on making the firm competitive.

III. COST-BASED QUALITY

Well-publicized studies a few years ago proved that companies whose products were perceived to have higher quality also had higher profits and bigger market share.[6] The conclusion is that quality pays, that it is a key to competitive advantage.

What happens when low defect rates like 500 or 50 PPM become common in an industry, as has been happening? Then, it's a new contest. The winners must have top quality—at a lower cost. Emphasis shifts to "quality for costs' sake"; that means looking for ways to prevent errors that generate rippling bad effects through the system. Techniques that serve this purpose include *fail-safing, robust design,* the *Taguchi loss function, control of changes,* and the *quality system audit.*

Cost of Bad Quality

Many prominent companies have estimated their cost of bad quality. Typically, it turns out to be 15 to 30 percent of sales. All that cash goes to pay for scrap, rework, rescheduling, overtime, and other internal disruptions arising from bad quality; and for warranty costs, returns, people's time to placate angry customers, and other external costs of bad quality.

A clarification: This is *not* plain old cost reduction in a new wrapper. The fixation of traditional cost reduction is on direct labor efficiency; in other words, work faster to drive down unit costs. But more speed often increases errors, and the errors often raise overall costs. Cost-based quality concepts rarely call for a faster pace; more likely, it would be slowing down or stopping to get the quality right. On the manufacturing floor at Compaq Computer in Houston, assemblers who spot a major flaw pull a red brake cable, which sets off sirens and flashing lights.[7]

Fail-Safing

The basis of fail-safing is a change in thinking about people and processes. The precept is that error and process failure are not the fault of the operator, because *it is human nature to be variable*. Good management requires doing everything possible to fail-safe the process from natural human variability. Then, instead of a nudge, a wink, and one more tired recitation of Murphy's defeatist law, we can cheerfully offer Murphy's antithesis: Anything that can't go wrong, won't go wrong.

Fail-safing often relies on some kind of device: timer, warning tone, "electric eye," alignment template, and so on. Office lights that turn off automatically when sensors fail to detect motion are an example. Masking tape to keep from painting over the wrong surface is a simple form of fail-safing.

While fail-safing isn't a bad term (doesn't emphasize the negative, like "fool-proofing" would), I like another term that I have heard around Eastman Kodak Company: *random mishaps*.[8] There always are some, aren't there? So, as a team, mount a massive assault on random mishaps.

Fail-Safing (Pokayoke) = Super-Fixing

While *prevention* includes fixing the process, fail-safing is *really* fixing it—a super-fix so it can't fail and cause cost or loss.

Fail-safing has been honed to a fine art in some top manufacturing companies in Japan. The Japanese word for it is *pokayoke*, which some Western companies use interchangeably with its English equivalent.

Start by identifying them. Then use all the tools of problem-solving to stamp them out.

A fail-safe process that copes with natural human error is a hardy, robustly designed process. While we're at it, why not robustly design the product too?

Robust Design

Consider a device that fails to work when it's damp or when it's dusty; a service that satisfies only regular (not drop-in) customers; or a management technique that tends to work only in a nonunion environment. Neither the device, nor the service, nor the technique is robustly designed. The cost is loss of a customer, or, in some cases, paying product warranty costs.

For robust product design to take place, the designer has to be in touch with users and uses of the product. One approach is for field service people to spend time with designers. Another is for designers to do a turn in the field, working with customers. For example, at Xerox, new-hire design engineers' first assignments are as field engineers or as manufacturing engineers. While robust design gets the designer thinking about customer losses, the Taguchi methods go further by having the designer consider *costs* of losses.

Taguchi Loss Function

The common view is that design's job is just to provide the functions the customer wants (in industry lingo, providing *functionality*). Genichi Taguchi has set the world of product design on its ear by convincing us that product designers also have responsibility for costs. Included are the cost of producing the product or providing the service, plus all losses *to society* that relate to the product or its use throughout the chain of customers and the product's life cycle. (More on the loss function in Chapter 10.)

Control of Changes

Some quality losses and costs are the inevitable result of changes. Each time something gets changed, bugs have to be worked out again. Quality improvement has to be restarted from a point some paces to the rear.

Thus, the total-quality organization must control changes. Specifically, it must control design changes, changes in the customer base and the supplier base, and sales-rate and production-rate changes. These are but a few prominent examples.

Good progress has been made in the area of design changes. One approach is clustering: Implement a cluster of changes all at once instead of allowing design changes to disrupt operations at any time, randomly. Clustering provides stable time periods during which employee-centered process improvement activities can flourish, IBM's version is called "JITER," for JIT *e*ngineering *r*eserve: Engineering guarantees stability of certain designs for X weeks or months, which allows operations—IBM's and its suppliers'—to hone in on improvement.

Other approaches impose limits. At Hewlett-Packard's terminals division, a policy for a new model of computer terminal was to allow only three engineering changes after prototyping. The intent was to make sure the product development team did it "right the first time."

Companies are also placing limits on number of parts, number of new parts, number of options, and number of suppliers. Fewer of each allows more concentration of quality efforts.

Limiting number of customers has the same benefits, but that sounds like turning down sales. For some first-tier suppliers—those whose first preference is for large, multiyear exclusive contracts—that is no longer a radical idea. The multiyear aspect (hang on to the same loyal customers and suppliers) pays big quality dividends—in the hands of firms with strong quality commitments.

Less obvious are the benefits of smoothing out the peaks and valleys in sales and operations. Business managers seem to have infinite toleration for the damage that is done by over- and underscheduling, feast-or-famine order booking, and get-it-out-the-door, end-of-period panic. Uneven, irregular operations results in quality of service losses as well as disruption to process stability. Vaughn Beals, CEO at Harley-Davidson (motorcycles) explains the connection:

> We quit jerking around our schedule (no changes for 30 days, a
> little for next 30, a little more for next 30). A main reason is quality.
> Because if we laid off a hundred guys, 400 guys changed jobs.
> And quality went to hell in a hand-basket.[9]

The cures include altering the way sales and managerial bonuses are paid—to emphasize steady business rather than end-of-period pile-ups. Another approach is to time promotions and set variable prices so as to shift demand from busy to slack periods. Making these changes requires marketing and operations—and perhaps finance and purchasing—to plan jointly. And there's the rub, especially in large companies.

In manufacturing, a small but growing trend is to produce certain standard items to a daily rate, which is a smoothed representation of actual sales. Smoothed rate-based production is the ideal setting for concentrated continual improvement in quality.

Where a fixed rate doesn't make sense, there is this option: Reserve a certain part of each day for certain star products or customers, then fill in the rest of the day with any and all jobs or walk-in customers. With at least some regularity and repetition, the process team, and all supplying processes, can reattack the same process problems every day until they are mastered.

A bonus of rate-based production is getting out of the mode of making a huge pile of an item based on a forecast; since forecasts are "always" wrong, the result is either too little inventory and a "hot-urgent" production order, or too much inventory and negative selling. By negative selling, I mean pushing unpopular items at cut prices upon customers who really want something else.

Quality System Audit

If we are to be concerned with extended quality costs and losses, then there ought to be an audit of quality throughout the system: a *quality system audit*. A few top companies now perform such audits, but I believe that virtually no Western company does it with world-class emphasis and involvement by senior management.

Two forces are acting to get that kind of involvement. One is the fast-growing practice of certifying and auditing the quality of one's suppliers or contractors. Senior executives of supplier companies get interested fast—when their chances of winning the large, exclusive, long-term contract hang in the balance.

The second force is public quality awards. The granddaddy is Japan's Deming Prize for quality (in several categories). Striving for one of the awards often has profound positive effects on people. One Japanese company president, who had a reputation as a one-man show, says:

> I have been president . . . for over 20 years, yet I had never had the kind of experience that I had while applying for the Deming

Prize. It was during that time that all of my employees became aware of what I expected of them. They understood the goals I set out for the company. They became dedicated workers, and all of them, acting as one body, tried to reach the same goals.[10]

In 1988 a similar set of National Quality Awards, also called the Baldrige Quality Awards, were offered in the United States. Because of the newness of the awards, only sixty-six companies applied. While three manufacturers won awards (Motorola, Westinghouse's Commercial Nuclear Fuel Division, and Globe Metallurgical), two prizes for service-sector firms and one for small manufacturers were not awarded. The Baldrige awards seem sure to become prestigious and visible, along with similar awards elsewhere; for example, the British Quality Award and the European Quality Award (which is being developed by the European Foundation for Quality Management)—to go into effect in the 1990s.[11] As prestige grows, so will executive involvement and quality leadership.

We have been talking about various kinds of quality audits done by outsiders. One reason for having such auditors in your plant is the hope of high marks that can be advertised.

True believers do not just go for external prestige and advertising copy. They make strong commitments for *internal* quality system audits. A complete audit program can include having the quality control staff audit some aspects of quality, heads of departments audit other aspects, and the company president doing still another personal and highly visible audit.

Internal quality audits are especially common among certain franchisers and store chains. Budgetel Inns is a good example. The Budgetel program includes daily audits by motel managers and head housekeepers, periodic visits by district managers, and official quality ratings. "Bad inspection scores," says Budgetel chairman Stephen Marcus, "are followed by lower occupancy rate like night follows day."[12] Managers' bonuses are directly tied to the quality ratings.

Official rating data come from guest comment cards, company inspectors, and secret shoppers. While comment cards are usually too hit-and-miss for a fair rating, Budgetel added an incentive to get guests to fill them in: a new color TV given to a guest monthly.

Presidential audits, which began in Japan, are rare (or nonexistent) in the West. When the company president does not undertake this task, the proof of a genuine quality commitment is missing.[13]

IV. SERVING THE CHAIN OF CUSTOMERS

When our thinking about quality expands to consider losses to *society* and quality audits of everything from nuts to soup in the cafeteria, we are on the right track. Professor David Garvin has helped us broaden our thinking in another way. He's told us that conformance to specs is only one of eight ways that customers judge quality.[14]

Multiple Dimensions of Quality

In that spirit, others are not content to stop at just eight items. My own expanded list numbers twelve dimensions of quality (Garvin's eight are starred):

*1. *Conformance to specifications.* Can be numeric specs, for example, package weight no less than 395 and no more than 405 grams; or yes-no specs, for example, bulb lights or does not.

*2. *Performance.* This refers to *grade* of service or product: degree of "home-baked chewiness" in a commercial cookie; clarity of TV picture; expertness of advice. When people are willing to pay more, it is often for better performance. Surveys reveal that performance is the number one way that consumers think about quality.[15]

3. *Quick response.* Often measured in delay or elapsed time: time wasted standing in a ticket line or clamping the phone to one's ear while on hold; delay in getting an order produced, filled, or delivered or a case heard in court; time-to-market for a new product or service.

4. *Quick-change expertise.* Costume changes in the theater, can size changes in a cannery, model-to-model changes in an auto assembly plant.

Does Perestroika Mean "Quick Response"?

Soviet women are more enthusiastic about perestroika and glasnost than the men. Because it's mainly the women who stand in the long lines.

—NBC interview (5/19/88) of a Soviet spokesman

THE WALL STREET JOURNAL

"I hope you enjoyed our hold music. I made the selections myself."

From the *Wall Street Journal*—Permission, Cartoon Features Syndicate.

*5. *Features.* Automatic focus in a camera, free coffee while you shop, airbag safety device in an automobile.

*6. *Reliability.* Car starts every time, keeps running for whole trip. In other words, reliability is failure-free operation *over time.*

*7. *Durability.* How tough it is or how long it lasts: a premium windbreaker jacket that can be crammed into a fist-sized bag and that will take 20 years of wearing, an antismoking cure that lasts a lifetime.

*8. *Serviceability.* Ease of providing a service or of servicing goods. An easy-to-clean oven, a typewriter with easy-to-access-and-change cartridge-style ribbons, a free complaint phone line.

*9. *Aesthetics.* Beauty, elegance, schmaltz, and other factors that appeal to the eye or other senses: an engine's full-throated roar, a greeting-card phrase that "tugs at the heartstrings."

*10. *Perceived quality.* Impression of quality based on things other than here-and-now evidence: loyalty to a brand of clothing, reputation of a judge for fairness.

11. *Humanity.* Providing services or goods with the right degree of friendliness, attentiveness, humility, honesty: service with a smile, machines that talk, waiters who know just when and when not to interrupt table talk.
12. *Value.* How much of any of the above dimensions of quality we get for the cost or price. In their ratings of the quality of life in a certain community, sociologists find out the cost of a kilowatt-hour of electricity, of police protection, of getting a tire fixed.

The four unstarred items are not just variations on some of the eight starred ones. They are basic and vital in their own right. For example, quick response and quick changes (items 3 and 4) are so important to customers that we should not permit them to be buried in the *performance* dimension (item 2). Moreover, *managing* for quick response and managing for fast changes each have their own sizable, still fast-growing bodies of knowledge—which are out of the traditional mainstream of thinking in quality management.

Humanity, item 11, is a necessary addition to quality concepts that in the past have tended toward the mechanistic.

Value, item 12, is always on the final paying customer's mind. The world-class company makes value a vital issue throughout the chain of customers. That is, each of us may continually improve service to the next process by wiping out costly waste and improving all the other dimensions of quality.

Extended Design Team

All the dimensions of quality need to be continually improved—in the eyes of the customer. One step is organizational: an *extended design team* whose members are in the chain of customers—final customers, marketing, design (product and process), suppliers, operations support, and involved employees.

The group works together to develop new products and services and to keep improving them. McKesson, a distributor of drugs and allied products, teamed up with independent drugstores (its customers) and, later, suppliers of its products. The initial reason was that the independents were being squeezed by the big chains, and McKesson's sales were falling. McKesson designed devices for collecting inventory data in the retail drugstores, and over time it developed and improved many related services. Suppliers were brought into the loop when it became clear that the stores' inventory/sales data had value for them as well: Suppliers can use the data to improve their production scheduling. All parties—customers, McKesson, and the suppliers—became much more responsive, with greatly reduced inventories and support staffs.[16]

The world's major automakers have forged similar alliances with their suppliers. The auto industry, and other industries as well, have several labels for what is happening. One is *simultaneous engineering*, in which car designers team up with their own manufacturing engineers, as well suppliers' design and manufacturing engineers. Formerly, each group worked independently; bad designs, bad quality, and high costs were the result.

In the McKesson case, troubles in the customer base triggered development of new services to customers. Do we have to wait for negative external events to spur us into action? Perhaps not—in those companies that have adopted quality function deployment.

Quality Function Deployment

QFD uses a series of matrices to link needs of external customers to internal processes. The needs go onto the matrices, along with ratings of importance to the customer and ratings of the competition.

Some versions of QFD have many add-on features and steps.[17] All versions seem to have at least these virtues: They oblige the product development team to reach out to the customer to define and rate needs, and they require that competitive analysis be done. That's enough to impress me. The added benefits of the matrices and other procedures are gravy.

Reduce Variation

Our earlier discussion of variation (item II, Prevention) was limited to simple variation. The new urgency over the matter has to do with awareness of "second-order variation": variation of one thing interacting with variation of something else. The two do not cancel out; instead there is variation pileup, which causes problem pileup (*tolerance stackup* is the engineering term).

Ford Motor Company has done a fine job of spreading awareness about variation pileup. Ford uses the example of a car door and a door frame. Say that the dimensions of every door and every frame

Continual Improvement—to a Point?

"We preach continual improvement around here. But now we are close to zero defects. So some of us can't help thinking, 'Is there really a need to push for still more quality?' "

My questioner was referring to a screen for a computer monitor. His plant coats the glass, cuts it, and curves it slightly. The customer, a major computer maker, was pleased: nearly perfect conformance to specs, which covered bubbles, bumps, dents, and scratches.

In my response, to a room full of plant employess, I said, "But your screens *do* have tiny bubbles, bumps, dents, and scratches. They are within spec today. But haven't specs in your industry been getting ever-tighter?"

The answer, of course, was yes. I went on to suggest that "if you don't improve and a competitor does," the customer could suddenly say to you, 'Sorry, contract canceled. Your quality doesn't meet our new tighter specs, and our second supplier's quality does meet them right now.' "

are within tolerances. None would be rejected in a quality inspection; it's *zero defects*. Still, the tolerance range allows variation within the range. Therefore, some percentage of the doors will not close right. Pick a door on the low (small) side of its spec and a frame on the high (large) side of its, and you end up with a loose-fitting door. Cold or hot outside air leaks in.

The variation-pileup problem gets worse as the number of elements increases. People employed in the process industry often like to say that "our process is a black art." The likely reason is variation pileup— large numbers of ingredients in a mixture, for example. In any industry, if performance at each stage in a long chain of customers is acceptable but not at the center of the spec, it adds up to trouble.

The cure for variation pileup is continual reduction in variation (going beyond zero defects, which is just a milestone, not an end). That is, keep narrowing the range of variability of the process. It won't do to just narrow the spec or tolerance limits. They are set subjectively. Variation of the actual process is the reality—and where the trouble lies.

FUTURE QUALITY

Since our concept of quality has expanded through four generations—corrective, preventive, cost-based, and customer-serving—in less than a decade, we may expect another generational expansion soon. Perhaps it will provide new thinking and breakthrough techniques for getting all employees to become "owners" of the continual improvement effort. If all employees assume that ownership—creating a large army of customer-serving quality improvers—the goal of *rapid* improvement is assured.

5

❧

Work Force on the Attack

WITH TOTAL QUALITY providing the core agenda, unleash the work force. Then sit back and watch the fireworks. If you did it right, you will have created an employee-driven *improvement engine* out of what was formerly seen as a wage-and-benefits sinkhole.

WHO MANAGES WHOM? OR WHAT?

We are not talking about treating people well and hoping for their cooperation in return. The be-nice-to-employees idea, which has re-surfaced repeatedly in the history of management, is passive and weak.

We aren't even content with the listen-to-your-people-for-a-change viewpoint. In the average firm—one that has not yet felt the quakes—the "people" do *not* have many good ideas for improvement, and their managers don't either. Many of the ideas of managers, as well as of their bottled-up subordinates, reflect narrow, wrong-headed views about what it takes to become excellent.

After enlightenment, all this changes: *All* employees get a full set of tools for solving problems—with the aim of serving the customer better and better. Throughout the organization, people own and manage their processes, with help from anyone else who has expertise.

89

Who's the Manager?

A visitor unexpectedly found out about employee involvement at a Westinghouse plant in Columbia, South Carolina, by asking an employee if he was a machine operator. "I used to be a machine operator," he answered. "I manage machines now."[1]

New Terminology for a Natural Work Culture

The employee-involvement (EI) earthquake has shaken old views about jobs and people and paved the way for enlightenment. The words we use must change, too (this is especially the case in English-speaking countries, since English is rich in word-symbols that take on different shades of meaning). Table 5–1 contrasts the pre-quake and enlightened terminology.

The column headings in Table 5–1 convey the message: On the left, the underlying view is that people are reluctant participators, problem solvers, or team members; they have to be coaxed. All the terms under "manipulative" represent good intentions, but they are simply an unnatural way to treat adults. Positive results and full commitment require getting out of the manipulative mode: Give employees the knowledge, the tools, and the *job* of solving problems.

I am not advising a purge of the words on the left. After all, changing a culture is a long transition, not a sudden happening. Also, the terms are not a set; each stands for a different concept that may or may not have a valued role in the cultural transition.

Table 5–1. *The Changing Work Culture—Terminology*

Manipulative	Natural
Employee participation	Employee involvement
Participative management	Managers-as-facilitators
Team building	Focused teams
Change agent	Trainer
Intervention	Interaction
Empowerment	Ownership

Beyond Participation

The oldest items on the list are employee participation and participative management. I recall the excitement over these terms in the early 1960s. Rensis Likert's *New Patterns of Management* was the inspiration. The back of the book listed over three hundred research works showing the power of participative management, study after study citing improved attendance and job satisfaction.[2] It bothered us (including me, a college student studying the Likert materials) that hard-to-measure productivity and profit effects were not central in those studies. But we had faith: If people were more satisfied, surely they would produce more, and profits would rise.

That faith was misplaced. Participation was putting a toe in the water. It meant having a say in where to place desks in the office or when to take vacations. There are plenty of hidebound them-versus-us environments in which even those meager steps would be break-throughs. Still, let's get on with it. First step is to set the goals and spread the word. Let everyone know that competitiveness requires employees to be on problem-solving teams and to assume process ownership. Make it clear that this means full involvement, not just small-issue participation.

The keepers of the jargon are in the universities—or just out as fresh-faced experts flashing MBA degrees. Part of this discussion is for them. I've found that people who make things work in the business world don't care so much about what you call it. Steelcase, Inc., the world's largest office equipment manufacturer, developed a world-class culture-change program, which included sending all supervisors through "participative management" training. We can quibble about choice of terms, but never mind—as long as the training emphasizes supervisors' role as *facilitators:* They advise and consult, and they facilitate change and improvement by knowing who to see and how to get things done.

Should supervisory training also teach about praise and positive reinforcement? Of course. We all should know about that.

I'm reminded of when one of my sons was in third grade. He was a dawdler, and yelling at him didn't do much good for the problem or for one's peace of mind. I tried positive reinforcement: He put on a shoe, and I made a big production of running to the freezer for a spoonful of ice cream, and running back and sticking it in his mouth. He said, "What's that for?" I said, "It's positive reinforcement." He said, "I *know* that, but what's it *for?*" I said, "For putting on your shoe."

My son's an adult now, and the shoe is on the other foot. He and his work team generate solutions to problems, and they hope their boss will be an effective facilitator. If so, the team showers the boss with praise, possibly even springing for an ice cream party at break; the team hopes the boss will keep up the good work.

I'm not suggesting complete reversal: employees evaluating and praising bosses instead of the other way around. In a healthy and natural adult work culture, it's a two-way street, each person evaluating and reinforcing the good works of each other person. An employee who says, "Nice tie, boss," should also freely say, "Nice work in digging up the information we needed."

Outside Assistance

While we want supervisors to be facilitators, some companies see fit to employ another, special type of facilitator: one who deals with person-to-person roadblocks, an expert in *team-building*. Or is it gang-building?

I have admiration for the skills of many of the for-hire facilitators, but they haven't understood the team-gang distinction; the companies employing them haven't either. Narrow the scope to product- or customer-focused team-building, and an outside facilitator can be of great service.

The executive or the outside observer sees a stagnant work culture as requiring the services of *change agents* doing *interventions*. Those terms have a loud manipulative ring (and I felt that way when I first heard them a couple of decades ago), more so than the other four terms on the left in Table 5–1. It is good to see them fading in use; today, companies are more likley to hire *trainers*. Trainers teach TQ, problem-solving, and so forth, and sometimes they train trainers. Armed with the tools of problem-solving, a focused team is inclined toward heavy-duty *interaction* to clear away obstacles and make things right.

Change agents, step aside; no interventions needed.

THE POWER OF OWNERSHIP

The final term on the left in Table 5–1 is word-of-the-year in management for 1989; *empowerment*. Everybody loves the word. It is used, often enough, in the same sentence with the last word on the right in Table

5–1: *ownership*. But the terms don't quite match up. A rental agreement empowers me to occupy your house for a time. Ownership? Well, that's different. Tell me more.

There is a lot to tell about ownership. It starts with transfer of something big, like quality. Operators are trained to take ownership of quality; they see it as real when in-process quality inspectors are eliminated or retrained for other work. This has happened in a thousand plants around the world.

In machine-intensive work, operators also assume ownership of preventive maintenance: lubricating, tightening and changing belts, removing access panels for cleaning and replacing components, and so forth. As operators learn and take over more and more of these jobs, staffing in the maintenance department shrinks—a sign of a real transfer of ownership.

In some companies operators also document the process, using words and diagrams. Engineers, supervisors, or human resource staff may help and advise; in any case, processes are scrutinized and improved as they are documented. One desired outcome is for operators to use the process sheets in training other operators. Another is for the documentation to serve as a base line for continual improvement.

Who Owns Process Improvement?

Operator ownership of base-line documentation for process improvement is not so hard to achieve. On the other hand, their ownership of process improvement is elusive. Lee Rhodes, formerly production managerr at Hewlett-Packard's Personal Office Computer Division (POD), has lectured a few times on his group's experiences.

POD was one of the first plants in the world, among computer manufac-

---

Revolving Door in Services

In much of the service sector, annual employee turnover averages 100 percent—and more. The easy cure: Raise pay.

Can't afford it? Okay, then how about a cheap solution: Make jobs more interesting. John Simmons (in the U.K.) has observed the connection: certain retailers with employee involvement programs that are able to retain employees even when wages are very low.[3]

turers, to break up assembly, test, and packaging and reorganize into focused flow lines.[4] Other steps included shifting quality to operators and training them in SPC and problem-solving; in addition, operators (with technical assistance) "wrote" their processes. Ownership was the key word for the management team.

Despite impressive early gains (e.g., throughput time and in-process inventory cut from three weeks to three days), the management team was dissatisfied; operator involvement was not up to their high hopes. Rhodes asked two questions: "Who owns process control?" and "Who owns process improvement?"

Investigation shed some light. Regarding the first question, operators were detecting when processes varied too much or were out of control. Then experts stepped in to find solutions, passing their recommendations up the line for higher managers to approve. First-line supervisors weren't involved, except to convey requests and pass on information.

Operator involvement in process improvement was even less. Operators didn't select projects, determine the improvement, or make approval decisions. For both process control and improvement, Rhodes ended up with much of the final decision-making—as it was in the old days before any of them had thought about focus and employee ownership.

The management team throught they knew why. H-P's managers generally come out of engineering, where their jobs are to analyze and advise, not decide. As managers, they tend to do the same. Real employee ownership requires breaking some ingrained behavior patterns—among managers as well as operators. It's not easy, but at least they pinpointed the roots of the problem.

It is a lesson for all companies to understand. We want take-charge employees who will make recommendations and decisions when they have the information and expertise to do so. We wish their immediate supervisors would be similarly assertive. If not, improvement will be sporadic, not continual and rapid.

Operators as Planners

Some of the EI problems identified in POD in 1985 have been resolved at Hewlett-Packard—and at other companies as well.

For example, Kodak's black and white (B&W) paper sensitizing group got operators involved in planning for the future. Much of the planning took place in a workshop held at a local hotel. The fifteen participants—line operators, process engineers, maintenance people, and product staff—had an overall objective: develop a future *vision* of B&W in which operators and staff people would be united as one team, with pride of ownership. One major subgoal was to totally restructure B&W operations and redo the floor plan.

After they completed the planning, it was time for a presentation to management. It wasn't the usual sober flip-chart run-through by one or two spokespersons in a company conference room. Instead, the group invited management to the hotel for a combined presentation and celebration, including balloons, funny costumes, a short skit, and prizes. Managers had to buy tickets.

Phil Stepkovitch, a workshop participant, had this to say: "If I sound excited to you, I am. . . . We delivered everything that management asked . . . and probably much more than they expected us to deliver. We even gave them recommendations about how to implement the plans."[5]

The group's thorough vision statement is seventy-four pages long. Among its provisions are the following:

- Advises devoting at least 10 percent of all time to developing capability.
- Recommends a "board of directors" for customer relations and another for supplier relations.
- Provides a time-phased plan for installing certain new machines and upgrading of some existing machines.
- Clearly specifies each group's responsibilities point by point— for example, regarding performance evaluation, housekeeping and contamination control, introduction of new technology, suggestions.
- Advises dividing responses and floor plan into two subgroups, each dedicated to a different Kodak internal customer.
- Recommends developing customer-oriented goals, performance measures, and accountability.

The document ends with a list of beliefs about the B&W group's expected attitudes, once the plan has been implemented. The impressive list is reprinted below, intact:

1. We have great operating principles and everything we do is based upon them.
2. People ask us our opinion and are interested in our ideas.
3. Innovation is everyone's job.
4. We finally know our customers and we know them on a first-name basis.
5. The main job of supervision is to teach and coach.

6. Everyone is responsible for our team, its successes and its failures.
7. We started small and kept building. It will never stop.
8. Everyone is committed.
9. The way we do work today is very different from the past.
10. We now have definite goals and we are working to achieve them.
11. All business information is shared with everyone on the team.
12. We are not stuck in the same job every day. We have flexibility and are asked to think.
13. Our job is to be team members. Therefore, we do what must be done.
14. We are involved in decisions that affect the whole business.
15. We now understand what it takes to run a business.
16. We share our knowledge and expertise with other team members.
17. We never realized there was so much to learn about our jobs and how important it is to the rest of the team.

TOOLS FOR AN EFFECTIVE WORK LIFE

Many other companies are in the middle of handing off ownership to employees. Each does it somewhat differently and has its own stories to tell about obstacles and successes. There is broad agreement on one thing: The employee has to own the *tools* of process control, improvement, planning, analyzing, decision-making, requesting, and presenting.

Those tools have been owned by experts and managers in the past. Actually, even experts and managers have been poorly equipped. They lacked statistical process control (SPC) tools, for example. The tools of SPC should be as familiar as your route to work; both are basic to an effective work life.

The main tool is a marker: pencil, pen, chalk, or felt-tip. It's for drawing a diagram, making a process sheet, writing an order, recording the team's ideas, and developing a plan or presentation. Most of all, it is the means of carrying out a new role, an addition to everyone's job: continually marking down what the process just did.

WHAT THE PROCESS DID

It is useless to talk about process control and improvement without data. It is easy and natural for each operator to record the data: what the process did—and didn't do. I'll describe four direct ways of doing this: incident board, check sheet, run diagram, and process control chart.

Incident Board

In one form of data capture, the employee writes a few words to describe a process problem. The one-liner goes on an incident board. A prominent display gets attention; so, at least in factories and offices, the incident should be written in big letters on flip-chart paper or large marker board. When the employee is out in the open—as in retailing, repair services, nursing, and construction—a big chart won't work; it has to be a log book or clip board.

I've seen several versions. They range from free-form to column formatted. In one factory, operators developed a display with four column headings: customer complaints (meaning *internal* customer— the next process), problems, solutions, and actions taken.

At one of Imprimis's plants (large disk drive manufacturing), operators record incidents on flip charts. Later, a team member enters the incidents into a computer by category. The output is a Pareto chart—a bar chart showing, in descending order, how many times per week each incident occurred.

Incident boards have weaknesses that may seem small but actually can be serious: It takes *time* to write a few words. Busy operators will tend to put off writing things down, and then forget to do it. They will write down big annoyances but not the little ones—which add up to big problems; and a question mark in everyone's mind is *which* problems deserve to be written down. Things like bad handwriting or even illiteracy also stand in the way. Check sheets correct for most of these problems.

Check Sheet

A check sheet comes with a prewritten list of common incidents. Operators just make a tally mark next to an item in the list. They meet to discuss and agree on what items to list and revise the list as things change.

Check sheet with trouble lights. Table 5–2 is a segment of a check sheet developed by one of the TEAM-BUILT groups at Physio Control. (Each of the eleven TEAM-BUILT lines has its own version.) Tally marks go under the appropriate week, so that week-to-week trends show. Just above the tally mark, an operator may write a couple of words of explanation (shown as squiggly vertical lines in Table 5–2). The sheet has two extra columns. One shows cost of the bad part—if the problem is with a component part; the other shows hours of rework, where a fault is fixable.

Physio's use of check sheets dovetails with its trouble-light and just-in-time system. Trouble-light switches are scattered among team members. An operator turns on a yellow light for a slow-down condition and red for a serious failure requiring the whole team to stop (red also summons help). Physio's JIT rules allow (usually) just one work piece between adjacent team members.

Thus, when a problem slows someone down, the next person runs out of work very soon. That requires turning on the trouble light and checking off the cause on the "discrepancy" chart; the lights go on several times a day.

Each team holds "huddle" meetings twice a week or as necessary. Before a meeting the team leader uses the check sheets to produce

Table 5–2. *Check Sheet at Physio Control*

Discrepancy	Unit Cost	Rework Hours	1–2	October 5–9	12–16
1 PCB documentation/workmanship/mechanical	18	5.0	⎨ ✓	⎨ ✓	
2 T/M conduit—broken standoff			⎨⎨⎨⎨⎨		
3 T/M paddle parts	22	2.3	✓✓✓✓✓		
.					
.					
.					
9 Workmanship error/missing parts					
.					
.					
.					
14 Rear panel paint					
.					
.					
.					
19 Defective switches					
.					
.					
.					
24					

two Pareto charts; see samples in Figure 5–1. One shows discrepancies by type and by cost of the part (for problems traced to a bad component); the other is by type and frequency of occurrence. These Paretos are the main agenda for the huddle meetings.

We can see from Figure 5–1 the likely main topic of discussion in the next huddle meeting: discrepancy number 6. It is the worst cost problem and second highest in frequency. The TEAM-BUILT group—operators plus response team—"brainstorms" the problem and, sometimes, solves it in the meeting. Otherwise, a few of their group, and perhaps a supplier rep, become a study team, which reports back weekly until the problem is solved. Then problem number 6 disappears from the check sheets, Pareto charts, and meeting agenda. A new worst problem (not quite as bad as the last) gets their attention.

Check sheets used this way—jointly with focused teams, trouble lights, and JIT—are a powerful tool for problem solving. The same

Figure 5–1. Pareto Charts at Physio Control

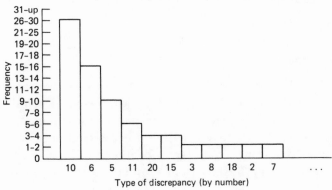

A. Cost and type of discrepancy

B. Frequency and type of discrepancy

approach will also work in services—processing ticket requests, for instance.

Check sheet in document processing. A ticket office might start by dividing its work—types of events, perhaps—into stars and nonstars, then set up teams (cells) for each. As an example, there might be a total of six cells, four dedicated to star events and two "fuzzy" cells for processing nonstars—low-volume work requiring special processing.

Each of the four "star" cells consists of a team arranged as a U-shaped cell, with processing in a strict person-to-person sequence, like an assembly line in manufacturing. A maximum of two documents might be allowed between each team member; when someone has trouble—document with bad handwriting, missing information, and so forth—the next person runs out of work and turns on the yellow light, which requires a tally on the check sheet.

A small but growing number of service firms have adopted some version of this formula for active, forceful employee involvement in data collection and problem-solving. One is New York-based National Westminster Bank USA, a subsidiary of National Westminster Bank PLC, headquartered in London.

At NatWest USA all officers and professionals go through a two-day training course, and everyone else, including messengers and mail room clerks, takes a one-day course. NatWest's quality measurement starts with data collection at the clerical level, since that is where detailed actions occur. An August 1987 survey of all the bank's 4,800 people and 134 retail branches showed the quick success of the data collection effort: Of those responding, 34 percent said they had been using check sheets since completion of their quality training.[6]

The check sheet displays data on a broad spectrum of problems; it's a shotgun approach. In most work centers, there is at least one standout problem that resists solution. It calls for a rifle approach—taking aim at just that one problem.

Run Diagram

First step in the rifle approach is to measure or judge the factor you are aiming at; then record the reading. One way to record it is on a run diagram, which is just a running plot of measurements, item by item or customer by customer, as the process continues.

Figure 5–2 illustrates. The factor of interest is missing or illegible data on sales orders "faxed" from the field to the international sales

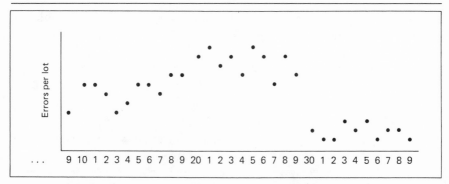

Figure 5–2. Run Diagram: Errors on Sales-Order Forms

office. The data-entry operator keeps track of errors and plots them on the run diagram. Errors are measured in number of missing items per lot of twenty forms.

In the example, the check sheet calls attention to itself from about day 18 to day 26, a time period when the error rate is rising. The operator doesn't wait for the problem to ripple through the company and come back in the form of customer complaints about late orders. She and her supervisor send a fax to all sales people warning them of the problem and its consequences. They follow up with a few phone calls. The upshot: A training session is added to the agenda at the next regularly scheduled sales meeting. Right after that, on day 30, the error rate plunges.

This is the kind of success story that should take place routinely in all firms—using run diagrams, check sheets, or any of the other tools yet to be described. The very high error rates in most of the services sector make it a natural target for heavy doses of these techniques.

Process Control Chart

The process control chart is the run diagram's better-known cousin. While not as simple to construct and use as the run diagram, the control chart is statistically precise. It has a center line (the recent process average), plus upper and lower control limits. The operator still looks for alarming trends (as with the run diagram). More than that, if a plotted point is outside either control limit, it tells the operator, *stop!* It's a rare condition. Find the cause, and get it fixed.

There's no point in expounding on the various forms of control charts

here, since a wealth of published information is available on the subject.
I'll just make a few general points:

1. It was hard to find *any* Western manufacturers that used control
   charts a decade ago, but now in some industries they are widely
   used. For example, all the world's major automakers use them
   and require most of their suppliers to do the same.
2. A control chart really does not control. Nor does it point to a
   probable cause of a process change. It just tells the operator
   that there has been a significant change. Still, the control chart
   is a powerful, important tool, because it tells what it tells clearly—
   no arguments—and it sounds its alarm while the process is still
   going on.
3. Most of the common forms of control charts use sampling—which
   is money-saving. In fact, it's doubly money-saving, since the
   operator's samples are small and frequent, not (as in lot sampling)
   large and after-the-fact—after costly mistakes have taken their
   toll.
4. Control charts are a godsend in government contracting and in
   heavily regulated industries, such as pharmaceutical and nuclear
   products. Contracts and regulatory policies have required use
   of the *worst* method of assuring quality: sampling inspections
   out of large lots. Discovery of lots high in defectives occurs
   much too late to control the process and avert high costs of the
   bad ones; also too late to have a reasonable chance of finding
   causes.

   It took a while. But now many agencies are accepting—sometimes enthusiastically encouraging—process control charts instead of lot sampling inspection. The savings to the contractor,
   the producer, and the public are enormous.
5. Related to this is what has been a catch-22 for some companies:
   "We want to slash waste by producing small lots. But we need
   large lots to sample out of." (Sampling formulas and tables allow
   sampling smaller percentages as lot sizes get larger.) Now, the
   shift away from lot sampling and toward control charts removes
   the obstacle to small-lot JIT production and shipment.

   Jim Litz, manufacturing vice president at McNeil Pharmaceutical Company, reflects the new thinking. He is leading a
   campaign to slash the production throughput time for his company's famous product, Tylenol. The old industry standard for that
   type of product was twenty-four days; the target at McNeil is

twenty-four hours. Inspection has been one of the big delays. In the future all suppliers will be SPC-certified and using control charts, so Tylenol plants may be able to eliminate most or all incoming inspection.

$TQ = R_x$ for Personal Health

The number one object of TQ surely should be our own selves, that is, our personal health. Medical breakthroughs are fine. But basic, proven techniques of process control and improvement, starting with good data collection, are scarce in the medical profession.

For one thing, there is a lack of simple record keeping on whether the patient gets better. For another, patient-history records—on incidence of medical problems and treatments—are meager, scattered, and widely varying in format. In those terms, raw materials in pharmaceutical firms, machines in well-run factories, and airplanes in well-run airlines get much better care than patients do.

Furthermore, the medical profession is stuck on *product-out* instead of *customer-in* quality.[*] In medicine, customer-in quality means provider and patients jointly working things out according to the patients' own, usually very high, standards.

---

6. Control charts may be used to monitor a wide variety of worrisome processes: sales losses, returned merchandise, and travel expenses, for example. Zytec, a manufacturer of power supplies, uses control charts to monitor its financial forecast, which has had to be watched carefully following a "buyout" by the company's new owners. (An attempt also to monitor cash flow with control charts was not completely successful.)

7. Computer software is widely available for control charting. It can accept sample data, make control-limit calculations, and print out blank charts for operators to record on. That's fine. Some computer aids go beyond that—to where operators just

---

[*] These terms are in use at Weyerhaeuser, the lumber company: They are saying, Let's not just worry about getting a quality product out the door—as we, the provider, might define quality; bring our customer in and become fanatical about getting it right by that customer's standards.

enter readings on a key pad, which triggers automatic plotting. That's okay, too. But some companies send the data directly to quality engineering, and that's not okay. If operators don't own the data, they are out of the process-control loop—the same sad situation that existed before the quality earthquake.

WHERE'S THE PROBLEM?

We have been talking about gathering routine data, and making data recording (and data ownership) a normal part of each employee's job. Everyone's job should also include improvement projects using special data. We'll consider five tools for this: process flow chart, Pareto chart, fishbone chart, lot plot, and scatter diagram.

Process Flow Chart

A simple, old-fashioned tool, the process flow chart, is a natural format for documenting the process. Boxes on the flow chart show actions, and the arrows show sequence. When a process team tries to flow-chart a complex process, they are likely to debate each box and arrow— and revise most of them several times.

Signetics, a semiconductor manufacturer, makes process flow charting an early step in each process improvement effort. "If we don't know what the process is, we can't improve it."[7]

One Signetics project was to improve the work flow. It required operators to figure out how they set priorities at each step in a complex process flow. For years, this problem had resisted efforts to be pinned down. After three tries, the project team had the process charted right. It was an eye-opener for the manager, who saw that operators had been interpreting policies about priorities differently from what was intended. Policies were restated, and operators changed their method of selecting lots. The result was a 30 percent improvement in work-flow efficiency.

The point of this example, and the reason why the process flow chart is on most lists of SPC tools, is that just charting the process often clears up problems.

Pareto and Fishbone Charts

What about problems that do *not* clear up through flow charting? What's next?

In most cases the problem needs further definition. Pareto and fishbone charts, also found in every SPC tool kit, are ideal for the purpose.

Pareto and fishbone are a cup-and-saucer-like pair. While they are becoming widely used, I think project teams tend to flit through them too quickly. In many cases, they need to be recycled, starting at a coarse level of analysis and proceeding to a fine and maybe a superfine level. Figure 5–3 is a deliberately trivial example, one that is easy to understand. (A nontrivial example of Pareto was shown in Figure 5–1.)

Incidence (coarse level). X has health problems—and doesn't need to flow-chart her life processes to pinpoint them. She gathers frequency

Figure 5–3. X's Health Problem

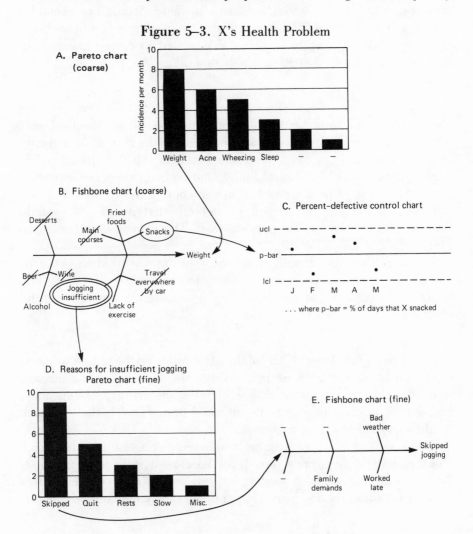

data on each problem and plots them in descending order as bars on a Pareto chart (part A of Figure 5–3). Weight problems dominate; they occur eight days per month. Acne, wheezing, sleep disorders, and others occur less often.

Causes (coarse level). The Pareto numerically highlights problem severity, but it doesn't say anything about causes. Next step is to make "weight problems" the spine of a fishbone chart, also known as a cause-and-effect chart. If weight is the effect, what are the causes? Main bones of the fish (part B of Figure 5–3) are labeled with answers: fried foods, desserts, alcohol, and lack of exercise. Three of those have secondary bones showing causes in more detail. For example, she succumbs to fried food in two ways: main courses and snacking.

"Okay," Ms. X says to herself. "I've zeroed in on the causes, but that doesn't tell me what to do about them."

Control chart. What should she do next? Set up one or more process control charts for causes (extremity bones) on the fishbone? Part C of Figure 5–3 shows how Ms. X might do that. It is a record of percent of days per month that she snacked. All the plotted points are staying between the control limits, and no bad trends are apparent. If a point were to plot above the upper control limit (ucl), it would tell Ms. X that she let herself go berserk that month. She would want to act decisively. But in what way? The control chart offers no hints. She's at a dead end.

The problem-solving path is not as short as we tried to make it. Let us see what happens if she does another round of Pareto and fishbone, instead of leaping all the way from coarse fishbone to control charting.

Incidence (fine level). Any of the extremities on the coarse fishbone chart can be looked at more intensively. Ms. X draws a line through what she thinks are lesser causes, circles the more pressing ones, and double circles the one to be attacked first. (This is the approach used by project teams at Signetics.)[8]

Ms. X double-circles "Jogging insufficient." She gathers data for a month, plotting them on a finer-level Pareto—part D of Figure 5–3. We see that she skipped jogging entirely nine times. Lesser causes are quitting too early, too many rests, ran too slowly, and miscellaneous.

Causes (fine level). Pareto's partner, the fishbone, comes next (part E of Figure 5–3), with "skipped jogging" as the spine. X isolates several causes (main bones), including bad weather, family demands, and worked late.

Still another, finer, Pareto-fishbone stage could come next. Ms. X doesn't think it's necessary. At this point she's ready to attack some of the causes directly:

- *Bad weather?* X decides to buy a rain hat and rain-resistant jogging suit she has been eyeing.
- *Worked late?* Time to talk to the boss, especially since the company supports "wellness" and being physically fit.
- *Family demands?* X thinks it simply boils down to better communication within the family: Who plans to do what and when? Easier said than done. Ms. X is thinking she ought to collect some evidence of how often communication lapses cause someone in the family to have to reschedule. The data could go on a superfine Pareto. Or should it be a lot plot?

Lot Plot

Sometimes a cause on a fishbone chart is worth investigating using a lot plot, which is a bar chart showing the "spread" of a set of measurements (a lot) taken from a process. The measurements might consist of samples from a lot shipped in from a supplier, or it could be all the items in a day's processing.

Time for a quiz. Figure 5–4 shows four lot plots.[9] Upper and lower specification limits are labeled *S*. What does each lot plot show about the process?

I hope your evaluations agree with these:

Plot A. Process seems capable of staying within specs, and it is centered nicely between the spec limits.

Plot B. Process is centered well, but is not capable; too many points fall outside the limits.

Plot C. Process is set too high. Looks like inspection has sorted out high-side defectives, which are costly in scrap or rework. Also, inspection device is calibrated wrong, accepting units that are just out of spec.

Plot D. Units from two different lots, one good and one bad, may have been mixed together.

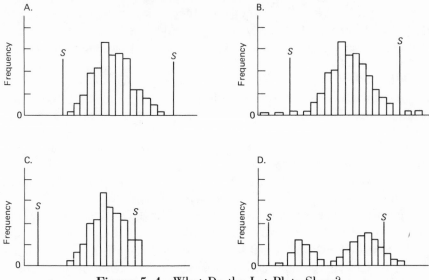

Figure 5–4. What Do the Lot Plots Show?

Scatter Diagram

Like the lot plot, a scatter diagram reveals things by its shape. What it reveals is whether the process factor of interest rises and falls in tandem with some other factor.

For example, do errors go up when it gets hot in the office? Looks like it in Figure 5–5. The shaded band spreading across most of the points shows that as temperature rises, so do errors. Among possible solutions, fans come to mind. It would be wise to check other possibilities on separate scatter diagrams: correlation of errors with humidity, for example. Maybe it's not the heat, but the humidity.

Scatter diagrams are easy to understand, a fine addition to the problem-solving team's tool kit. (And it is *not* necessary to inject statistics,

Figure 5–5. Correlation of Office Temperature with Error Rate

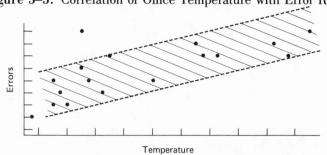

Temperature

such as correlation coefficients, into the analysis. The diagrams tell enough by visual inspection.)

Visual Control and Management

A striking feature of the tools we've discussed, compared with conventional management tools, is *they're visual*. As profound as any of the lessons of the eighties is the discovery that visual devices can take over much of the management of company operations. Managers making use of the visuals include operators, teams, supervisors, professional experts—and manager-managers.

My point is that the plotting of data about processes and problems *makes people managers of their processes*. Knowing that vital up-to-the-minute data is always on display in work areas and in team meeting rooms, experts and managers tend to spend more time in those places interacting with operators and current problems.

TOOLS FOR QUICK RESPONSE

The visual methods we've considered for watching the process are general—helpful on a wide spectrum of problems. It's time to look at special tools, namely a few that attack delay and foster quick response.

Response Ratios

In gauging their progress in quick response, many firms have gravitated toward the same approach. I'll call it the *response ratio,* which is a ratio of actual time to minimum time for work to flow through the processes. (Some companies turn the ratio upside down and end up with a percentage.)

One semiconductor manufacturer has a goal of 3 to 1: Three minutes elapsed time for every minute of actual processing (when value is added to the wafer or chip); the two minutes of delay are queue time, move time, and so forth. The company's past ratio might have been 50 to 1 or 100 to 1, and the plan is to chip away at the ratio: 30 to 1, then 20 to 1, and so on, relentlessly aiming at the 3 to 1 goal. (Note: I would want to ask the company about the unit of measure. Is it one die, one wafer, or one lot of wafers? In wafer fabrication, if it's one wafer, 3 to 1 is a properly ambitious target; otherwise, perhaps not.)

Should we expect much employee involvement as the company pursues its 3 to 1 goal? I think not. How can an individual or small team relate to a quick-response measure for the whole plant?

Fortunately, the quick-response ratio is a versatile tool. It can work for a single machine or a cell, where it has a much better chance of affecting people's work lives. At the employee level, where we may call it the *micro-response ratio,* it is more meaningful if expressed in pieces instead of in minutes.

Assume four clerks are in a four-station cell processing invoices. Each of their desks, plus tables in between, is piled high with invoices waiting their turn for processing. The clerks do a quick count and find 400 invoices in the flow. Since only four can be worked on at one time—one for each clerk—the response ratio is 400 to 4 or 100 to 1. That's 99 in a state of delay for each invoice being worked on. Intolerable!

The team works out a plan: No more than four invoices shall be allowed per desk, including one in process. To make the rule stick, each desk gets a three-high stack of in-basket trays. Bottom tray is green, middle yellow, and top red, and the rule is to fill them in that order. If the red tray already holds an invoice, the preceding clerk has to stop, or move over to help at the next desk. (The rules apply whether the daily invoice load is high or low. On busy days the supervisor pitches in, or the team works overtime.)

Someone may refer to the color-coding as "kindergarten stuff." But the team insists on it. They favor its clarity and discipline. And they'd like people to notice and ask about it, because in cutting the invoices in the flow from 400 to 16, they have slashed throughput time 16-fold!

In a factory, unlike an office, a quick reduction from 400 pieces to 16 would not be so easy: too many obstacles, such as machine breakdowns, rework, model changeovers, and late arrival of parts. A factory team would want to commit to cutting the ratio in stages—for example, as is shown in Figure 5–6: The current average is 400 pieces among the four work stations. The plan is to be at 200 pieces after two months, 100 after six months, 50 after nine months, and 30 after twelve months. They put the time-phased plan on large poster board, sign their names, and mount it on the wall. The team uses the tools of data collection, analysis, and problem-solving to meet the plan. They lean heavily on other resources, such as maintenance and manufacturing engineering, to overcome delay problems. Like the invoice team,

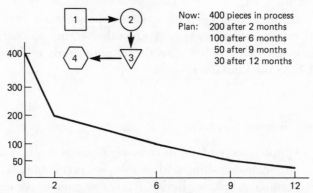

Figure 5–6. Plan-Driven JIT *(Planners: operators or JIT team)*

they may use fixed trays to keep queues from growing—the *kanban* system.

Kanban

These days, *kanban* (a term from the Japanese) is used broadly; it refers to about any visual device that strictly limits length of a waiting line and authorizes work. The invoice team's kanbans were the green, yellow, and red trays.

Today, most assembly of mainframe computers, large copiers, mass spectrometers, and certain other bulky, nonvehicular products is done on "kanban squares," which are boxes lined off on the floor with tape or paint. It is common to allow one or two large squares for final assembly and a smaller nearby square for each major subassembly and component assembly. The focus is on getting a unit onto and off a square quickly, with no delays and perfect quality.

Before kanban squares came into use, it was typical for an assembly floor to be choked with units in final and subassembly, most of them stuck in a state of delay for one reason or another. Under the discipline of kanban squares, things *have to* be made to work—harmoniously from one process to the next. In the new mode, some companies are hard put to figure out what to do with all the empty floor space.

Literally translated, kanban refers to a visible record, such as a card. When cards are used as kanban, they must be printed with part number, source, destination, and quantity. If there are six cards for a given part number, they allow no more than six units, or six containers of the part.

Squares on work benches, designated openings in rack storage, and labeled recirculating containers are other forms of kanban. Container-kanban may be labeled with detachable cards or identification plates riveted to the container.

The Human Side of Kanban

Kanban is a simple mechanistic device, right? It is really much more. It is an aid to team-building and employee involvement. Consider the usual nonkanban situation: Between any two successive employees, the time delay—represented by inventory—is uncontrolled and usually large. With so much time separation, people cannot see themselves as a team.

Kanban, on the other hand, permits only a small time gap (e.g., the time for one, two, or three work units to move forward). It's almost like a bucket brigade, or like rapid-fire touch-passing in basketball.

Kanban is also known as the *pull system*: I grab the unit from the kanban square on my left and work on it; the now-empty square "pulls" more work onto it from you at the preceding work station. It pulls,

---

Self-Directed Work Groups

Square D Corporation's medium-voltage switchgear plant has its work force organized into "self-directed work groups." A group is thirty to forty people, including a "product production manager" and a materials analyst. (Materials people formerly worked for the materials department, an overhead group.)

It works like a charm in two new "bus-bar fabrication cells," which are linked by kanban to final assembly. Since kanban schedules itself, the cells don't have to worry about coordination with their customer, final assembly. They just keep up with the flow of kanban, apply for overtime as needed, and focus on quality, training, and hiring. Next step is for the groups to set their own goals and do their own performance evaluations.

because that's the rule: Fill the empty square, so you don't cause the next process to come to a halt.

Processes and people are tightly connected under pull. Not so under the push system, when work is pushed out according to a schedule, work orders, intermittent batches or lots, or the pace of a conveyor.

Wait a minute, you might say: Does a conveyor push, or does it pull? Or is this a chicken-or-egg question?

Actually, it's a good question. Until recently, conveyors always pushed. That, at least, was the general feeling: "No time to think; here comes another unit." Or, "Not enough time to do it right; let 'em fix it in rework." Charlie Chaplin, in *Modern Times*, knew the feeling.

The onslaught of total-quality thinking is making such views obsolete. In major appliance and automotive companies, it is now common for assemblers to have access to line-stop switches (or ways to uncouple the work from the conveyor's movement). Under the new rules assemblers are to stop (or slow) the line to get the quality right. The assembler, in other words, has control of the "pull" rate of the conveyor—no more relentless pushing of goods forward by an unseen outside force. The pull system, in other words, is partly a state of mind, a feeling of being in control.

While kanban is excellent for controlling process-to-process delay, something different is needed for process changeovers: carefully orchestrated speed.

Quick-Change Artistry

Stage crews are famous for their quick-change skills. I've also admired convention services people in hotels where I conduct seminars. They seem to arrive *en masse* at exactly 4:30 (or whenever the seminar is scheduled to end), and they have a banquet set up almost before I can gather my papers. But the best-oiled change machine in the world surely is the pit crew in an auto race. It can change four tires, fill the gas tank, wipe the windshield, and squirt Gatorade in the driver's mouth in seconds.

Now, in most manufacturing industries the same quick-change concepts are being applied to machines, dies, molds, work pieces, loading and unloading, and quality adjustments. In many cases changeover or setup times have fallen from hours to single-digit minutes.

The quick-change concepts can get detailed, but I'll mention four general ones, the first being a special case:

1. The ideal is *no* changeover—which is possible for some star products having volumes high enough to justify their own dedicated equipment (e.g., a surgical room just for obstetrics).
2. Tools and equipment are devised specially for quick-change purposes. Air-cushion rollers to move scenery on a stage or heavy dies at a machine are examples. Where quality tests and adjustments are part of the changeover, operators have their own gauges and portable test kits and are trained in their use by quality technicians.
3. The setup person (or team) and all setup devices are on hand and ready at the instant changeover is to begin. (Changeover hand tools hanging on pegboards attached to the machine have become a common site in today's better factories.)
4. If access space permits, changeover is a *team* effort: The team is practiced, all members know their assignments, and they perform in parallel. This usually requires a base crew, plus others borrowed from nearby jobs whenever an important changeover is scheduled. The team may need time-phased sequence charts, practice time, and synchronized watches.

Today, unlike ten years ago, whole new classes of diskette-driven quick-change machines are on the market. One can also buy quick-change clamps, rollers, and other accessories to mount on existing machines. Engineering textbooks now treat the subject, which they didn't do formerly.

Notwithstanding what's for sale, most improvements are operator-driven. An early step often is for operators to videotape present methods. First improvements usually are rearranging, relocating, and providing places for things. (For example, provide movie theater patrons and airplane passengers with plastic bags for their trash.) Such simple, commonsense changes often can cut changeover time (including cleanup) in half.

Next, after the easy changes, look for ways to modify equipment: Operators dream up the ideas, engineers draw the blueprints, and toolmakers alter the equipment (e.g., trash pouches designed into theater or airline seats.) Modifications involve either taking away or adding to:

- *Taking away*. Remove or immobilize unneeded adjustment cranks, knobs, buttons, and switches. For example, if a keyboard is being used just for alphabetic characters, devise a cover for top-row numeric keys. This *prevents* unwanted changeover (from alpha to numeric) and makes the general-purpose keyboard a special-purpose one.

Taking away is suitable for *most machines*, because most are equipped with things the buyer doesn't want, but that others might. So after purchase, the equipment buyer should always look for features to blank out. (If needs change, put the machine back the way it was.) Besides speeding up changes, taking away also prevents errors: wrong settings and unintended changes in settings during operations.

- *Add to.* Add guide tracks, locator pins, alignment devices, glides, stops, and the like. These are what you don't get when you buy the machine or the building. And you don't want to pay the maker for customizing it for your special needs. You do it yourself—and then redo it every time your needs change.

FAIL-SAFING

Sometimes there is a thin line between achieving quick change and fail-safing. Much of what is taken off or added on for speedy changes also prevents random mishaps. Also, fail-safing and quick-change study methods are much the same.

Fail-safing, however, has a broader range of purposes, all of them preventive: prevention of defects, nonconformities, overspending, wasting time, late arrival, entering wrong data, breakdowns, overloading, omitting steps, operating before warmup of lubricants—the examples are endless. So are the methods of fail-safing: governors on engines, error subroutines in computer programs, and warning lights on dashboards, for instance.

Fail-safing can be elaborate but often isn't. In Durban, South Africa, at a Toyota engine plant, it was important to make sure all engine bolts were properly torqued down. Three operators had the job; and, to make sure, three quality control people did it all over again.

Someone came up with a simple fail-safing device that eliminated the duplication: a dollop of paint in the torque wrench sockets. When operators tighten the bolts, traces of paint show up on bolt heads, making it easy to detect any that were not torqued.

While engineers and toolmakers are often involved in fail-safing, sometimes there is no need. The photos in Figure 5–7 refer to a commonsense, fail-safing method that engineers (like myself) would be unlikely to think of. The example is from a Ferguson TV plant on the outskirts of London, England.

The problem was that TVs were getting damaged when the conveyors stopped or jerked: Being front-heavy (the center of gravity of solid-state TVs is well forward of center), they toppled forward onto their faces.

The engineers got the project. They designed a new type of carrier to replace the plain wooden pallets. It featured side bars to hold the TV sets upright when the conveyor stops. The cost to equip the whole plant with these fancy fail-safing carriers: 250,000 pounds sterling (over $400,000). Ray Canton, director of production—and an ardent advocate of simplicity—said, "No way!"

Canton reassigned the project to operations. Their fail-safe solution was strips of velcro cemented to the old wooden pallets, and bean bags velcroed to the strips. The bean bags raise the front of the TV, which shifts the center of gravity backward. That keeps it upright. The cost: negligible.

Figure 5–7. Conveyor Line at Ferguson TV

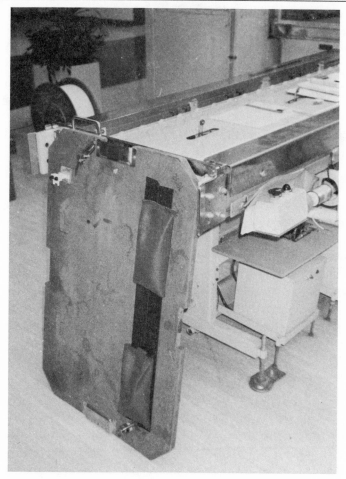

Figure 5–7 *continued*

TOTAL PREVENTIVE MAINTENANCE

A common by-product of quick setup and fail-safing improvements is making equipment work better and break down less often. Just as the world-class company wants zero defects, it strives for zero break-downs.

The set of methods for moving toward that goal is called total preventive (or productive) maintenance (TPM). New books and writings on the subject cover mostly familiar ground: classical PM, as presented in standard plant maintenance books. The only really new concept—

which is the all-important foundation of TPM—is that the operator assumes responsibility, and ultimately comes to feel a sense of "ownership" of the equipment.

It starts small. For one thing, the operator takes charge of keeping a thorough machine history, which is used for the classical PM purpose: Feed history into computers, which churn out advice on replacing components before failure or wear-our.

For another, the operator takes over small PM tasks, such as lubrication, cleaning, and tightening. Maintenance technicians teach and monitor, much as quality technicians do under total quality. They help upgrade the operator's technical capabilities—until, perhaps, the operator really *is* a technician. This is important to the future of business and industry in view of the scarcity of technicians in an increasingly technological society.

Operator duties may also include: controlling or knowing the availability and adequacy of spare parts; knowing, using, improving, and maintaining machine manuals, drawings, and maintenance checklists; and knowing how to request maintenance assistance and how to do an equipment study and make a presentation.

TEAM ATTACK—IN EVERY INDUSTRY

The tools of process control and improvement that we have considered (and others not considered) are for all jobholders. While those tools can work wonders, we should not forget the message of Chapter 2: The best tool is close connection and communication along the chain of customers.

The soundest approach of all is a combination: a focused team fully involved in data collection and problem-solving. We've examined a few cases in this and earlier chapters. But sometimes it is hard to see how to get the right people together.

Distribution

Consider, for example, my friend who drives for a grocery wholesaler. Call him Terry. Terry rages about waste and inefficiency. He tells me, for example, about how sheet metal lining inside walls of trailers sometimes gets torn. The jagged metal rips every pallet load of goods as they are loaded. Wasted food litters the trailer floor. Sometimes the rip gets written up and fixed promptly by the shop, but often it doesn't.

Terry can go on for an hour recounting the improper ways that trailers get loaded. For example, heavy items on top squashing boxes of potato chips on the bottom; high pallets for store A loaded next to low pallets for store B, so that at the first stop sign the high one falls over and creates a mess.

Terry tells me, as well, about drivers dumping loads of "mispicked" stock into dumpsters when grocery store people say, "We didn't order that." I also hear about flocks of birds that keep watch in the loading area, hoping someone will fail to shut a trailer door. It happens all too often, spreading bird droppings all over the trailer and its load.

The solution to these problems: Organize a few teams and get them plotting data and holding brainstorming meetings. A team might include a dispatcher, stock picker, loader, driver, shop mechanic, and store representative. Their work sites are geographically scattered, but no matter. The company needs to make time for them to get together, if only a few times a year.

Between meetings, each team member gathers data, perhaps on check sheets. Some team members meet in pairs daily in their normal jobs (e.g., driver and loader); the telephone is available for all others. As people communicate, they work out solutions to problems. Where possible, team members implement the solutions; otherwise, they prepare proposals and make presentations on their ideas.

Airplanes

It's hard enough to get truck drivers together into chain-of-customer teams. It is much tougher for airline cabin crews, who live out of suitcases and have to introduce themselves each time they fly. While most airlines make use of check sheets, the hitch is that the data are examined and acted upon by people other than those who record them.

Figure 5–8 shows two of the check sheets used by Delta Airlines. (Delta is a good example, since its crews record more data than most other airlines.) The "defective catering unit placard" applies to a rather major, specific problem. It probably gets the job done rather well. The "cabin service supply request" is a long list; it won't get much attention when the flight is full and the attendants are run ragged— *and when the worst problems occur.*

Do we have a "no-EI" situation here? It need not be so. With creativity and persistence, and perhaps some trial and error, process

Form 0412-80476
PLACARD 5-83
SP 170

DELTA AIR LINES

DEFECTIVE CATERING UNIT PLACARD

☐ FAULTY PLUG
☐ WILL NOT HEAT
☐ LEAKS
☐ OTHER _____

☐ LATCH/DOOR BROKEN
☐ BRAKES DO NOT HOLD/RELEASE
☐ CARRIER BENT/WARPED

REMARKS: _____
_____
_____

FLIGHT # _____ DATE _____ SHIP # _____

STATION: _____   STATION PARTS TAG/
SHIPPING TICKET # _____

DELTA AIR LINES

CABIN SERVICE SUPPLY REQUEST   0412-80731
REQUEST 5-86

FLT/DATE _____ / _____

STA _____ F or Y or LG (circle one)

	QUANTITY		QUANTITY
* PLASTIC GLASSES	____	PEANUTS	____
* FOAM COFFEE CUPS	____	*COFFEE — JAR/PILLOW	____
* PLASTIC COFFEE CUPS	____	*CREAMER	____
SPOONS	____	*SUGAR	____
STIRRERS	____	*SWEET N' LOW	____
TRAY LINERS	____	SALT/PEPPER	____
TABLE CLOTHS	____	TEA BAGS	____
LINEN NAPKINS	____	CHOCOLATE	____
* COCKTAIL NAPKINS	____	SANKA	____
* BUFFET TOWELS	____	PLAYING CARDS	____
• COCA-COLA	____	LIQUOR - FORMS/ENVELOPE	____
* TAB	____	*SHOPPING BAGS	____
* DIET COKE	____	JR WINGS	____
* 7-UP/SPRITE	____	FUN TIME BOOKS	____
* DIET 7-UP/SPRITE	____	FIRST RIDER CERTIFICATE	____
* GINGERALE	____	TIMETABLES	____
• TONIC	____	SUPPLY REQUEST FORM	____
* CLUB SODA	____	KNIFE	____
* BLOODY MARY MIX	____	ICE TONGS	____
* TOMATO JUICE	____	BUFFET TAPE	____
* GRAPEFRUIT JUICE	____	HEADSETS	____
• APPLE JUICE	____	ANACIN/TYLENOL	____
• ORANGE JUICE	____	DRAMAMINE	____
OLIVES	____	BAND AIDS	____
LIQUOR KITS		FREQ. FLYER APPLICATIONS	____
KITS TO DEPLANE:		ICE	____
_____ _____		*EMPTY TRASH	____
_____ _____		F/A KIT	____

(*) DENOTES ITEMS AVAILABLE (LIMITED QUANTITY)
AT THESE STATIONS:

BTR   CSG   FWA   MLU   PHX   SRQ   TOL
CHA   DAB   MLB   MOB   PNS   TLH

NO SUPPLIES AVAILABLE: BDA   MCN   NAS

Flight Attendant _____ Agent _____

Figure 5–8. Check Sheets at Delta Airlines

control and improvement can be a part of work life for anyone—flight attendants included.

Perhaps chain-of-customer team meetings should be held right after some (not all) trips; the team might include one or more representatives from the flight attendants, gate attendants, catering and cleanup crews—maybe even a volunteer passenger. One item on the team's agenda would be design of forms that are more service-oriented—for example, number of times a problem or complaint occurs. The current forms concern supplies and equipment, not errors and complaints. Another agenda item might be modifying the employee performance rating system to include contributions to improvement.

WHEN EMPLOYEES ARE INVOLVED . . .

When the work force mounts an attack on variation, error, waste, delay, and other evils, as outlined in this chapter, it transforms the company. Rates of improvement (if there are any to begin with) take off. Without involvement of the whole, improvement is in the hands of too few people, whose interests tend to be narrow and poorly directed.

What about firms that have always tried to be improvement minded? In the absence of employee involvement, they can only watch the growth of another type of waste: enlarged staff departments and extra hierarchical layers. In recent years, companies of all kinds have seen fit—or been forced—to cut out layers and lop off overhead. Too many of them did so without rolling out an EI crusade, which leaves *nobody* to mind the controls.

Enough companies have done it right, however, to make an impressive list. Those firms have few layers and smaller staffs, and remaining experts' and managers' lives are forever changed for the better. They have hundreds of allies—the front-line employees—in the cause of process control and improvement. They have access to detailed on-the-spot data about important goings-on, so that decision-making is easier and less risky. They have good reasons to go to where the action is on a regular basis, which keeps them closely in touch with the workings of the business. And their traditional narrow outlook is replaced by breadth of understanding of the effects of one thing on many others in the chain. Those with ambition are well served by the experience.

6

∞

The Learning Organization

IN MY HASTE to relate, in the last chapter, the powerful message of an unchained work force, I didn't say how to get there from here. Also, nothing was said about how long it takes. That's a lot like asking how long it takes to become an educated person. The obvious answer is, You don't. You just keep learning.

It is the same in a healthy, improving business. All employees, from CEO to bottom-scale new-hire, get on the path of continuous learning and don't ever get off. To see where we're going with continuous learning, it is necessary to see what we are escaping from.

NO LEARNING

I recall this from a motivational speech I heard years ago. An indignant employee was saying, "But how can they lay me off? They need me. I know my job inside out. I have thirty years of experience." Answer: "No, you don't. You have one year of experience repeated thirty times."

The audience laughed. A clever punch line. But not one that made people uneasy, not one that required any definable action.

These days, many of us would react differently to that line. It exposes a raw nerve, addresses a devastating flaw. It describes the organization that won't (or wouldn't) let its members learn. Probably it is the organization you work for.

You may argue that your firm is different. It has always sent managers and staff experts to seminars, paid their dues for education-oriented societies, and subsidized night classes at the local college. Moreover, you may say, your company has a large training staff, and all first-level employees go through a formal training program, followed by on-the-job skills training.

If so, you are above average, but that is not enough. If it were, you wouldn't be so anxious to have your senior people take early retirement. Your experts are up-to-date all right—but in just a single specialty. After X decades of employment, your people have a permanent set of blinders on. They don't see themselves in a chain of customers; in fact the customer is "the problem," maybe the enemy.

Regarding your first-level employees, formal training is narrow and brief—a one-shot deal. They are expected to stay in their skill category and leave control and improvement to the experts.

ROOTS OF WORK RULES

It is easy to find reasons why employees get pigeonholed. Spectacular successes at Ford Motor Company in the 1920s electrified the world, and it didn't take industry long to learn that one of the secrets was *division of labor*: Break a big job into many small ones. To paraphrase Henry Ford, Man number one puts the bolt in the hole, but does not put a nut on it. Man number two puts a nut on, but does not tighten it. Man number three tightens the nut.[1]

With jobs so trivialized, just hire unskilled warm bodies off the street at minimum wages, and they can be up to speed the first day.

Man the Ladders!

Bill Rutledge, former executive vice president at Emerson Electric Company, was inspirational change master when the company kicked off its just-in-time crusade in about 1984. He liked to tell Emerson audiences of a job titled *climber-peeker*. A small company acquired by Emerson had inventory piled so high that the jobholder climbed ladders to peek over the top to see what was there.

Nothing need be spent on training. Keep the employee in that job forever, and nothing ever need be spent on training.

In time that pat formula for low-cost production fell apart. Those little jobs became entrenched. The company gave job titles to each one (bolt putter? nut turner?) and hired costly staffers to maintain the system: Wage and classification experts studied the jobs and set different wage rates on each; time study analysts timed them; production controllers counted output so the paymaster could pay efficiency incentives. If there was a union, it put its stamp of approval on all of it: a contract grounded in work rules.

In another setback, the system's originator, Ford Motor Company, nearly went bankrupt; its production lines kept turning out basic black Model Ts while the market began to demand variety. The industry had to figure out a low-cost way to produce sporty models with rumble seats and luxury models with endless options.

The answer was *not* to train people and go for versatility and flexibility. In a misguided attempt to hold down costs, narrow specialization was preserved. The modified system was to group people by specialty (e.g., drill press operators in one area, subassemblers in another) and have them build the proliferation of component models, sizes, and colors in large lots or batches, which went into low-cost storage. Industry stocked up.

Batch manufacturing made factories big, wasteful, and enormously complex. Experts of all kinds were hired (cost accountants here, inspectors there). Costs went up, but the batch system was not seen as the problem.

Every attempt to rein in costs had the opposite effect. Producers installed bigger, faster machines, which drove labor costs down but usually just filled stockrooms faster and fuller. It also created needs for specialists to manage the new costs: installation, tooling, setup, maintenance, process planning, inventory records, machine scheduling, and so forth. Stop-and-go factory life, revolving around batch production, is stop-and-go for the growing staffs of specialists, too. Between batch runs, the experts retreat to their offices (to their own kind).

What I am saying is that batch production created needs for non-value-adding specialists who gravitated into specialities. Once grouped that way, we protect territorial rights and seek to learn (if at all) in our own specialty, not someone else's. Since much of the service industry has copied manufacturing, right down to processing documents in batches and suffering customers to wait in long lines, it suffers the same problems.

Frederick's Fault? (I)

It's popular sport to blame Frederick W. Taylor, father of scientific management (circa 1900), for the excesses of specialization. It's true that Taylor advocated "functional foremanship"—a foreman for every specialty. It never caught on.

That does not whitewash Taylorism. But much of the specialization trend is traceable to later events. Following World War II, marketing people moved into high positions; later financial people took over. Neither group knew much about production, engineering, quality, scheduling, maintenance, and so forth. They delegated those things to growing layers of specialists who had free-wheeling authority.

Business schools and fast-growing professional societies certified the specialists, who carried their ways into banking, health care, government, and elsewhere.

To summarize, the system of no learning and hemmed-in work lives was developed to keep costs low. We tried it for seventy years. It has been an outright failure. Today, the highest costs are in plants and offices that cling to that system. Training costs are tiny compared with the costs that grew to avoid training. Time for a sharp reversal—everyone a learner, and a teacher as well.

STANDING IN YOUR CUSTOMER'S (SUPPLIER'S) SHOES

And what should we learn? No problem there. The earthquakes that have rumbled in all the business functions provide a full curriculum.

For lower-level employees, first step—because it requires little preparation or materials—is cross-training: You teach me, I teach you. Then we switch jobs, often—and extend teach-learn-switch to the whole team.

Cross-Training in Cells and Flow Lines

Cross-training is easy and natural when focused cells or flow lines—natural teams—have been formed. As a start, adjacent people in the work flow can easily train each other and trade jobs.

Frederick's Fault? (II)

Frederick Taylor is the father of work study: improving and timing the work, after first breaking it into elements—the division-of-labor idea. Perhaps this is why he is sometimes blamed for the modern problem of narrow skills.

Not fair. Division of labor has never been the problem. *Of course* it makes sense to divide up the work. The error is in keeping people chained to a singled divided task. Today's approach is still division of labor—made wholesome by adding cross-training, job switching, and process control and improvement responsibilities.

A supervisor told me that his people, who are in a cell, don't want to switch jobs. I told him that if his employees do not switch, the work place retains all the disadvantages of division of labor, namely, utter boredom, low self-worth, and use of just a small fraction of one's talents; low pay, too. I pointed out, in addition, that without switching a major benefit of forming cells is lost: People who don't learn their customer's or supplier's jobs cannot effectively team up with them for joint problem-solving.

Cross-Training across Distance

Sometimes cross-training has distance to span. Next process might be in the lab, the kitchen, the back loading dock. Or perhaps it involves a massive machine that cannot be located next to you or your group. It may be in the next plant, yours or your customer's. In those cases, special measures must be taken to keep knocking down the chimneys that rise around separated groups. Here are several examples, the first being the extreme case of plant-to-plant distance to span:

- Robinson Nugent, Inc., a producer of electronic components, has developed a "Partners in Quality" program of employee education. One part of it has Robinson Nugent employees and customer representatives exchange plant visits with key customers. The object is see-for-yourself awareness of how to better serve customers' needs. One major customer is Xerox, and the visits have inspired Robinson Nugent employees to put up signs and wear T-shirts proclaiming, "I'm part of the Xerox team."[2]

Other companies are following similar reasoning: Slow day coming up? Let's *not* send our employees home. We'll put them on a bus to learn something at the next plant.

In a few cases visiting employees do a turn on the production line at the next plant—seeing what happens when they try to use their materials in the customer's process. Exchanges of phone numbers follow, so that makers at one plant and users at the next can keep in close touch and resolve problems quickly.

Employees can also make good company representatives at trade shows—to see what's new that they could use or should learn more about. And why stop with trade shows? Where possible, send your people on tours of a competitor's facility.[3]

- Lechmere, Inc., a twenty-seven-store retail chain, has faced labor shortages in many of its store locations. Its plan, now in operation at several stores: pay by number of jobs learned. A cashier might fill in selling hardware, and a clerk might learn to drive a forklift on the back dock. Incentive-based cross-training was first tried out in a new store Lechmere was opening in Sarasota, Florida. Productivity soared, which cut total labor needs. The store also enjoys higher work force stability: 60 percent of employees are full-time, versus 30 percent for the company's stores still under the old system.[4]

- An office furniture plant has four processes: sheet metal, welding, painting, and final assembly. The last two, painting and assembly, produce "to the order book." Since the same order book governs both processes, one would expect them to be closely synchronized; yet their schedules, shifts, and priorities never match. They operate almost as two different companies, though they are on the same floor of a single building.

  The solution to their poor coordination: setting up a "SWAT team" of about ten assemblers who learn how to hang and remove parts from hooks on the paint chain, to clean paint guns, and so forth. When paint is in trouble—lots of repainting (it happens often)—the SWAT team rushes to the rescue. The absence of team members cuts output in assembly, but that's not bad. It is good, because problems in paint soon cause assembly to run short of painted components anyway.

Lend Me Your Best

A focused group should not be too independent and aloof. When demand is great, it will need to borrow labor from another focused group—and will want to lend its excess people when demand is down. But when you borrow from the next team, do they send their top people—the experienced who can fit in easily? Not on your life. You get the dregs.

That's the way it is—and the way it was at the Sittard (Netherlands) plant of Philips Components Group, a site consisting of seven product-focused plants. One manager broke the cycle; he lent his *best* people. At a managers' meeting others commented on his unusual action. He explained that he did it so that other managers would do the same for him. They did. Now it's standard practice.

Does it really matter? It does indeed. When another team is shorthanded, *they are in trouble*—failing to meet commitments. They *need* your best person, and you don't. This isn't just being nice to a fellow supervisor. It is doing the right thing—period.

- Hotels and motels experience surges of activity several times a day. Employee flexibility is badly needed. Yet the lodging industry (the major chains, at least) did what manufacturing did: chained everybody to a job classification. Laundry people launder, maids do rooms, housepersons vacuum halls and replenish linen supplies in the mech room, convention services staff set up and tear down conferences, and so forth.

  Problems occur all the time: equipment broken down, shortages of light bulbs or clean towels, convention services short five people. Cross-training and job-switching would help. A couple of housekeepers switch with two people in laundry, see the problems from another viewpoint, and quickly the towel shortage problem is resolved—without buying more towels. House "boys" sometimes drive the airport shuttle van and help set up chairs in conference rooms.

  Embassy Suites is one of the few lodging companies that makes a serious commitment to employee development—and a more flexible, knowledgeable work force. Typically, about 25 percent of Embassy's total employees are in company-sponsored training for a better-paid job. Passing a course does not move the employee right into the new job but does result in an immediate pay raise. If, say, a housekeeper passes the course for a front-desk job, pay goes up 25 cents an hour, and the housekeeper gets chances to fill in on the front desk.[5]

At the Marriott Hotel in Toronto, I was surprised to walk by the coat-check room in mid-morning (after the rush) and see the coat-check lady at a sewing machine. I guessed that she was hemming cloth napkins that had come undone. She is a versatile employee. Just what the lodging business needs.

- At General Electric's jet engine parts plant in Bromont, Quebec, every office employee is required to spend one day per month in the shop—a different task each time.
- The "process" industry is rife with examples—even in mining. Cypress Minerals Company in Arizona has shaken up the industry a bit with its new labor policies. In the aftermath of a clash with the union, the company slashed job classifications from 240 to nine and now offers miners raises for learning multiple jobs.[6]

In pharmaceuticals, those manning the big mixers, the smaller tableting machines, and the long packaging lines are separated because of great size and shape differences among the three processes. The same is true in the sheet-coating industry: Chemical solutions are prepared in mixers in a separate room, with pipes carrying the solutions to massive coating machines. Today, in both cases, leading companies are switching people and cross-training; one sure outcome is new ways of looking at problems, which are likely to improve process yields. It's a "new" idea in those industries—one whose time has come.

Crossing Organizational Lines

In these last examples, job switching would not take place weekly, daily, or twice per shift—as is done on some production lines. Instead, a pair from solutions and coating might trade jobs for six months or a year—maybe longer—because the technologies are quite different and not easy to master—and (probably) organizational lines are being crossed.

Usually, where organizational line-jumping is concerned, it is just a short hop: from sales to credit department, for example. Companies should also actively support a certain amount of "long jumping"—say, from plant maintenance to computer programming, or from assembler to technical writer (for the occasional highly literate assembler). This allows good people to pursue their preferences and career interests. It is valuable in its own right for inspiring people to generate novel ideas.

Multiyear Career Changes

New thinking about human development applies as well to technicians, professionals, and managers. Instead of cross-training and frequent job changes, it is multiyear career changes.

I recall going through the job interviewing mill as an about-to-graduate engineer years ago. First concern among us job-seekers, of course, was how the interviewer rated us; but we also rated the companies.

The Great Japanese Secret

There's little talk of Japanese management any more. That's partly because it is old news. It is also because those who wrote about it stressed the least important things—like quality circles and consensus management.

There is, however, one consistent strong belief among the early writers on Japanese management and those who wrote later about the real strengths, which were in quality, JIT, equipment policies, . . . and in *development of the broad view.*

Some of us Westerners, when we want to feel good about ourselves, point to Japan's gross underuse of half its human resources—the feminine half (who are generally excluded from influential occupations). Is the Western practice of pigeonholing people so much worse?

Japan may resolve its cultural weakness. It is much easier for the West to resolve its failing, which is noncultural: It is just a matter of adopting continuing programs of cross-training and cross-functional shifts of people. Until then, the broad view remains as the great Japanese strength, and the Western weakness is the lack of it.

Fellow students said, "If AT&T makes an offer, take it," citing AT&T's great, two-year management-training program.

That was a mighty commitment to training—in that era. No longer. The AT&T program, and lesser ones back then, just put you down for a few weeks or months here, then a few more there. You dabbled.

In most companies, employees do not even have the chance to dabble. Take a job as a buyer, and you're stuck—a buyer for life. Same for secretaries, bartenders, systems analysts, and forklift operators. To change occupations, you have to quit and start over at the bottom of the other one.

It's a woeful thing to do to an employee, and an appalling waste of the employee's *many* talents—kept bottled up by denial of the chance to learn other parts of the business.

Cross-Training Signboards

By now, cross-training has a good start in many, if not most, of the better-known manufacturing companies, though it is still unusual in services. But too many starts stall later, when things get busy. To make sure that cross-training "has legs," the plan needs to be emblazoned on the wall large enough for all to see. (Part of the power of visual management is that it publicly proclaims things that otherwise might get conveniently pushed aside.) Figure 6–1, photos from Milliken and Company (textile manufacturing), shows what I mean. (Milliken is a winner—along with Xerox Corp.—of the 1989 Baldrige Quality Award.)

Figure 6–1. Cross-Training at Milliken

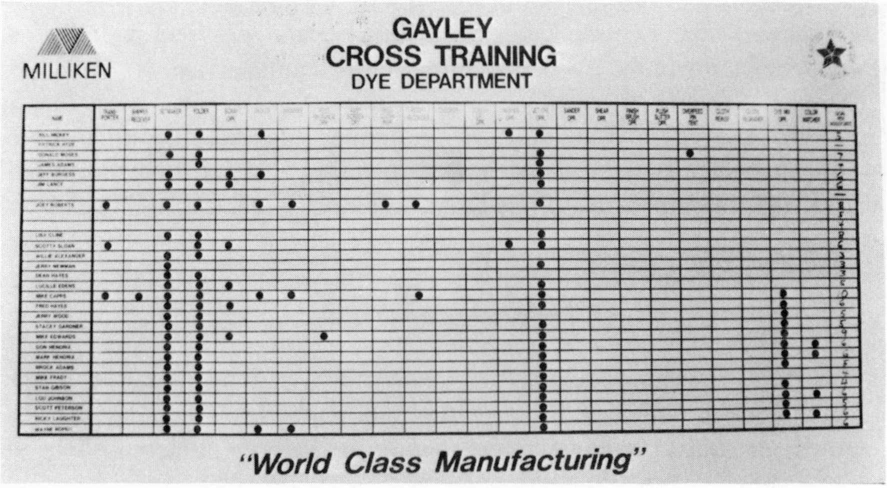

Figure 6–1 *continued*

The first photo, from the Gayley plant, names twenty-seven "associates" (Milliken doesn't use terms like employee or worker) and shows, by dots, jobs in the dye department that each is qualified for. Job names include transporter, shipper/receiver, setmaker, folder, spray operator, packer, and wrapper. Handwritten numbers in the rightmost column show the "goal per associate"; that is, the number of jobs each is committed to master.

The second photo, from the Humphrey plant, displays "vital signs" of progress and also the cross-training plan and status for the twenty-three listed associates. The status board is in three colors (not detectable in this black and white photo): green dot for home job, red for in-training, and blue for qualified.

These cross-training signboards show up now and then as I visit plants and offices around the world, but I don't see them nearly often enough. I'll not be satisfied until they are as common as safety reminders. It's just good management.

It is also good management to formalize the cross-training. Free-form "you-teach-me, I'll-teach-you" training may be okay for small firms that operate fluidly, but larger businesses need to tighten up.

FORMAL TRAINING

A complete learning program must teach, test, convince, and tie closely to implementation. It must be continuous, since evolving technologies, products, and management knowledge are facts of life that affect all businesses. A critical aim is to make everyone an expert in process control and improvement, but the core of the learning program is basic job skills.

Outside Assistance

Job skills range from basic (how to read) to applied (how to type) to specific (how to type a company requisition). Basic and applied job skills have gone downhill in recent decades in a few countries, notably, the U.S., Canada, and the U.K. At last, there are flurries of activity to fix the problem. Employers are teaming up with trade schools and community colleges, often with government funding.

General Electric got training help from ten organizations in and around its plant in Fitchburg, Massachusetts. GE had revamped its turbine business and needed to phase in seventy new machinists. The local chamber of commerce and the city development commission helped coordinate the effort; a state institution granted $128,000, and the regional private industry council kicked in the same; a community college trained the GE trainers and arranged space for the next training phase; a state agency screened more than five hundred applicants; another agency helped get dislocated people into the applicant pool; and the International Union of Electronic Workers offered support. Recruits received 176 hours of lecture and hands-on evening instruction over an eleven-week period. Training included blueprint reading, math, instrument reading, and use of lathes, grinders, and other machines. Four months of on-the-job training followed.[7]

Since agency funding is limited, it pays to be aggressive in seeking it—as Toyota was in the State of Kentucky. Governor Wallace Wilkinson found, after his election, that *most* of his state's share of federal training money is committed to Toyota.[8]

Among other imaginative ways of funding training, twelve small companies pooled their resources and organized the Texas Quality Consortium. The Consortium provides training on quality improvement to member companies.[9]

Inside Institutes

When a company is large enough, it can afford its own training institute. Many of the well-known companies have done so. For example, IBM has had training institutes of several kinds for years, inasmuch as retraining has been an IBM religion. McDonald's long-standing Hamburger University has played a central role in its success. General Electric's Crotonville management institute and Motorola's manufacturing institute have been acclaimed in recent years. Budd Company, supplier to the automotive industry, plans to invest $1 million in a training center having a focus on quality improvement.[10]

Companies that can't afford an institute have to rely on a variety of training resources. The important thing is to have a commitment, a budget, and a complete plan. Peter Drucker states that training has been the secret of success for the "four (or five) tigers" of Southeast Asia—South Korea, Taiwan, Singapore, and Hong Kong (and perhaps Thailand):

> What these countries did was quite new. They took an American invention of World War II—it was called "training" and it enabled the U.S. during the war years to change pre-industrial, unskilled people into efficient, high-productivity workers—and turned their unskilled and low-wage people rapidly into highly productive but still low-wage workers whose output could then compete in the developed markets.[11]

Accompanying the growing commitment to training is a better grasp of how to conduct it. Clear expectations about what is to occur in each process provide a firm foundation.

Process Specification for Training

Frederick Taylor, defended earlier in the chapter (twice), must be cited once more. Taylor advocated the "one best way." It's a fine idea. There *is* one. We shall never be able to discover what it is, but continual improvement is the search for it; when we get close, conditions (designs, customers, etc.) change, and we have to start the search all over again.

Meanwhile, at each step in the quest, the process has to be defined, recorded, stated, drawn—or otherwise specified. The process specs are the basis for training.

Where possible, the specs should be visual: templates, video screens, photos, sketches, diagrams. At a Westinghouse Transportation Division plant near Pittsburgh, video screens just above assembly benches tell assemblers just how to build the many different assemblies. At the Tektronix Portables Division, assemblers lay a finished circuit board on a template as a quick check on whether every component is correctly placed.

Practice Makes Perfect

A few years ago, Honeywell subcontracted with Mitsubishi Heavy Industries to produce torpedoes. On a visit to Mitsubishi's plant in Nagasaki, Honeywell production employees noticed that some operators did not use torque wrenches.

"Why?" they asked.

"We don't need them," was the reply.

"Oh? Why not?"

The Mitsubishi supervisor called for a demonstration. Pick an operator, he said. One was picked, and they all went to a table of different sized bolts and nuts. The supervisor said. Pick one. One was picked, whereupon the operator installed the bolt and tightened the nut with a common wrench *by feel*. "Check one with the torque wrench," said the supervisor. It was checked and was fine.

The supervisor explained how it was possible: The operators *practice*, and once in a while they recalibrate themselves.

At Valeo Thermique Company in La Suze-sur-Sarthe, France, producing auto radiators and air conditioners, instant cameras are available in the work centers—like production tools. Employees take photos of things such as correct machine setups and orderly work places. They post the photos for all to see—and follow.[12]

All-Inclusive Learning

Learning for total quality covers not just the process but also all the people in the process, sometimes including suppliers and freight carriers. This all-inclusive view of organizational learning applies as well in low-wage work as in high-wage, high-skill work. Examples of those two opposite cases, plus a few comments on training outsiders, follow.

Training at a maquiladora plant. At Eaton Corporation's Condura "maquiladora" (Mexican plant supplying a U.S. sister plant just across the border) assembly plant in Matomoros, Mexico, all new hires, from clerks to assemblers, take a two-hour introduction-to-quality course before going to their job assignments. That is only the beginning of

Table 6-1. SPC Training, Condura Plant

Hrs.	Introduccion a Calidad / Introduction to Quality — 2 Hrs.	Estadistica Basica / Basic Statistics — 12 Hrs.	Interpretacion De Graficas / Chart Interpretation — 2 Hrs.	Estudios De Capacidad / Capability Studies — 4 Hrs.	Tecnicas De Solucion De Problemas / Problem-Solving Techniques — 6 Hrs.	Aceptacion De Ajuste De Maquinas / Machine Setup Acceptance — 4 Hrs.
Operator	Required	Req./Opt.	Req./Opt.		Required	
Q.C. Inspector	Required	Required	Required	Req./Opt.	Required	
Supervisor	Required	Required	Required	Required	Required	Required
Technician	Required	Required	Required	Required	Required	Optional
Engineer	Required	Required	Required	Required	Required	Optional
Manager	Required	Required	Required	Required	Required	Optional
Administrative	Required	Optional	Optional	Optional	Required	

136

their training on quality and continual improvement. Table 6–1 shows the full set of training courses that are required or optional, depending on jobs. Visual evidence of use of the training is up on the walls in the form of spec sheets, data sheets, and control charts. [13]

Condura's hundreds of production employees, paid $1.40 an hour, know more about quality and problem-solving than CEOs, presidents, and graduate engineers in most companies. The kind of training provided at Condura should be available in all firms to all jobholders: mail sorters, stock pickers, data-entry operators, retail clerks—anybody. People who hold low-wage jobs with questionable job security are double-damned if they also are denied the satisfactions of being able to solve job-related problems.

Training in a precision machining plant. In 1986 TRW's Steering and Suspension Division, consisting of four plants, began a total reorganization into cells. A year later, in the flagship plant in Sterling Heights, Michigan, six cells were organized and eight were left to be done. Employees who were still outside the cells were in sixty-eight job classifications; those inside the cells have just *one*. Cell operators do job setting, inspection, salvage and repair, general labor, machine oiling, forklift operation—and run all the machines in the cell.

Jobs in the first cells were filled by voluntary transfer; 80 percent of the plant's 550 hourly employees, represented by United Auto Workers, applied. Why would they volunteer? Because the union and com-

---

Management Sheds Its Work Rules

The eighties saw three great labor phenomena. First came forced pay cuts. Then it was bartering for elimination of work rules. Finally, the clouds of doubt dissipated, and the new labor structure became clear: Earn higher pay by learning more skills, mastering more jobs.

When the business press reports on yet another company that has managed a wholesale wipeout of work rules, it calls it a "labor concession." And it is. But it is, even more, a management concession: An admission that job classification—sticking people into narrow slots—has utterly failed. Work rules came from management; labor just got accustomed to them.

pany had negotiated a contract providing higher pay for more jobs mastered in the cells: Lower-paid people could qualify for higher pay. The union rejected two earlier versions of the plan but accepted a third one that also provided for retraining and supplemental unemployment benefits.

The plant reorganization was costing an average of $73,000 per cell—$20,000 of which was for training. (TRW also committed an average of $397,000 per cell for machine rehabilitation.) Operators received forty hours of classroom training in six modules: print reading, tooling and machine setup, gauging and gauge calibration, preventive maintenance, SPC, and quality auditing. Operators were certified upon passing mastery tests.

On-the-job training followed, mainly via job rotation; operators trade jobs every four hours. Cell operators also sat through ten more classroom modules, covering materials handling, safety, writing requisitions, cleanup, lubrication, coolant maintenance, product specs, routings and files, and just-in-time. They also learned how to write work-center operating manuals.

Results: Scrap rate fell from 8.5 percent to 0.7 percent, and most of that was destructive testing. In-process inventory plunged from 36,000 pieces to about 900.[14]

Training your suppliers and carriers. It has become commonplace for first-tier companies—Northern Telecom, Du Pont, and numerous others—to invite suppliers to SPC training sessions. These companies have the know-how and feel a sense of urgency in getting their suppliers up to speed. Now second-tier companies are taking the message to their suppliers.

One example is Globe Metallurgical, a producer of silicon metal products for the auto and other industries. Globe invited five major suppliers to its training in Beverly, Ohio. Then Globe's trainers visited all five suppliers' plants and trained both their salaried and hourly employees. Globe left the suppliers with training materials, blank charts, and even calculators.[15]

In the U.K., the Hubinger affiliate of Heinz has developed a "Partners in Perfection" program aimed at bringing the whole delivery chain under its own rigorous quality control. The program includes an orientation on total quality, mandatory for drivers at the contract carrier firm. Hubinger has a strict follow-up procedure to make sure the message is having its desired effect: ultra-clean trucks, all spills cleaned up at the delivery site, good truck maintenance, and so on.

Multifaceted Learning

Since part of learning is being convinced to use what you learn, any old training approach *won't* do. Best approaches have the learner see things from several angles. Putting it differently, if you read a book about statistical process control and are wholeheartedly sold on it, you still probably won't go do it. If you also see a video on SPC, attend a seminar and browse through case studies on it, sit through a classroom simulation using it, and visit an office or plant where everybody does it with wondrous results displayed on visual signboards, you may decide you can't put it off any longer.

The Bible contains many stories about people who were freed from their doubts when confronted by miracles. Enough minor miracles— notably in quality improvement and response-time reduction—have taken place in industry to provide good evidence to build into company training.

THE TRAINING/LEARNING COMMITMENT

The same convincing evidence that becomes part of the training also serves to pry open company purse strings to fund the training. How far must the strings be opened? A report by the American Society for Training and Development, "Gaining the Competitive Edge," recommends that firms spend at least 2 percent of payroll on employee training and development. That may be significant, but it's not world-class. In 1988, Hewlett-Packard spent 5 percent *of its revenue* on training.

Investment Down the Drain?

In the early part of the eighties, when the great need for training was just dawning on us, I used to hear this comment: "Yes, we ought to do it. But how can we afford to spend all that money on training? Some other company will just hire away those we've trained."

I don't hear that any more. There are several reasons why the objections have fallen aside: (1) "Everybody's" doing it. (2) It works; and it's risky not to do it. (3) Training costs are low compared with most anything else. (4) There has been a knowledge explosion: an enormous outpouring of things everybody in every firm ought to know (we didn't train in the past partly because we didn't have good subject matter).

(5) Employees see the value of it for themselves and the company; they are flattered that their employer is willing to invest in them and proud to work in a "class outfit"—which makes them less likely to bolt.

If those are the main reasons for businesses to commit to training, what are the employees' reasons to commit to learning? The fifth factor above, pride, has something to do with it. A more important factor is livelihood.

Learning for Livelihood

Lower-paid people are, under the system of pay for knowledge, eligible for higher pay for more skills mastered. That helps take care of short-term needs. In a world of business turmoil—mergers, consolidations, restructuring, plant closings, migration across oceans—many employees are more concerned with the long term: What if I lose my job? Am I re-employable at a decent income?

Prospects are bleak for someone whose only experience is feeding parts into a spot-welder or documents into an optical character reader. For someone with a skilled trade who has received regular wage increases for years, re-employment at a similar wage is dubious.

Now is the time to do something for personal employment security: Make a weak resume strong. Every new skill mastered adds a line on the resume and opens up another employment track. These days, multiple job skills alone may not open the right doors. What will is job skills, plus knowledge skills: lines on the resume citing number of hours of training in SPC and problem-solving, evidence of active use of control charts and fishbone diagrams, number of improvement projects completed, number of individual or team suggestions approved. These kinds of skills point to a versatile person who's comfortable with continuous learning and can contribute to continual improvement.

Personal security for professionals is gained the same way: more breadth in the resume. Someone experienced in continual improvement who served a few years in sales, a few more in human resources, and in recent years as a line supervisor is well positioned: groomed for a higher management job, a likely survivor in case of company layoffs, and attractive to another company as well.

P. Bruce Walker, plant manager of a Dow Chemical plant producing aspirin, says, "I finally realized that I can go into any operation in the United States and cut 20 percent to 25 percent of the costs and have the people love doing it." Walker made this statement after seeing his plant succeed, following a few false starts, in finally getting "on a road of continuous improvement."[16]

I believe him. Sounds like an employable guy.

NO FAILURES, NO MISTAKES

We have been talking about developing a new kind of employee, whether line operator or staff expert: a master of several parts of the business who is fully schooled in the techniques of control and problem-solving. With a whole company of such super-employees, little improvement projects go on all over.

We should understand the great difference between many people working on numerous small projects and a few working on an occasional big one (and everyone else a bystander). If the big project fails, people resign and others are let go.

In the multiple-small-project mode, the whole concept of failure is altered. Failure doesn't even seem to be the right word, since the projects are not large or costly. When the outcome of a change isn't right, and the team has learned another lesson, it regroups and tries again. Isn't that the spirit of continual learning and improvement?

7

❦

Attack on
Nonobvious Wastes

WASTE REDUCTION is great sport. When the objects of waste reduction have previously been admired, we may take special delight in the sport—like throwing a pie in the face of an authority figure.

Things held in prior esteem that we shall attack include: selling the unwanted, order tracking, automating the waste, taking it out of one container and putting it into another, analyzing the waste, costing the cost reductions, costing the bad quality, and reporting the utilization and efficiency. All of these are common practices. We shall see why each is totally or partially wasteful (it may not be obvious) and what to do about it.

We start with a waste that directly touches the customer: trying to get the customer to buy something not wanted.

PROMOTIONAL WASTE

My own rough guess is that half the time, money, and energy in sales and marketing goes for promoting what customers really don't want. Some of that kind of promotion results in a sale. Isn't that success? Isn't it good for the company?

Negative Selling

No. It's *negative selling*. Hurts repeat business. Transforms potentially loyal repeat customers into flighty ones whose first preference is *not* to do business with you.

The waste of negative selling arises mostly from designing and making goods or offering services that aren't in tune with the market. There are many causes, but it is ridiculous to simply say it is bad market research and bad forecasting.

The greatest cause is the slowwwwwwwww pace of responding to customers. Sales doesn't check with key customers often enough; thus, it is slow to find out about changing needs. Order processing is in batches, so that orders booked one day may still be in a pile on somebody's desk days later. If design work is required, same problem in design. When the order (or customer, in the case of a human service) finally gets to operations, all the now-familiar operating delays add to the problem: queues, delays to accumulate full loads, multiple handling steps, wait for inspection, data entry, storages, rework, equipment failures—the list is lengthy.

It is normal in many businesses for the need and the final response to be days, weeks, even months apart. By then, the customer's need goes away or changes; sometimes it is a 180-degree change: from euphoria over the product to we-can't-give-it-away. So the sales staff tries to talk the customer into a substitute item. Or a competitor makes the sale (perhaps through its own promotion of something the customer really doesn't want).

What happens to servers (the serving company, plant, shop, or department) who have been prepared to deliver what the customer *used to want*? They are idle, unless marketing can attract customers by negative salesmanship. What happens to the goods produced to satisfy what the customer *once wanted*? Cut the price. Have a sale. Flood the airwaves and print media with ads. Tell the customer, as car dealers often do, that "We are overstocked—and ready to *deal!*"

The other side of negative selling has to do with quality—or the lack of it. It includes selling goods or providing services that are not right. It also includes after-sale schemes of correction: warranties, liberal returns policies, and service contracts. A Gallup poll, in summer 1988, tapped the views of U.S. consumers. Over half said service contracts are a bad idea, something they should not have to pay extra for.[1] The best service contract or best warranty in the business *sometimes*

Warranty or Quality?

"Absolutely positively . . . or your money back" sounds good. And it is. But not excellent. Excellence is when you or I buy the product or service because *we know* it will be good or do what it is supposed to.

McDonald's doesn't need to put a warranty on its box. Nor does Kleenex. Nor Ethan Allen (furniture). In the rare event of a clinker, I know I can speak up, call, or write and get satisfaction—without warranty paper.

First time my mother visited Nordstrom after moving out here (Seattle area) she was awed; the stores are so nice, with a pianist in tails playing at the baby grand. But my wife, who has shopped there for several years, says, Yes, the stores are nice, and sure, they are wonderful about returns. But I shouldn't have to take things back all the time. In other words, she is saying, If only their goods were as good as their service.

Nordstrom is excellent in sales and service. Compared with its competitors in the department store industry, Nordstrom is perhaps good, maybe superior, in buying, quality control, and supplier development. In those matters, compared with the world's best across *all* industries, they are only average. (Note: Nordstrom is still my favorite store; my wife's, too.)

is offered by the best company. On the other hand, it might just be a desperate act to shore up slipping sales (another version of negative selling).

Talented marketers and smooth-talking sales people live and die on negative selling. Companies just die on it—especially if their competitors have found the path to positive selling. That path is one of quick, error-free, flexible response throughout the many links in the chain leading to the final paying customer.

The point is that a sale is not a sale. There are bad sales that yield only revenue. And there are good sales that bring forth revenue, repeat business, and praise about your service, passed on to others by your loyal customers.

Allegiance

Do companies see the distinction between good and not so good sales? It seems not. In pressing for excellence, CEOs of a few large, well-known companies have made this statement: "We will be number one or number two [in sales] in all of our businesses." The rest of the pledge is that any business that can't gets sold.

The commitment to excel in these firms is above reproach. The unit of measure, sales volume, is the problem. It isn't hard to make sales grow: just cut the price, raise the ad budget, and send out more sales people. But sales growth for growth's sake has its day of reckoning.

The firm that wants to be a dynasty, not just a flash in the pan, should court the customer's *first allegiance*. Sales, like profits, fall into place thereafter.

First allegiance of the customer comes from continually improving in the big four competencies—cost, quality, flexibility, and quick response—*and making the customer aware of it*. In other words, marketing teams up with the rest of the organization to achieve internal excellence, then crows about it in the market place. That is *positive selling*.

WASTE OF TRACKING THE ORDERS

Next on our list of wastes is order tracking, which has three purposes. One is to find out the status of an order for somebody—perhaps a final customer. The second is to accumulate cost data. The third isn't a real purpose; it just follows from the way the work is scheduled: everything treated as a special case.

Order Status

A fine company that I like to do business with—perhaps you do, too—is Federal Express. But I recall a week in fall 1985, when several incoming FedEx letters arrived at my office days late. It was the week of a rare, bad snowstorm that brought many activities to a halt in my part of the world (Seattle). I made several phone calls trying to get delivery. In each case, Federal Express's order-tracking system performed admirably. It told me exactly where my late letter was. The letters weren't lost!

From my standpoint as customer, they may as well have been. I didn't want to know that the letter was put on the delivery truck in the morning but that the delivery run was not completed and the letter was now safely back at the FedEx plant. I just wanted my mail.

Federal Express spent an enormous sum setting up its elaborate order-tracking information system, and it continues to pump operating cash into it. (United Parcel Service has been planning to invest in the same kind of system.) Would the money be better spent on more trucks and drivers? I thought so in fall 1985. Now, after years of subsequent on-time pickups and deliveries—without fail—I don't think FedEx needs more trucks and drivers.

So the question is this: If deliveries are "always" fast and on-time and there are "no" late orders to track, why not eliminate order tracking?

I realize the issue is not quite that simple. The same computer system keeps track of customers' names, addresses, and account numbers and handles billing. Also, perhaps customers feel a sense of security just knowing that FedEx tracks all orders—a marketing benefit.

My point is that order-tracking systems normally are associated with *failure and delay*. Reliable, quick-responding factories, mail services, government agencies, financial institutions, or other businesses should, in most cases, spend their money on something more useful.

Tracking Costs

That brings us to the next purpose of tracking: adding up cost, operation by operation, as orders go from place to place. Most manufacturing

---

Thousands Saved

When response becomes quick, the order-tracking system goes to the scrap heap. And what are the savings?

- At the Tektronix Portables Division, lead time was cut from about twenty-five weeks to less than ten days, at which time the company's finance people gave the go-ahead to cease material tracking; that eliminated 25,000 material transactions per month (labor transactions were wiped out as well).[2]
- At the Hewlett-Packard Disc Memory Division, slashing lead times led to elimination of 100,000 inventory and labor transactions per month.[3]

firms of any size have installed computer systems to do that; some large "paperwork factories" do it, too. Many plants (but not many whole companies) have, in the last few years, quit tracking orders, which at the same time brings progressive costing to a halt. They are plants that have cut production lead times from weeks to a few days.

Instead of building cost in small steps, those quick-responding plants just do costing twice: once when the raw materials come in the front door, and again when the final product is finished and going out the back door. In other words, the computer just sums up the purchased material costs for the completed unit and adds a share of total labor and overhead. The material costing part of it is called *backflush* costing: Flush back through the product's bill of materials to capture all the purchased components used in the end product.

Everything a Special Case

The third point about tracking is that it usually forces star products or customers to suffer the same heavy-handed scheduling as the specials. That doesn't make sense, because star products can be routinized.

There are several versions:

Rate-based scheduling in seasonal production. In this scheduling method, the production rate rises in stair-step fashion as the seasonal

---

Cost of Chaos

In a typical big bureaucratic company, if a customer or client wants information about an order, a mad scramble ensues. First problem is *finding* the order in the confused, delay-prone system. The computer-tracking system is vast and impressive but bogs down in the chaos.

The same system that can't provide order status to the customer also fails to deliver the facts to its own managers—facts about costs, for example.

It's tough to cost chaos. And how do you cost delay? The quick-responding, delay-free company that has steered its way out of the confusion mode finds costing to be a piece of cake—and timely advice to customers, too.

peak approaches. Say that in August the rate is 1,000 cases per day, and in September it rises to 1,200 per day (number of shifts of capacity is raised accordingly). The rule is, in September, make 1,200 each day and stop; no overproduction allowed (unless there was unavoidable underproduction the previous day). *Nothing* is to be irregular: All purchasing and receiving is geared to the rate, which permits ordering by contract and a monthly invoice—no purchase orders and hardly any other transactions.

This is the just-in-time formula for seasonal businesses. The purpose is not to eliminate finished goods, since the idea is to build for the seasonal peak. Rather it is to set forth a regular rate that earlier production stages can synchronize to; that eliminates stage-to-stage delays, transactions, work-force disruptions, and cost; also, purchased and in-process inventories plunge.

Rate-based scheduling in nonseasonal production. Same as the seasonal method, except that very few finished goods build up. The rate is close to the actual sales rate. How close? Stanley Hardware uses the *weekly wash system.* Roughly, that means making this week the wrenches, saws, and hammers that were sold last week—with some adjustment allowed. In one area it's weekly wash plus or minus 35 percent. Stanley can accommodate that much change, because it carries extra machine capacity—especially extra packaging machines, which are not expensive.[4]

There are many businesses like Stanley that have rising and falling—but continuing—sales of certain items, or certain components. *Those items should be wholly or partly scheduled by rate, not by separate work-order transactions.* When MK Electronics in the U.K. set up a pilot work cell to produce a certain high-volume model of wall receptacle, it converted from work orders, with 1,600 transactions per week, to a rate in which there was just one transaction per week.

Actually, changing the rate weekly is too often. Today, some companies, such as Harley-Davidson, Physio Control, and CalComp, set a rate and stick to it (except for extraordinary events) for a month. In volatile-demand situations, two weeks is about the lower limit. If a firm changes the rate more frequently, it will be responding too often to false signals of a fall or rise in demand, which increases the likelihood of running out or having too much of a certain item; then it's back into the panic mode.

Rate-based scheduling for components only. In companies with a V-shaped product structure—a few components going into many end products—the few components should be rate-based, with final production to customer orders. At Stanley Hardware, a hardware item itself may be considered a component, which can be packaged in many different ways. A good system—for star hardware items—would be to schedule their production to a longer-term rate (e.g., a four-week wash system) and schedule packaging to customer orders. Better yet, it might be able to schedule 60 percent of its packaging to, say, a two-week rate, and schedule the other 40 percent to actual customer orders. (This is similar to Benetton, the apparel company, which dyes 75 percent of its clothing to a rate and the other 25 percent to up-to-the-minute orders coming in from retailers all over the world.)

Rate-based scheduling for part of the day. At Avon, West Germany, the day shift operates to a regularized plan; unplanned demand and problems are handled by a cadre of *trained* on-call employees. Avon adopted this sytem to meet its commitment to deliver within six days of when its door-to-door salesperson makes the sale. (It also halved the changeover time on tubes that supply cosmetic materials to packaging machines, so that it can run smaller orders economically.) Sales patterns for its cosmetics are volatile, but at least the first shift may be operated in a highly simplified, routine manner.

In many businesses, it pays to set aside a few hours each day (or shift) to process the star products or customers; then "open the doors to anything" the rest of the day. I have found this way of scheduling to be widely applicable in the process industry—where, in some cases, it must be modified to something like running the stars every Monday and Thursday.

In still other businesses the ideal schedule has a few star items repeating at regular intervals, with gaps in between filled in with specials. Over coffee at a public seminar in Chillicothe, Ohio, two men from Kenworth Truck were telling me about trying to schedule their massive rigs, which have a prodigious number of options. I asked if there were big-ticket, hard-to-get options. They said, yes, two in particular: the new "pillow-cushion" suspension system and the "cab-over" cab design; they couldn't make enough of them.

Okay, I said, then they become the core of your schedule. The schedule has those two main modules on a repeating rate, and anything else fitted in between. The schedule sequence might be (where P is for pillow-cushion, C for cab-over, and A for anything):

$$PAAACAAPAAACAAP \ldots$$

With P and C on predictable schedules, all their component parts, made and bought, can be planned well in advance, which is an excellent, partial cure for a bottleneck problem. Also, with P and C regularized, the sales force can be told accurately what the availability of pillow-cushion and cab-over trucks will be.

WASTE OF AUTOMATING THE WASTE

Simplifying to get rid of order tracking or other waste is a cost reduction. It also reflects a *change in the way we think about progress and modernization.* It isn't modern to automate the order tracking; it's modern to stop the order tracking cold.

Few of our economists, political leaders, and business press writers have been sufficiently exposed to that thinking. Nor have many of our top executives. Their vision of a progressive office or factory is the magazine photo of an AGV (automatically guided vehicle) named Herman delivering the mail; or a multistory, narrow-aisle, computer-controlled storage system that directs a mechanical device to put away at random and remember where—for later automatic stock picking; or hundreds of units on a powered conveyor, propelled forward to the next machine untouched by human hands; or bar-code readers for internal data collection that, by implication, permit sharp cuts in the budget for pens and pencils.

Why Is It Waste?

Each of those kinds of automation has some worthwhile uses—but not many. They are examples of *automating the waste*: Stock handling, storage, and data collection add no customer value to the product or service—only cost. In fact, the money spent on them denies funds for improving the value-adding or customer-serving operations themselves. We'll consider some of the well-known examples of devices that often don't add any value:

- *AGVs.* Some of the big sledlike AGVs I've seen in auto assembly plants and paper mills seem okay. They follow tracks, but the tracks can be changed without major expense. They move heavy loads that cannot be lightened (a car is a car, a roll of paper is a roll). They span distances that cannot always be shortened. And they don't need a driver.

On the other hand, AGVs that handle mail and small electronic parts are foolish toys. They encourage large-quantity batches of mail and parts, which inject delay and inventory. They discourage moving the process at point A closer to the one at point B. In other words, they inhibit breaking up the functional departments and creating cells and flow lines.

- *Automated storage.* Some AGVs deliver into a highrise, automated storage system, and later fetch parts from it. The storage systems ensure that plenty of delay is inserted between the value-adding processes. Good plants that installed centralized, automated storage systems in the 1960s and 1970s ripped them out in the 1980s. They tore out smaller carousel storage systems as well.

  I am talking about storage of semifinished parts (or piles of documents in process, for that matter). A general rule of just-in-time production is: Keep the materials where they are made—in small amounts. If the quantities are so large that one is tempted to put them into automated storage, that shows inflexibility and bad coordination with the customer at the next process. The material handling industry has begun to respond to the need for efficient handling of *small* quantities. An example is a new type of mini-automated storage rack that becomes a part of a machining cell; parts made in small lots sit in mini-storage for hours—not days or weeks—until they are summoned by the next cell or by the final assembly line.

  A valid use of automated storage is in distribution warehousing: products ready for sale. As marketing and the other business functions unite to better serve the final customer, however, distribution warehouses are being shut down and shrunk in size.

- *Conveyors.* When its purpose is to free the hands for stuffing envelopes (document conveyor) or stuffing components, a conveyor is fine. On the other hand, when a conveyor stretches across distance, it is waste. And when a conveyor spans necessary distance, but lacks spacers (or rules) to ensure that most of the conveyor is empty, it is moving waste and injecting delay.

  Consider a conveyor ten meters long (about thirty-three feet) between point A and point B, and assume that operations A and B each take one minute. Say the conveyor's maximum capacity is thirty pieces and that it is loaded. That means each piece leaving A spends thirty idle minutes on the conveyor before it reaches B. The response ratio (delay time to work time) is 30 to 1.

But if A and B are well synchronized, the conveyor should hold *just one* piece: the piece that's on its way to ensure that B's production is not interrupted. Allowing only one piece on the conveyor cuts the response ratio to 2 to 1, and speeds up the flow fifteenfold! Time to clean out your conveyor.

At CalComp's Anaheim, California, plant, they did more than that. In creating fourteen focused plants-in-a-plant, they tore out the conveyors and replaced them with pushcarts. Nothing is bolted to the floor any longer, which allows the flexibility to constantly reconfigure, change, and improve.

Overhead conveyors are particularly odious. They make plants inflexible. The conveyor becomes part of the structure, often too costly to tear out or to move.

A conveyor, floor or overhead, with little or nothing on it seems to make people uncomfortable. The same is true of storage openings. There is a compulsion to fill them. And never mind the extra cost and delay represented by the extra idle units!

- *Bar-code readers.* Bar-coding goods in and shipments out of the building is a reasonable idea. With a few exceptions, that's where bar-coding should start and end. Bar-coding *inside the building* generally means orders are being tracked and labor costs are being progressively added—two dubious practices. Some bar-coding captures data about process failures that is better put up on large signboards—for all to see and worry about!

  I have seen worthy uses of in-process bar-coding. For example, Physio Control, a maker of defibrilators, uses the twin-parts-tray system; bar codes on trays identify the parts. When the empty twin goes back to stores for refill, bar-code wanding identifies the backup stock location *without error*. This is an example of a fail-safe device. Many of the small parts—resistors, capacitors, and so on—look alike, and it is vital in the medical products business to be sure the right ones are installed.

Productivity and Cost

While productivity in manufacturing has been improving smartly in much of the world in recent years, the same is not true in the services sector. Stagnant productivity in services is "especially puzzling," as the *Wall Street Journal* put it, "given the extraordinary explosion of computer technology . . . in the last decade and a half." Nobel-laureate economist Robert Solow suggests "the cynical explanation . . . that all that computer capacity and word processing is producing information that nobody needs."[5]

The explanation is not really a cynical one. New technology usually doesn't work well. Even if it works technically (and often it doesn't), even if there are people who know how to keep it running (often there aren't), the new technology usually won't pay off. The reason, as we have seen, is that it is likely to be used to do something wasteful.

While the greatest wastes show up in the form of delays and inventory, let's not forget the continuing cost to keep the technology operating. In highly automated factories, the maintenance department doesn't have much time to devote to productive equipment—things like upgrading, overhauling, replacing components before failure, and modifications for quick setup. They are too busy trying to keep the non-value-adding conveyors and storage apparatus running. In highly automated offices, there may not be much time for coordinating people, products, processes, and customers; everything is thought to have a technological fix—in the hardware or software.

Broken Machine to Monitor Broken Process?

I once found myself admiring the transformation that had taken place in a plant producing computer memory products. Lead times and defects had been driven down by orders of magnitude, and employees used marking pens to record "discrepancies" on large flip-chart sheets.

They also showed me the bar-code system operators used to enter data on material usage, work completed, and other activities.

Oh, oh. They're still feeding the computer, I thought. Too bad they didn't spend that money on productive operations.

My negative reaction became double-negative when I glanced at the three entries on the discrepancy sheet. One described a problem with a certain piece of production equipment. Another noted a problem with a bar-code reader. The third referred to a problem with a bar-code control device. Two out of three were problems with equipment that doesn't produce anything having value for the customer!

CONTAINER-TO-CONTAINER WASTE

Some years ago, one of my clients, a food products company, brought me to its largest cannery. Half the plant was for can manufacturing, the other for food canning. (Today the company buys its cans instead of making them.) Can bodies were made at a rate of nearly five hundred per minute on each of seven production lines, which dumped them in a jumble into "jumbo" storage units—*not* directly to can-filling.

Wait a minute, I said. Why put them into the jumbos and then take them out again for conveying to the canning machines? One reason was that can-making operated three shifts a day, whereas canning was generally two shifts. Size changeovers in can-making and product changeovers in canning also interfered with synchronization.

Still, I asked, Why send every single can into the jumbos and then out again? Doesn't this rough handling damage some of the cans? It definitely did.

My suggestion was to send most of the cans most of the time directly to canning, and send only the overflow to the jumbos. It is not much of a mechanical engineering problem to devise a system of conveyor diverters and shunts that will accomplish this.

That may seem to be an unusual case, one of those shocking lapses in common sense that can be found in any organization. It's not. Needless extra handling and storage—dumping into a container or rack only to take some of it out the same day—is commonplace. It is the norm in manufacturing, hospitals, offices, restaurants—any business that uses materials and supplies. Never mind that it makes no sense.

Gradually our top companies are breaking the bad habit. The most common point of attack is the interface between a supplier and a user. The two parties are agreeing on a container that works for packing at one end, shipping in between, and use at the other end; sometimes the container is returnable to the first party for recycling.

At Hewlett-Packard, Vancouver, Washington, engineers designed a special type of oblong cardboard box with perforations at one end. The box is for small purchased electronic parts. Suppliers are to ship their parts in those boxes, which go right out to H-P's assembly lines. By tearing off the end of the box at the perforations, assemblers can use the boxes as parts trays on their assembly benches.

The old practice, still normal in most companies, is to dump out of the supplier's container into a company storage box, later into an internal delivery container, and finally into a tray at the work site. Some items have to be counted at every dump point. Most sites handle thousands of items the same wasteful way year after year.

WASTE OF ANALYZING THE WASTE

With so much waste just lying around waiting to be wiped out, where does one begin? Some would say, start with broad-gauge analysis. Thousands of activities go on all the time in even a modest-sized business. Find out where the wastes are, which are worst, and which should be tackled first.

One popular analysis tool dates back to the beginning of scientific management at the turn of the century: the process flow chart. The analyst follows each product through all steps, including those that do not add value. Each step is a line on the flow chart, and five flow-charting symbols visually capture five different kinds of activities:

○ — A value-adding operation

⇨ — A move or transport

□ — An inspection

D — A delay

▽ — A storage

If the flow chart shows five operations, ten moves, three inspections, six delays, and six storages, that makes thirty activities, only five of which (the operations) add value. Time to attack the twenty-five havens of waste, the worst ones first.

In today's challenge-everything mood, we have to question broad-gauge analysis itself—using flow charting or any other technique. Big Business has relied too much on professional analysis, which adds overhead cost, not value to the customer. The employee involvement enthusiast might say, Keep the analysts away. Teach the employees, singly or in teams, to do micro analysis to smoke out waste, delay, and variability in their own operations. Strive to have hundreds of little improvements going on all the time, not a few grand projects led by analysts.

Actually, flow charting, which comes in several variations, is a versatile enough technique to be used for a small-scale study by a work team. Other tools (Pareto charts, fishbone, etc.) for use by operators in improving their own operations are presented in earlier chapters. Micro-response ratios, explained in Chapter 5, are especially useful.

Though operating teams should do most of their own analysis, professional analysis sometimes is needed to help jolt a company out of its complacency—just to get an improvement effort started. In that case analysts might help by presenting stark, broad-gauge figures on waste— in the form of macro-response ratios, flow-chart data highlighting the delays, competitive analysis information, and so forth.

Analysts also have the kind of knowledge needed in company training, of which there is much to do. Many analysts already have shifted into training as their main pursuit.

Finally, in most companies there are some complex issues that cut across the work spaces of several operating teams. The role of analysts is not to retreat to their computer terminals and run business simulation models. Simulations are fine, but not if done in isolation, away from operating people. The proper way to attack boundary-crossing problems is to bring together representatives from each affected work area. The analyst may serve as coordinator and may also run simulations *for* and *with* the group, as needed. Some of the new graphics simulation packages allow simulations to be understood by others besides the analyst.

WASTE OF COSTING THE COST REDUCTIONS

There is more to say about analysis. In small companies, if someone thinks of an improvement or gets a formal suggestion approved, it's done and that's that. In large companies and government agencies, there is one more step. Analysts do a study to find the net savings,

---

When Cost Reduction Raised Costs

Professor Thomas Vollmann tells about the company that levied an annual target for cost reduction on its manufacturing engineers. They were evaluated on how much they could save by redesigning products and processes. "Unfortunately," according to Vollmann, "this led to products being poorly designed in the first place"!

The company wised up. Now it considers that type of cost saving to be evidence of bad original design (unless the technology in the design improvement was not available at the time of initial design). The company's new emphasis is on bringing new products on stream with as few later changes as possible.[6]

which contribute to the year's cost-reduction target. The last step costs money and adds nothing of value.

There was a time, a few decades ago, when waste-reduction techniques were in wide use, but cost-reduction programs did not exist. We have already partly seen the method: The analyst (could be an operator trained in the old *work simplification* methods) does a process flow chart, analyzes it for wastes that could be cut out, then flowcharts the improved method. Net savings go into a summary box at the bottom of the chart—like the following:

Symbol	Before		After		Net Savings	
◯	5		5		—	
⇨	10	2,500 feet	2	40 feet	8	2,460 feet
☐	5		1		4	
D	5		1		4	
▽	5		0		5	

The improved method eliminates eight transports and 2,460 feet of travel distance, four inspections, four delays, and five storages. No one needs to see the savings in money to be impressed. Yet today, large firms require net *monetary* savings.

The requirement to "dollarize" savings sneaked into business and industry a few decades ago. I cannot trace the history of it. Let's just say that at some point, cost-oriented thinking (and people) took control of operations, and companies added a layer of analysis—analysis by cost. Over time, cost savings drove expression of savings in other terms into the background; the background took on the catch-all term, *intangibles.*

The improvement effort also took on the new name, cost-reduction program, which had annual targets, like charity drives. Managers developed a love-hate feeling about the programs. They hated to be driven. On the other hand, cost reduction gave cost-sensitive managers in cost-focused firms a way to cover their rear ends: "During my two years as general manager, my people saved $97,850.22."

George Graham, senior vice president and director for quality at Texas Instruments, says (of TI's team and project improvement effort), "Don't ask me what the total annual dollar savings are because I don't know. We primarily are interested in the commitment of all TIer's to the process of continuous improvement."[7]

It's time to tear the cost-reduction charts off the walls. Uncosted waste reductions go right to the bottom line just as surely as costed ones do.

Managers: Wean yourselves off the dollar sign (or pound, franc, yen, etc., sign).

WASTE OF COSTING THE BAD QUALITY

The points just made about costing the cost reductions apply as well to costing the bad quality. I must hasten to say, however, that *cost-of-quality* programs, as they are called, have been valuable. They got the attention of senior management.

The history of cost of quality (actually, cost of *unquality*) is fairly short. It dates back to the 1960s,[8] but industry did not do anything with it until the quality earthquake of the 1980s. Small numbers of managers became aware of severe quality problems in their companies and needed a way to shock other managers into the same realization. The method was to add the four costs associated with bad quality: prevention, appraisal (inspection), internal failure (e.g., rework), and external failure (warranty costs, returns, etc.).

A book by John Groocock shows us TRW, Inc's., calculations for 1983. As a percent of sales, its cost of quality was 7.27 percent (1.37 percent for prevention, 3.19 percent for appraisal, and 2.71 percent for internal and external failure).[9] Many famous Western companies arrived at percentages a good deal higher than that. (Japanese companies never were attracted to cost of quality.)

Seeing that 7 percent, or 10 percent, or more of sales goes down the drain did indeed create a stir in the executive ranks. Books, articles, speakers, seminars, and consultants continue to agitate on the same theme.

Plenty has been done to fix quality weaknesses. Plenty more needs to be done, especially in medium and small manufacturing companies. Then there is the services sector—still with notoriously high error rates. For those companies that haven't done anything about their bad quality yet, estimating cost of quality would help break the ice.

What is *not* wise is to carry on with cost of quality. It should not become a reportable item in the accounting system, nor should it be used for evaluating performance. Bad quality should be controlled at the source (fix the causes of variability and error), not "by the numbers."

WASTE OF REPORTING THE UTILIZATION
AND EFFICIENCY

Planning and controlling equipment and labor by the numbers is yet another poor practice. I am talking about machine utilization and labor efficiency reports.

Sins Committed to Keep Machines Busy

Oftentimes, people who manage high-priced machines—from mainframe computers, to nuclear magnetic resonance (NMR) scanners, to industrial equipment of all kinds—really don't. The machines manage them. The machines cry out, "FEED ME!" like the giant potted plant in "Little Shop of Horrors."

Planners, schedulers, supervisors, and managers dutifully scrounge up work to feed to the machines. They may get marketing into the act—to "scare up some orders. . . . Find *something* to keep this costly equipment running." Here are a few examples of what happens.

- In computing, information systems staff are praised if they can get jobs off people's personal computers and onto the hungry mainframe. Never mind the user's preference.
- In medicine, physicians are implored to generate patients for the scanner and help fill hospital beds. Never mind about patients' real needs.
- In metalworking, schedulers are called upon to keep the big fast new multiton machines busy and avoid running jobs on the older, slower machines. Never mind that the prodigious amounts run on the fast machines make stockrooms bulge.

In the supermachine case, next step is to sell off the older, smaller machines. That makes the denominator in the equipment utilization formula (capacity used divided by maximum capacity) smaller. Like magic, the utilization rate rises, and managers collect their "attaboys" and "attagirls."

These days, multiple slow machines are often treasured: Each can be set to run a different class of product—to be turned on just when the customer has a need and to make only what the customer wants.

Not long ago, the machine utilization report was one of the centerpieces of capacity management. Today's thinking is that the report drives people to do dumb things—to keep the machine running—and turn a blind eye to the negative effects: overproduction, rework and

---

The Skating Rink

A manufacturer of communications gear had made the transition from bulky electromechanical to small electronic products. In one of its huge plants, new production lines were fitted into small spaces alongside shops crammed with largely idle metal-forming machines. The company's edict: Sell the old machines.

A few of the plant's managers protested, to no avail. Shops were emptied as over one hundred machines (punch presses, spot welders, drill presses, lathes) were sold, at ten cents on the dollar, or less. There was nothing to do with the empty space but rope it off, whereupon it became known as "the skating rink."

Later on, as the cost of outside machining soared, the protesters said their I-told-you-so's, and some even suggested buying a few of the machines back: Put them on the new production lines, each machine dedicated to making just one part at the point of use.

But it was too late. No one sells old machines and then buys them back.

---

obsolescence, lack of time for machine maintenance, sale of valued older machines, and so forth.

Harley-Davidson (the motorcycle maker), recognizing the negatives, was one of the first companies to take the bold step of eliminating its machine utilization report.

Isn't the report necessary at least for projecting needs for additional capacity? No. That can be done simply and effectively by an annual capacity survey confined to critical and bottleneck machines. No need to make it a monthly event, complete with data entry, computers, reports, and all the other costs.

Unproductive Efficiency

Do these points about equipment also apply to labor? Well, yes, except that labor is a more complex resource, tricky to manage. Unlike machines, humans get paid and they vary in motivation. Performance-reporting issues get scrambled with pay and motivation matters.

Let's try to unscramble the issues—just look at how business tries to measure labor performance. The measures are either labor efficiency or labor productivity. Often the two terms are used interchangeably, but technically they are different: Efficiency measures speed—when working (it requires a formal labor standard). Productivity is looser— just quantity produced divided by "clock" time, which includes all delays. In other words, productivity is a blend of labor utilization (is the operator kept busy?) and speed of production.

Productivity. Since productivity includes delays not the fault of the operator, it is imprecise and unfair as a measure of labor performance—or of the supervisor's ability to get labor to perform.

Productivity is not even a good measure of how everyone is doing in keeping people busy and the enterprise productive. Productivity is simply too gross a measure to lead to solutions—too gross to prod operators or managers to fix problems.

It's necessary, of course, to keep output data. When Coach Leatherware, a maker of fine ladies' handbags and other products, adopted cells in its Manhattan factory, it also put up chalk boards with hours of the day marked off. Each hour an operator enters the number of handbags completed, plus remarks about problems. While the plant still retained much of the old work-order system, its days are numbered. Scheduling is just a daily rate, and the control is just meeting the rate hour by hour—not the traditional productivity measure.

Data on hourly completions have to do with *current* performance.

Robot Productivity

T he robotic assembly line at _____ Company is certainly impressive. Tour guides proudly showed me videos, next to each robot, displaying real-time data on number of component insertions (productivity).

"Whoa!," I said. "Seems to me that output of the robots is exactly the same as that of the whole assembly line, which, of course, you keep track of."

A quick-thinking tour guide explained: "That's true, but we get a lot of Wall Street types on plant tours. They are impressed by all the data displays."

(This is a true story.)

The system isn't world-class unless there are data leading to continual improvement, including tracking the separate causes of halted production: machine breakdowns, unclear plans or specifications, key person missing, process out of control, lack of materials, production out of synch with demand, long setups, and others. Many of these are the data that go up on large charts in the workplace. When the specifics are on display, operators, technicians, and managers can see from the data what has to be done, not just if there is a problem somewhere.

There is one valid use of a productivity measure: in scheduling. Schedulers *must* know how long it usually takes to produce something or provide a service. That is, they need to know the work time, plus typical delay time (usually delay time is much greater than work time). But don't call it productivity; call it the output rate, or the task time. Collect the data through an occasional audit, and *don't* allow it to become a data collection and reporting *system*.

Efficiency. Efficiency is speed of labor—when working (formally, it is standard time divided by actual time, or actual output divided by standard output). Labor hates it. Always. People simply don't like to be watched, timed, and measured repeatedly; an audit once in a while is okay. (Tying efficiency to incentive pay is another matter, addressed in Chapter 9.)

Efficiency reporting is expensive. It costs a good deal more than productivity reporting, because efficiency is based on formal time studies, which require time-study technicians or engineers.

Further, for all of its precision, efficiency fails to measure or accomplish what it is supposed to. Both numerator and denominator in the efficiency formula have weaknesses:

- The stopwatch (or other timing method) is the precise part but most labor standards actually are negotiated—for these reasons: The supervisor or labor representatives don't want the standard to be too tight, and the analyst wants to keep the peace.
- People being measured have ways of making the measure come out *their* way. One tactic is deliberate peer pressure to assure that output is X percent below standard (lots of documented studies confirm this). Another is to make sure of overcounting the output.

Enter the Customer

Finally, and most important, what do the measures—utilization, productivity, and efficiency (UPE, for short)—have to do with serving the customer? If they worked well, they would at least drive the cost down, and cost is one of the customer's main concerns.

They *don't* work well. The sad history of UPE is that it drives cost up! Many of the costs once were hidden or ignored ("just overhead costs"). Now they are out in the open, and they are huge costs. And we know how to drive them down—certainly *not* by UPE reporting.

The customer's other wants are quick response, flexibility, and quality. But utilization and productivity promote "busyness," which in most cases lengthens lead times. Busy resources are making and doing what they will, not what the customer wants *now*. Efficiency permits still less concern for lead times, since its focus is just on speed *while working*.

Finally, there is no room for quality and flexible response in the UPE formula. In fact, quality just slows the pace, and flexibility means too many interruptions.

It may be a bit of an exaggeration, but here is a Far Eastern view (exact source unknown)—a very customer-oriented one—about managing capacity:

> *The ideal state of a machine is idle but ready; the ideal state of an operator is idle, but ready and alert.*

8

⚬⚬

Minimal Accounting
and Noncost Cost Control

M UCH OF the old house of cost management has already caved
in. More will go, and a new spartan structure is rising. Judging
by my large file of 1987-dated references, that is the year when leading
companies and the accounting community defined the new structure.
Those references include a book with a telling title: *Relevance Lost:
The Rise and Fall of Management Accounting.*[1] We can summarize
the profound changes in terms of management accounting's two main
purposes:

1. *Tactical decisions.* Accurate costs of each product or service
   are needed for pricing, bidding, and go/no-go decisions, but
   conventional cost accounting yields only rough costs. Often they
   are way off. Time to send the old system to the dust bin. New
   ways of organizing resources and spreading overhead costs allow
   us to do so.
2. *Cost control.* Some say that the cost system was not originally
   designed to control costs.[2] Its purpose was number 1 above (along
   with meeting legal requirements). Today, we have a full set of
   controls on the *causes of cost.* Controlling causes is much more
   effective, and, in the words of Professor Thomas Johnson, "unlike
   the distant, often distorted financial echoes of those causes that
   appear in traditional cost and performance reports."[3] The traditional approach—the whole cost-variance system—gets scrapped.

As we saw in Chapter 5, the new one is largely visual: operators plot causal data on large signboards in the workplace.

At first, the impetus for bringing down the creaky cost structure was the opportunity to simplify inventory accounting. That was quickly followed by the same thing for labor reporting.

INVENTORY ACCOUNTING

Just-in-time (JIT) production began to spread worldwide in about 1980. In many cases, time to convert purchased materials to finished goods fell from weeks to days.

Having done that, a natural question was, Do we still need our elaborate inventory accounting system? First answers from the accountants were yeses. Then, on further thought, maybe not. Finally, on checking with auditors (which might have taken months), the cheer went up. No! There's no need!

The firm's accountants, along with the auditors, must ensure that the value of inventory on the books is correct. It's a legal requirement. When in-plant inventory drops by, say, a factor of five, the job of valuing the inventory is likewise reduced. In fact, since many JIT

Pay Points

In the old days, when delays were normal everywhere, most companies tracked order progress and cost (labor, overhead, any new materials) at numerous pay points between first and last operation. Today's best firms employ many new techniques for cutting out delays and directly controlling costs; thus, the cost system with all its internal pay points is mainly for legal reporting purposes. How many pay points will satisfy the auditors? Time will tell, but a rule of thumb is about one per two weeks of lead time.

And where should the pay points be? A good candidate is a place where the work is stuck a while in a state of "capture." Examples of capture operations are electronic circuits plugged in and tested for a day or two, or cultures growing in a petri dish for days or weeks.

plants and even offices make some use of the disciplined kanban method—every piece in a standard container holding a fixed quantity placed in labeled locations—counting the inventory is simple and quick: accuracy with ease. Better yet, in a total kanban system (as at Harley-Davidson) don't count at all: Kanban keeps the quantities fixed, so the auditors accept a fixed count for inventory valuation purposes.

When converting raw material to finished goods took weeks, accounting had to put a value on semifinished inventories held at scattered stock points. The 1970s offered advanced methods: data-entry terminals, perhaps with bar-code readers, disbursed around the plant. The computer can know the amount of semifinished stock at every location, and the accountants take it from there. But slashing conversion time to a few days makes the terminals and bar-code readers excess baggage.

Or are they? What about all the other data collectible on the same terminals?

LABOR REPORTING

For every operation or job, someone wanted data on not only inventory but also things like labor consumed, material wasted, and machine downtime. For efficiency's sake, we told ourselves, why not collect most of the data on one system—generally one *computer* system? So data-collecting computer systems—in factories, health care, insurance, banking, retailing, overnight mail, and elsewhere—grew. And grew. And grew. In companies like Federal Express and McDonnell-Douglas the computer systems department is a huge company unto itself. The cost of computer support for operations begins to rival, or even exceed, the payroll in operations.

Challenge and Change

In progressive companies like Hewlett-Packard, Omark Industries, and Harley-Davidson, people began to ask why. Why the elaborate system to track direct labor, when it is only a small portion of total operating cost? (On average in manufacturing, direct labor is only about 15 percent of product cost, down from over 50 percent a hundred years ago.)

People were ready to chuck labor reporting. One problem: Nearly every firm used direct labor as the basis for allocating overhead cost to products. As Andy Nicholl, material manager at Caterpillar put it, "We manufacture base hours; we sell tractors."

Most firms still do allocate by direct labor "base hours." But a steadily-growing number don't. Some have wiped out direct labor as a separate cost category. Plants in electronics (e.g., Hewlett-Packard and Texas Instruments) were first to do so, since direct labor is usually less than 5 percent of product cost in that industry. Companies in metalworking are doing it too. That is, they treat direct and indirect labor as a single type of cost, which wipes out a category for detailed labor reporting.

Don't those trends open the door to abuse? To out-of-control costs? Let's take a look.

The Cost of Costing Direct Labor

I recall a room full of people at Andrew Corporation, which makes and sells telecommunications products. While I was on the topic of excessive reporting, two people in the back of the room started whispering and nudging each other. I knew who they were. They were two machine operators; all the others were managers and staff professionals.

I stopped and asked, "What are you two whispering about?" One replied that the company had just put in a big new system that schedules production, tracks inventory, and collects all kinds of data. He explained that "we have to clock in on every operation": ID badge goes into a reader, which brings up a menu on the screen; the operator completes the clocking by typing the part number. After finishing the operation, "we clock out" by keying in the quantity successfully made. "I must have clocked in and out eighteen times yesterday," he said. "Some days I think we spend as much time clocking as working."

"That's right," added the second operator. "Some operations take only two minutes, and it takes longer than that to do the clocking!"

That opened the subject for debate. The heads of production control and management information systems were in the room; they admitted to having doubts about all that labor reporting, too.

Those kinds of grand projects tend to take on lives of their own. Andrew benefited from the no-nonsense wisdom of two machine operators who aired their doubts in the right setting. Other companies have not been so fortunate.

Or was it just good fortune? I think not. It was good management— in that Andrew had the sense to invite the two operators to the session.

Still have doubts? How about another example?

Closing the Books

In the spirit of cutting valueless transactions, Texas Instruments now closes its books only quarterly instead of monthly. Managers no longer have to react to profit and loss statements twelve times a year. And, regarding the infamous end-of-the-period push, operations and sales people only have to ask "Why are we doing this?" one-third as often.

Too bad that regulations in the U.S. and Canada (but *not* in most other countries) require P&Ls quarterly. Otherwise, companies in those countries might see fit to report just once a year. If what critics say is true—that subservience to frequent P&Ls makes Western managers short-term thinkers—maybe yearly is often enough.

At the Portables Division of Tektronix, study revealed that direct labor amounted to only 3 to 7 percent of production cost. Even so, for each production line, direct labor was reported at every operation—forty to sixty labor transactions. By rough estimate, the cost "to record, process, correct, and analyze" each labor transaction was probably more "than the actual value of the labor per operation"![4] Based on that shocking revelation, the division acted quickly. Labor reporting ceased, which eliminated about 35,000 labor transactions per month.

Direct Labor *Plus*

Related to all this is the employee involvement (EI) issue. EI is, by definition, *involvement in things other than direct labor*—ideally *heavy* involvement in other activities. Non-direct-labor roles include things that indirects, managers, technicians, and professionals have always done. These include teaching, learning, moving materials, loading, setting up, and moving equipment; also, preventive maintenance, data collection, data diagnosis, problem analysis, presentations, advice, placating customers, and implementation of new methods.

To make room for those activities, CalComp's plants run seven hours a day instead of eight. That allows time for operators to do other productive things, including holding daily process improvement meetings.

Abolishing the direct-labor cost category is not done just because it has become a low percentage of total cost. The main reason is the new belief that nobody's job should consist *only* of direct labor.

SIMPLE, ACCURATE PRODUCT COSTING

The changes we've been talking about are not minor. They reverse the trend of choking off essential operations by layers of staff support— like jungle vines that wind round and round an imperiled tree. As we strip off the vines, *real* costs of goods and services are laid bare. Some vines come off easily. Deliberate actions strip away the rest. Before seeing what those actions are, we'll look at examples of how out-of-whack the cost system became.

Over- and Undercosting

What is the cost of making a product, such as a box of pencils, or performing a service, for example, making a sale? The usual way to find out is to add up the direct costs—direct labor and materials— and throw in a factor for overhead. It is not always easy to find the direct wage and material costs, but that is a small problem compared with the overhead factor.

These days, overhead costs are often three or four, sometimes seven or eight times greater than direct labor costs. With overhead so large, small errors in spreading it around can mean big errors in costing goods and services. Tables 8–1 and 8–2 illustrate.

Manufacturing TVs. A manufacturer of TV sets makes one large-volume standard model and many low-volume models. Table 8–1 shows costs for the standard TV and a typical low-volume model—in this case a swivel type. Material cost is $50 for both models. Assembly labor is also the same, $50, for both. The accounting system applies 500 percent overhead to the direct-labor cost, so estimated overhead is $250. Total accounting cost per unit, then, is $350. This is the case for both standard and swivel models.

Everyone in the firm who has ever given it a thought knows better. The swivels and the other low-volume models are a disruptive pain in the neck; each small order is a "special" requiring all sorts of paperwork and special support. "We *can't* be making money on them," is the prevalent viewpoint.

Table 8–1. *Costing a High-Volume and a Low-Volume Product:*
Television Sets

	Standard, High-Volume, 5,000 yearly		Swivel, Low-Volume, 100 yearly	
Accounting unit cost, where overhead = *500% of direct labor:*				
Direct material		$ 50		$ 50
Direct labor		50		50
Overhead		250		250
Total cost per unit		$350		$350
True unit cost:				
Direct labor & material		$100		$100
Actual overhead:				
Design engineering & design changes	$80		$250	
Planning, scheduling, expediting	6		40	
Storage & handling	4		30	
Accounting & order tracking	5		50	
Purchasing & distribution	15		50	
Plant, equipment, & general	70		140	
Total overhead		$180		$560
Total cost per unit		$280		$660

Accounting conducts a special cost audit to see how much overhead
support each model actually receives. Sure enough, a swivel is far
more demanding. For example, it takes twice as much "plant, equipment, and general" cost per unit (including cost of space and management); and it absorbs ten times more "accounting and order tracking"
cost.

Based on standard accounting methods, the two models have been
priced the same, at $400. At that price the firm has been losing
$260 for each of the 100 swivels sold! Same story for its many other
low-volume models.

Now, with a much better idea of true costs, the firm takes three
steps:

1. Ups the price of swivel models to $599.95; judiciously adjusts
   prices of other low-volume models as well.
2. Still losing money on swivels (and some other low-volume models),
   so mounts a crash cost-cutting effort. The plan is to set up low-
   volume assembly cells, each for a different family of models,

Table 8–2. *Costing a High-Volume and a Low-Volume Service: Title Search in a Law Office*

	Residential, High-Volume		Commercial, Low-Volume
Accounting unit cost, where overhead = *500% of direct labor:*			
Title transfer fee		$300	$ 300
Direct labor		100	100
Overhead		500	500
Total cost per unit		$900	$ 900
True unit cost:			
Transfer fee & attorney's time		$400	$ 400
Actual overhead:			
Administrative support	$60		$160
Research assistance	30		220
Office equipment, including mainte- nance contracts	60		110
Building and office fixtures	70		250
Utilities	10		40
General (communications, insurance, etc.)	50		250
Total overhead		$280	$1,030
Total cost per unit		$680	$1,430

and each equipped with assembly and test devices and a small amount of visually replenished parts; when an order for, say, a swivel comes in, the cell team (could be one person) assembles, tests, and packs it—with no handling, storage, paperwork, or accounting transactions.

3. Lowers the price of standard TVs to $349.95, with the expectation that new markets will open up (perhaps in discount stores) and sales will spurt. As volume grows, scale economies will drive overhead costs per unit still lower; sales will jump again, and profits, too.

Lawyer's title search. For Table 8–2, just change a few words. The point is the same. A title search for residential property, which is high-volume business, takes the same lawyer's time as for low-volume commercial business (assuming the same property values). Accounting calculations, based on applying the same amount of overhead to both types of title search, show that they cost the same, $900.

They don't. The bottom half of Table 8–2 shows "real" overhead costs, based on a careful cost audit. Residential title searches are much less costly: $680 versus $1,430. The firm is now armed with good information for pricing the two types of service. (Actually, in law offices costing has an additional complication: each attorney has a different overhead rate.)

These two examples are not out of the ordinary. Management accounting audits in a variety of industries are showing a systematic bias: "The low-volume products are consistently under-costed and the high-volume products over-costed."[5] What can be done?

Zap the Overhead

One action is to partly or wholly shift an overhead function, like quality control, to the operators. The cost of the function plunges, and any costs of operators doing it apply directly and accurately to the products made or services provided. Other candidates for this treatment, besides quality control, are:

- *Scheduling.* Let the work schedule itself. Examples are a first-come, first-served waiting line; kanban (when a labeled empty container appears, fill it); and min-max order filling (if down to the minimum amount of French fries, load another batch into the fryer). No schedulers or computer scheduling needed.
- *Production control.* Operators manage the flow of the work themselves. No staff or computer resources needed for production control.
- *Preventive maintenance.* Operators clean out and lubricate machines themselves. No preventive maintenance staff needed.
- *Storage and handling.* Operators maintain their own small stocks of materials and supplies. No stockkeepers or material handlers needed.
- *Purchasing.* Operators reorder their own materials and supplies. Buyers have given them phone numbers for calling suppliers directly. Buyers stay out of routine ordering.
- *Training.* Supervisors and operators train other operators. No trainers needed.

And so on.

Contained (Product-Focused) Costing

Of course, this is exaggeration. Can't have *no* trainers, *no* material handlers, and the rest. The world-class company greatly reduces their numbers, but some remain, and their costs need to be charged to products accurately. One solution is to take staff-support people out of the overhead departments. Reassign them to a product manager's team.

In 1984 I did some work for a company that manufactures a line of wire products. The company's components division was tucked away in its own building. Outside suppliers were a big headache, and all corrective actions had to go through central purchasing a few miles away, a clumsy procedure. I learned that purchased materials for components were unlike those used in the company's main wire-making divisions. The logical answer seemed to be to reassign one buyer to the components group, which would transform that buyer from an overhead person to a member of the operating team. Also, the buyer's salary and expenses would be direct-costed to the products made. The company's purchasing department vetoed the suggestion; few companies were ready for that kind of action in 1984.

By 1989, such shifts of overhead people had become common. A number of manufacturing plants do as electrical and electronic controls producer Allen-Bradley does: assign a buyer-planner as a team member in each of several plants-in-a-plant.

Other kinds of costs usually charged to overhead accounts include energy, supplies, supervision, and depreciation of equipment and space. Often these can be switched to contained (product/customer-focused) costing, which is a natural step after reorganizing into focused cells and flow lines.

Government Work

Say that a manufacturer forms a separate team to handle all contracts with the state. The team consists of one production cell plus a dedicated support group. The support contingent includes contracting, design, buying, accounting, scheduling, shipping, computing, and other staff, as well as space, files, desks, phones, and a small computer. Likewise, the production cell has its own resources. The team's facilities, energy, and people are dedicated to state contracts. Direct and support costs still have to be carved up and charged to *each* contract, but at least they are not intermixed with work for the city, the county, commercial accounts, and so forth.

Progress Payments

In just-in-time's formative years, people in government contacting would say, "But why cut inventory? The government pays us for it as we buy it." Those progress payments cover the *price* of the materials. But every pile of inventory is layered with costs of waste, delay, and overhead. The contractor company that understands this will do everything in its power to get into the buy-for-immediate-use mode.

I picked a governmental example deliberately. Regina Herzlinger comments on costing problems in medical care and their adverse effects on government medical payments. She blames the medical care's functional structure:

> Because the dispensing of a service usually cuts across many functions, cost accounting and billing become horrendously complicated. The absence of accurate cost-accounting data forced the federal government to derive its [medical payment guidelines] through econometric analysis.[6]

Government contractors have fits over problems of allocating costs. And government auditors agonize over potential abuses. The news media regularly inform us of prestigious companies being prosecuted for illegally charging the government for work that should have been charged elsewhere. It's a problem of "rendering unto Caesar what are Caesar's; and unto God what are God's."

Best solution to this rendering problem is *focus*—the dedicated-office, dedicated-plant formula. Without focus, it is a frustrating battle of trying to assign costs to tangled mixtures of resources, orders, and customers.

Allocating Shrunken Overhead

Direct costing shrinks the overhead pool, but doesn't wipe it out. More changes are needed to more accurately sprinkle remaining overhead around. The concepts considered below can be applied in the period-cost mode, or used as guidelines in as-needed cost audits.

Overhead by lead time. One way to assign overhead is by lead time, which means time elapsed through all operations, including all delays. Hewlett-Packard, Greeley Division, may have been the first to do this. (And, starting in 1984, I was advocating it in my seminars—timidly at first, then forcefully after I heard about firms that did it successfully.)

The method is simple. Here's how it was done for a time at Zytec, a small maker of power supplies.[7] (Zytec has since moved on to a different approach—but has *not* gone back to the traditional burden-rate approach to costing.) Periodic samples of power supplies are tagged—see sample in Figure 8–1. The tags hold date and time data used to compute average throughput time for each model of power supply. Those averages, plus monthly data on units of each model shipped, yield a factory overhead rate. Table 8–3 illustrates. In the sample month, thirteen models of power supply were produced. PS404 gets the most factory overhead, 18.9 percent. Its average lead time, 4.5 days, times 500 units shipped in December equals 2,250 "lead-time-units." Dividing 2,250 by 11,875 total lead-time-units for all models yields the 18.9 percent overhead rate.

When Zytec needs a cost—say, for negotiating with a customer—it uses the percentage figures. Assume, for example, that total factory overhead is averaging $200,000 per month. PS404's share is 18.9

Figure 8–1. Zytec "Thruput" Tag

| Coil 70107640 |
| Xfmr 70107600 |
| P/S 94003421 |

THRUPUT TAG

	DATE	TIME
Coil Start		
Coil Finish		
XMR Start		
XMR Finish		
PS Start		
PS Pack		

Table 8–3. *Lead Time-Based Overhead Rates*

Product	Average Lead Time in Days	Units Shipped in Dec.	Lead-Time-Units Shipped	% of Total
PS101	1.0	2,000	2,000	16.8%
PS102	1.5	1,000	1,500	12.6
PS201	6.0	50	300	2.5
PS202	7.0	50	350	3.0
PS301	4.0	100	400	3.4
PS401	3.0	600	1,800	15.2
PS402	2.0	400	800	6.7
PS403	3.5	300	1,050	8.8
PS404	4.5	500	2,250	18.9
PS501	2.0	100	200	1.7
PS601	3.5	200	700	5.9
PS701	2.5	70	175	1.5
PS801	7.0	50	350	3.0
			11,875	100.0%

percent, or $37,800. For December's shipping total of 2,250 units, that is $16.80 (37,800/2,250) of factory overhead for each PS404.

The method is simple, fair, and accurate. The power supply model that creeps through the plant in a stop-and-go seven-day trip (e.g., PS801) is fussed over by overhead people for that full time period. Handlers handle it. Stockkeepers put it away and take it out again. Expediters and others juggle its priorities. Accountants value it. Managers get calls about it. The one-day model (PS101) zips through the plant, scarcely seen or sensed by overhead people.

The same idea applies to companies specializing in information processing: banking, accounting, engineering, libraries, mail handling, and thousands of other activities. The greater the elapsed time to process a loan approval, the more overhead support it takes. So, why not allocate overhead to information-based work that way? (But *don't* apply the lead-time method to human clients or patients. They pay enough, in anger and frazzled nerves, when they have to wait. A patient would *not* like to see a line on a bill saying, "General overhead charged at $3 per minute × [15 minutes processing + 48 minutes waiting . . . .])."

Costing in the process industries. People in the process industries say, We're different. When it comes to costing, that's often true. When the process is up and running, it disgorges (rolls, sheets, liquids, powders, etc.) in torrents with little labor in attendance. The extraordinary costs—costs other than material—are during changeovers: changes in size, density, color, grade, chemistry. Changeovers involve engineers, technicians, chemists, operators, supervisors, schedulers. Changeovers also produce scrap—sometimes a great deal of it—until the process is stabilized.

The issue is how to charge labor and overhead costs to products. How about doing it according to number of production runs per year— since most of the costs are related to start-up of a run? Very bad idea! It would discourage running the star products more often in smaller lots, to approach the customer-serving ideal of making some every day.

Some process-industry firms allocate by direct labor hours. That seems roughly okay since both direct labor and operating overhead occur for about the same reasons: start-up problems. But it requires a separate, costly system—one operators are sure to resent—to collect and charge labor to products. Also, in the process industry direct labor as a percent of product cost is nearly always too low to be a stable basis for overhead charging.

A few firms have made a step in the right direction: They allocate factory overhead to products by production quantity, for example, liters or square feet. Still, by that method, the trivial many (the extras), which require heavy support, will not receive a fair share of overhead. The important few (the stars) will get too much overhead. In most cases that overhead method needs to be modified.

I suggest a "quick-and-dirty" approach. Table 8–4 illustrates. Three product groups are shown. Group A are star products—a few items that sell in huge quantities per year. Group B are the starlets, and Group C are the many extras. For the sake of simplicity, we may assume they all have the same material cost: $100 per thousand square feet. We assume also that, as an average across all products, for every $100 in materials there are $30 of labor and operating overhead (direct labor, technical support, depreciation, utilities, etc.). But to assure that Group A, the easier-to-make products, gets less overhead than average, we make a minus adjustment of $20. We leave Group B alone, and make a plus $20 adjustment for Group C.

How are the adjustment factors determined? Quite arbitrarily—

Table 8–4. *Allocating Labor and Operating Overhead in the Process Industries—Adjustment Factor*

	Average Material Cost per Thousand Sq. Ft.	Average Labor + Operating Overhead per Thousand Sq. Ft.	Adjustment Factor	Estimated Cost per Thousand Sq. Ft.
Group A	$100	+$30	−$20	=$110
Group B	$100	+$30		=$130
Group C	$100	+$30	+$20	=$150

around a conference table. Accuracy isn't so important—and may be impossible by any kind of audit. Making sure that Group A gets less and Group C more is what is important.

Costing in human services. There is a surprising parallel between the process industry and certain kinds of human services. Organizations that process patients and clients—legal, medical, consulting, accounting, etc.—have big start-up costs. Later processing of the same client is simpler and takes much less overhead and direct processing. That is especially true of "star" patients and clients. They cost less, on average, per visit and could be billed less. Stockbrokers and car rental agencies *do* price that way—by volume of business.

Purchasing overhead. Some elements of overhead are special cases. Purchasing is one example. At Zytec, the purchasing people held meetings to find an accurate way to charge their costs to products. First question was, What causes us work? An obvious answer was number of items to be bought: the more items, the more work. For costing purposes, that translates to: the more purchased items *in a given model of power supply*, the more work. So why not charge purchasing department overhead by number of bought items in a certain model?

But wait a minute, someone said. Something else causes us work: supplier lead time (as distinct from operating lead time). The long-lead-time suppliers are the unreliable ones; buyers have to prod them all the time, and then they may deliver lots high in defectives. Also, during a long lead time there often are order changes, cancellations, substitutions, and lots of expediting.

The method the team came up with was this: For a certain model of power supply, add the lead times for each purchased part; the sum is the basis for costing.

Say, for example, that there are only two power supply models, A and B. If A's additive lead time is two hundred weeks, and B's is three hundred, A gets two-fifths of the purchasing department's costs, and B gets three-fifths (weighted by volume, as in Table 8–3).

The Zytec team was delighted with their creation, partly because it places cost pressure where it counts. Their costing method may prod engineering to design new models with more common purchased parts and fewer total purchased parts, which cuts many costs. The method also may urge purchasing to find or develop suppliers with shorter lead times (purchasing can help by providing suppliers with better demand information, longer-term contracts, and so forth).

Standard versus special costing. Zytec's purchasing and accounting people did their own innovative cost study. At least one other company is charging purchasing overhead to products in the same way. The method may become a standard textbook approach, one that other companies can "pull off the shelf" without the need for their own cost study.

Closer to being accepted as a standard approach is assigning operating (factory) overhead to services and products based on lead times. It seems correct for many kinds of businesses. The reason is that both costs and delays (lead times) fall as a result of almost any improvement in support of operations: Make machines run right, use common parts, cut setup times, shorten distances, take discounts on time, get orders processed quickly, and so forth. Lead time as a basis is often suitable for general management and sales overhead as well.

Perhaps new standard approaches will arise for costing other staff support, such as design, maintenance, power plant, and janitorial. Still, in many firms some staff areas won't fit the mold. So special cost studies may become commonplace.

Activity-based costing. Some schools of accountancy—from Harvard to Portland State—have developed new courses that teach students about doing customized cost studies. (This is quick response by our educators to a pressing need.) The method being taught is called activity-based costing—or, sometimes, causal-based or work-based. It starts with brainstorming. Key people from the staff department meet with someone from accounting to answer the question, "What causes us work?" Whatever they agree it is—so-called *drivers*—becomes the basis for assigning costs to products or services.

A case study, "Hewlett-Packard: Roseville Networks Division,"[8] describes one of the first and most extensive uses of the activity-based method. The cost system was conventional—direct-labor driven—until 1985 when the accounting team, with plenty of input from others, developed a new set of drivers. An impetus for change was accounting's discovery that design engineering didn't believe in or use accounting's numbers; they had developed their own cost model, called MAKE (*m*anufacturing *k*nowledge *e*xpert).

The team changed to a new set of drivers later in 1985, changed drivers twice more in 1986, once in 1987, and twice in 1988. The changes were mostly in the direction of more drivers—relating to number of parts, number of insertion slots in insertion machines, volume of component usage, number of assemblies, number of solder joints, and so on. Engineers using the cost data to make design decisions could be victimized. For example, at one point an engineer became a local hero by making a design change that slashed reported product costs. A hero, that is, until the next round of cost-driver changes, which caused reported costs to "go through the roof."

Kyle Black, engineering project manager, said, of all these changes, "My initial reaction . . . was anger . . . I wanted one set of numbers that I could rely upon." Later Black came to feel that the ongoing effort had been beneficial in that accounting, R&D, marketing, and manufacturing had worked together and developed valuable understanding of each other's work.

As the cost-driver system evolved, did it become more useful? One engineer, Fred Huang, wondered: "We could improve the model to capture more costs, but we would risk it becoming too complex to understand and hence use."

Costing long-term activities. In decisions about drivers, activities having a payoff out in the future are special cases. Cooper and Kaplan cite research and development (R&D) for new products as one example. They suggest *not* allocating such R&D costs to *present* goods or services;[9] doing so would yield costs that are unfairly high (unfair for management purposes, that is; the legal accounting requirements are another story). The same reasoning applies to costs of deliberately holding excess capacity for potential future business growth.

COSTS AND BEHAVIOR

Some of the pioneers have used their innovative new costing methods for more than just a check on prices, bids, and go/no-go decisions. For example, lead-time-based costing gives Zytec an incentive to drive out delays, which at the same time reduces overhead (e.g., stock handling) associated with delays. And, as we've seen, Hewlett-Packard, Roseville, provides design engineers with data showing how product costs go down with fewer parts in a product, which can induce engineers to simplify designs.

Better Behavior with Better Cost Data?

These are behavioral uses of cost data. Industry's experience in recent decades in using cost data that way has been sad, even tragic. Part of the reason is that grossly inaccurate cost data have been used. We've looked at hypothetical examples: the TV manufacturer and the law office. The error was charging overhead to goods and services based on direct labor. In manufacturing, that has caused companies to buy machines for hundreds of thousands of dollars to save a few hundred dollars per year on direct labor. It was cost-driven behavioral manipulation gone amok!

In the face of the flagrant cost inaccuracies of the past, it's a wonder that more plants didn't shut down and more companies go under. Part of the reason that all businesses did not choke on their bad numbers is that companies know they must price based in part on what the market will bear, not just on markup from cost.

Actually, there is no good reason for costs to be ultra-accurate. For pricing and product-line decisions, roughly accurate costs are good enough. For those purposes, I think a cross section of managers could do an almost-good-enough cost audit in a meeting room using only their experience. After all, our costing systems in the past, relying on numbers, often didn't even have the signs (minus and plus) right.

Now that we have found ways to make costs fairly accurate, is it a good idea to use costs to drive behavior? Only under certain conditions, such as for giving a hard nudge to an important customer-serving objective, such as quickly slashing delays, number of parts, or errors.

- *Example 1.* In a company whose design options have been growing explosively for years, maybe it makes sense to put new, *real* cost data before the marketers and designers.

Losing an Industry

The memory chip industry, once headquartered in the U.S., is now nearly owned by Japan. On hindsight, a key reason for the migration appears to be the cost system.

Early low-density chips (e.g., 16K) required high direct labor but little overhead, compared with later high-density (in the 256K range) chips. The latter require costly clean rooms and armies of technical and engineering staff.

During the transition, low- and high-density lines sometimes ran side by side in the same plant. The conventional cost system laid a heavy overhead burden on the low-density chips, because overhead was charged based on direct labor; the high-density chips, with little labor content, were charged little for the overhead that actually was theirs.

With pricing set in the market, memory chip makers in the U.S. found prices for low-density, commoditylike chips to be too low for profitability. The "strategic" decision: drop them.[10]

That was just the beginning. The cost system continued to irrationally decimate the product lines of semiconductor makers, always attacking the high-volume products first.

How many other industries or companies suffered the same sad sequence?

- *Example 2.* In a human services setting in which waiting time has become intolerable, it may be useful to provide servers with new cost data: "It costs us $40—in overhead and lost business—for every minute a customer has to wait." (Just like documents or widgets, humans waiting have to be provided waiting space and amenities, and that's overhead; other overhead costs tied to waiting include handling complaints, cancellations—"I'm leaving; I've waited long enough!"—and rescheduling.)

Driving Behavior the Wrong Way

Now for the negative side: Staff work is supposed to help improve the value of the end product or service. Sometimes, however, cost data from an activity-based cost audit can end up driving staff people to add cost or decrease value. The following example[11] concerns an inventory control department:

> *Cost auditor to department head:* "What determines the time required to process an incoming shipment? Does it matter if the shipment is large or small?"
>
> *Head's answer:* "The time to process an item depends on number of times it is received, not on size of shipments."
>
> *Next question:* "What other factors affect your department's work load?"
>
> *Answer:* "Three other people disburse material to the shop floor, and again, volume is not an issue; it's number of times material is disbursed."

The answers become the basis for a new method of charging inventory control costs to products made: by number of lots handled. That seems accurate—for pricing. If used for driving behavior, however, that costing method would put an overhead-cost penalty on small, frequent deliveries in and out of the stockroom. It would favor large batches, which pile up all over, incurring the high overhead costs associated with stocks made out of phase with demand. It is exactly opposite to the world-class goal of frequent, small-lot movements of work—just-in-time and in synch with customers' needs!

Note: In the earlier discussion of costing in the process industry, allocation of labor and overhead by number of production runs was rejected for the same reason.

Cost Audits, Not Cost Transactions

When business people hear about simplifying operations, cutting data collection, and fixing the cost system, their usual reaction is appreciation and joy. One attendee at a 1986 seminar of mine had a mixed reaction. He told me he sees the value of it all, but his company relies on the traditional system for a special reason: They buy distressed manufacturing companies, impose full cost reporting, do complete cost analyses of every operation, and then apply the cost-cutting ax. This turnaround formula has been highly successful. So, he asked, how could his company even think about eliminating the reporting?

I have rarely been so eager to answer a question. I told him I had been "waiting three years" for someone to ask a question like that. I was so excited I almost forgot the answer!

My response was, "But do you have to *recost* the same operations again and again, day after day, all year long? That's what the cost transaction system does! Why don't you just do cost audits?"

I explained that audits would give them far more accurate product costs than they were getting. Audits would also be much cheaper, since cost data for go/no-go decisions (promote a product or kill it) are only needed yearly or less often. Pricing and bidding decisions come up infrequently as well. So throw out your factory cost system and just do cost audits as needed. My questioner was intrigued with the answer, to say the least.

But there is more to cost management than go/no-go, pricing, and bidding decisions. I am not thinking of profit-and-loss accounting, which is a legal necessity, not part of cost management. (P&L accounting is based on gross periodic expenditure data. It does not usually require operation or product cost data.) Rather, the other part of cost management is control: control of cost and performance.

We have seen how the cost system can drive behavior in exactly the wrong direction: less control and higher costs. It is exceedingly hard to devise a cost system that will not push a few cost factors the wrong way, and if a company *does* get the system working just right, it won't last. Conditions change, and needs to revise the cost system will tend to be overlooked. (The wrong-headed system of allocating overhead by direct labor hours persisted for decades!)

Are there better ways to control costs than the cost system? There are indeed. We consider them next.

CONTROLLING WHAT CAUSES COST

Unnecessary cost comes from bad design, poor quality, unpredictability, delay, adversarial dealings with suppliers, narrowly pigeonholed employees, and the customer-out organization. Under each of these terms is a long list of subcategories of unneeded cost. For every item, the management earthquakes of the eighties have provided solutions: direct controls on the multitude of causes of cost.

Variable Costs

The most important of the direct controls are those in design. The new approaches are designing products and services for the customer, quality, delay and cost minimization, and fewer parts and suppliers, and also minimizing the need for new resources. New policies, techniques, and ways of linking designers to customers and to suppliers pave the way. This is *cost-impact management of the design function.*

A second set of direct controls is the vast array of mostly new techniques and concepts used in the trenches and largely operator-centered. They deal with cross-training, data collection and analysis, total quality, preventive maintenance, quick response and quick setup, and cells and flow lines, to name a few. For each, large signboards display the pace of continual improvement. The signboards are at or near the action, not in middle managers' conference rooms or buried in computer sheets or files. The displays don't monitor or control so much as they inform, teach, lead, and motivate. Moreover, for the most part, they are not periodic, such as monthly or weekly; they are on-going.

The third type of direct control deals with the other large category of so-called variable cost: cost of purchased items, including all the costs of poor performance by suppliers. The costs go down when suppliers get their acts together—which means axing their wastes. The buying companies' role is called supplier development or supplier partnership, an abrupt about-face from the adversarial approach of the past. For their part, the suppliers have at their disposal all of the world-class concepts. Some suppliers are aggressively putting them to use—and

---

Dispersed Accounting

The new cost-cutting engine is driven mostly by visual signboards in the workplaces. Since traditional accounting is hardly involved, the accounting department is much reduced in size (another big overhead cost reduced).

For better service to customers, still more accounting department changes are needed. Why, for example, should the department house accounts payable and accounts receivable? The two may work side by side, but they have nothing in common. Forward-thinking accountants, like Alan Vercio of Texas Instruments, see a better way: Move payables to purchasing and receivables to sales. That puts each accounting subgroup right next to its customer—next process in the chain.

not being timid about letting their customers know about their new competencies.

Fixed Costs

Then there are the fixed costs—which really are not fixed, especially for the continually improving company. As a result of the controls in design, operations, and the supplier base, many of the fixed costs evaporate. World-class improvers shut down stockrooms, dispose of forklift trucks, tear out racks, sell off containers, and get rid of equipment to track inventory and "clock" each labor transaction. If all cylinders are firing properly, the result is the "incredible shrinking plant" with less investment in space and equipment—even while sales soar.

Expenditures on *new* equipment and automation also must be controlled—but not pinched off. New acquisitions are often made because the old machines don't work well and because of labor and quality problems. Those are often bad reasons, since there are many ways to make big improvements with existing equipment and labor. Improving what you have comes first—before investment in more equipment or automation.

Budgets and Expenditure Authority

Let's not leave the wrong impression: Penny-pinching is not the answer. The world-class company doesn't hesitate to spend on the many little needs and the occasional big one that can make an impact.

The poorly run company hesitates all the time. It hesitates because only certain high-level people have spending authority, and they have learned to doubt the numbers that come from feasibility studies. It hesitates because most low-level people with good ideas are confused about or give up on getting the funds even for low-cost items, like an essential hand tool.

To help keep the improvements flowing, some companies are giving operating teams a small budget or petty cash fund; at one company, it's $20 a month per employee. Team members may go to the local supply store to buy paint and brushes, a rubber hammer, or presentation materials.

At Imprimis's plant near Oklahoma City, PEP (personal employee participation) teams learn budgeting as part of their extensive training. Now that they know the ropes, team members lose their hesitancy about getting attractive improvement items into the budget. They also help keep expenditures in line on a daily basis; for example, budget-watching employees, concerned about going over budget through costly overtime, have elected to bear down and catch up without overtime.

In the same vein, at CalComp's Anaheim plant, plans are in motion for operators to have the authority to approve payment on supplier invoices. Since quite a few of their suppliers deliver daily "just-in-time," it makes sense to simplify the invoicing.

Quantum Medical Systems has already greatly simplified its invoicing. Quantum turned over the buying and handling of twenty-five cable assembly items to one supplier, who delivers just-in-time right to Quantum's shop floor. Billing is monthly instead of weekly, and Quantum pays if the invoice amount is within about 2 percent of Quantum's informal records. That approach cuts clerical time for checking, correcting, and matching shipping paper and invoices.[12]

What about authority to make a big purchase? An A. T. Kearney study shows that top companies push spending authority down to the division level—so the division can act fast when there is a need. The study compared 200 top-performing companies with lesser performers of the same size. In the top companies, division managers' spending authority averaged about $20 million, which is ten times higher than that of the other group of firms.[13]

Casting Off Cost Controls

We have been summarizing methods used by today's top companies in controlling the causes of cost—via continual improvement and total involvement, including making prudent expenditures. If a company is using the full set of new controls, *it does not need to rely on cost itself for management control.*[14]

Few companies are ready to accept this. Business has relied on costs so long that it cannot yet imagine getting by with just direct controls on causes. Business also cannot imagine using costs just for making product-line and pricing decisions and not for cost control.

Thus, most companies that have visual charts on the walls—showing continual improvement in lead times, setup times, and so forth—still have their cost systems intact. In fact, several are busily devising multiple-driver, activity-based cost approaches. Few are satisfied, for example, with simple approaches such as charging operating overhead to products by lead time. And, for those who want to use cost for control, a cost audit once or twice a year won't do. It has to be a transaction-based accounting *system* with monthly reports and reviews (and gripes that the accounting system still isn't right).

Simplicity will, I think, prevail in the long run. Right now, activity-based costing is a new toy, which everybody wants to play elaborate games with.

REPLACING CARROT AND STICK

Controlling what causes cost is logical, direct, and effective. It replaces the ineffective conventional approach to cost control, which is carrot and stick: a limp carrot and a thin stick. The cost-variance report was the thin stick. It said, Cut your costs, or else. But it offered no specific hints as to how. The limp carrot was the pay and reward system—again not tied to much that was specific and clearly worthy of reward. Pay and reward is changing too, as we see in the next chapter.

9

⽗⽷

Pay, Recognition, Celebration

MONEY TALKS. Money is also easily squandered. Part of the earth-quakes in accounting and employee involvement are in the ways people are rewarded. The innovations, as well as renewed enthusiasm for old approaches, include both monetary and nonmonetary rewards.

PAY AND OPPORTUNITY

Mary Kay of Mary Kay Cosmetics leads cheers and gives away pink Cadillacs. Bruce Engel of WTD Industries (sawmills) passes out $50 bills. Thomas Melohn of North American Tool and Die interviews every prospective employee—and helps iron out problems in his people's personal lives. Lincoln Electric Company (welding machines) pays huge wage incentives for output.

These companies have success stories to tell about their motivated work forces. There are many more such stories. They all are different, and they leave us somewhat confused about motivation and reward.

Pay for Knowledge

I am confident of a few things, however. One is the soundness of *pay for knowledge*. Since employee involvement *requires* that operators become multiskilled, the pay system must conform.

Say that base pay is $8.00 per hour. Operator masters the first job, proven by passing a test of mastery, and the wage goes to $8.25. Sits through the firm's forty-hour course covering a dozen topics (including SPC, problem-solving, and teamwork) and passes the test; the wage is upped to $8.40. Masters a second job, and the wage rises some more.

Just a few years ago pay for knowledge was unheard of. Now it is a fast-growing phenomenon. Among the users are many companies with labor unions, largely in the automotive industry. So far, the action amounts to tremors—not 6.8 on the Richter scale—which is to be expected since pay is a sensitive, emotional issue for all of us.

Pay for knowledge is not just for front-line employees. For professional, managerial, and staff support people, it becomes *more pay for learning more parts of the business*. Far too few companies are getting this done, even though we have heard over and over how effective this policy is in top Japanese companies. (Ouchi gave the topic ten pages in his 1981 book, *Theory Z*. I devoted three pages to the matter in my 1982 book on Japanese manufacturing.[1]

Pay for Knowledge + Comparable Worth

Pay for knowledge has appeal for a contemporary social reason: It may help quiet key arguments against pay by comparable worth. The objections have to do with disruptive labor-supply effects of comparable worth, as it is usually conceived.

The Feds, Too

Pay for knowledge is not just for the private sector. The U.S. Defense Logistics Agency (DLA) is running a "skill-based-pay" experiment covering 1,600 employees at the Defense Depot in Ogden, Utah. First step is to reorganize the work force into teams focused on a total product, service, or process. All team members get the chance to learn all jobs, with pay tied to mastery. If successful at Ogden, the plan will be extended to the DLA's other five depots.[2]

Comparable-worth pioneers have mostly used job classification as its basis: Classify all jobs based on "content" of the job (that approach is now the law in Ontario, Canada). The method pushes up pay for office jobs, many of which are dominated by women. At the same time, it makes jobs like nursing, machining, plumbing, carpentry, trucking, factory work, garbage hauling, and many others relatively less attractive than they are now. Since people tend to prefer to work in nice temperature-controlled offices, other kinds of work suffer losses of applicants. Society is the loser (companies, too) if it can't attract enough people into those occupations.[3]

Job classification systems have been a miserable failure. They have pushed people into narrow-niche jobs and kept them there, letting them rust. I recall my own frustration at a time early in my career. I was an industrial engineer. A few of my projects involved unit-record (punched-card) equipment—predecessor to business computers. Computers came along shortly thereafter, and I learned some programming. I was eager for a career change—to become a computer systems analyst, where I thought the future lay. No way. The job classification system says NO to lateral career shifts.

The system also requires a large staff of classification specialists, creating an overhead empire in the human resources department (HRD). HRD should, like all other staff units, be lean and mean; its focus should be on hiring, training, and genuine human resource development. Ironically, its role in job classification makes HRD an accessory to the crime of failure to develop human resources. A worthy concept like comparable worth should not taint itself by associating with one so unworthy as job classification.

Here is a better idea: Press for comparable worth, but with pay for knowledge as the basis. It works like this: Mary X, a trainer in HRD, starts at a modest base pay; it is the same as the base for many other jobs in the company. Mary can earn step increases, but gets a good raise—after three years or more—only by making and mastering a career shift: perhaps to purchasing, sales, computer programming, or operations; it's a lesser raise if the shift is from training to recruiting. The person is paid—based on knowledge—not the position.

To be sure, this system won't help certain acute shortages, such as in nursing. The comparable-worth law must be written to allow market-based pay in occupations for which there is a proven chronic shortage; for nursing that has been the case for decades—in many countries.

Comparable Opportunity

On the surface, comparable worth is a pay issue. Just below the surface, there is a riptide surging in another direction: It is the seething anger of women—plenty of men, too—who are stuck in a dead-end job. These are bright, ambitious people, many with a college degree or at least some college. (U.S. Census statistics show that half of all service employees in the U.S. have some college education; in manufacturing the percentage is slightly less.) They took, say, a clerical job, and can't get out.

By itself, comparable worth will not do much for the many people in this fix; nor will it do anything for the companies they work for, which are guilty of squashing human potential. The combined system, comparable worth *and* knowledge (CWAK), ensures that people have plenty of chances to move into new career tracks; and the system pays those who are good learners.

So, employees, CWAK for your opportunities. And managers, CWAK for employee development; it's your company's future.

SELF-WORTH

In between pay and opportunity lies another issue. It is self-worth, or personal gratification. As badly as employers have mishandled monetary rewards, they have done worse in providing the intrinsic rewards of feeling good about oneself.

Involvement as Its Own Reward

Old-style efforts, called participative management (or, from the receiver's point of view, employee participation), were weak. What it amounted to was an offering: "In our magnanimity and benevolence, we, the company, shall offer you, the employee, a chance to participate"— but not in anything meaningful. As was noted in Chapter 5, employee involvement (EI) is much more: It's ownership of your own process and its quality, team ownership of your team's cell and its output, and continual improvement in serving the customer at the next process.

Barcy Smith, at Xerox's New Build Operations Division, says:

I went to team meetings once a week, beginning in January 1987. They asked for my input to get things going. They even sent me to Illinois to check out a company and a line they were considering.

It's a very different feeling from just being an operator. Now, I help design workstations, help make design changes on the parts.[4]

Tim Dellapenta, machine operator at Prestolite Electric, says:

I like the new freedom. Before, engineers bought all our equipment. Now we make recommendations. We used to call a [maintenance] man; now we do most of the preventive maintenance, and we're reducing downtime. Now I am responsible for getting the product to the customer. It's more than just a job with me now. It's a commitment."[5]

In contrast to Smith's and Dellapenta's remarks, I heard more typical comments from a man who drives a truck for a distributor. He was grumbling about his firm's practices in buying a large fleet of new trucks. "There are a hundred different kinds of seats, but they don't ask any of the drivers what they prefer. And most of the drivers have back trouble of some kind."

Furthermore, he said, most of the new trucks they choose are under-powered; they creep over Cascade mountain passes at ten miles an hour, which stretches the trip and gets the driver home an hour or more late. "No drivers were asked about that. They say it's for fuel economy."

Fuel economy may be a good reason—one the drivers could only agree with had they been involved. Ten or twenty years ago, we would have taken the company to task for its failure to inform the drivers. Today, the failure is in excluding drivers from helping to choose the equipment. The reason for including them is not simply to allay gripes and hard feelings. Rather the purposes are positive: (1) to *improve the decisions—for the company as a whole* and (2) to provide personal gratification to the drivers who had a hand in the improved decisions, which encourages further involvement in the improvement effort.

Welcome Mat for Staff Experts

Jobs in engineering, public relations, advertising, and other areas of expertise might seem to be inherently fulfilling. Often they aren't. Professional and staff people have plenty of those days when they hate to go to work in the morning—same as clerks and factory opera-tors. Ask staff people about their jobs, and you hear things like: "We're out of touch with reality around here." "Just going through the motions." "A Mickey-Mouse job." "A big, impersonal bureaucracy."

The barrier-busting themes of this book pave the way for staff people to achieve greater personal gratification; here is how:

- Staff people who are let out of their offices to team up with front-line employees on mutual concerns are closer to the customer, the source of revenue, the reason for the firm's existence. That's reality.
- In this mode, staff people come to be welcomed by line employees—welcomed for their knowledge and expertise, which is a gratifying change. In the old system, staff advisers were too often resented and sometimes ridiculed for unrealistic "ivory-tower" advice.
- Experts who learn to work with other kinds of experts, and who take career-change assignments, find they are more effective, that the chain of customers is better served. That raises feelings of self-worth.

RECOGNITION AND CELEBRATION

It's nice to be able to pat oneself on the back. Some can thrive on that, but most of us need and appreciate occasional strokes from team members, supervisors, and the company.

Unique leaders like Thomas Melohn and Mary Kay have their own special way of showing appreciation. Most managers, indeed most parents, teachers, social workers, team members, and close friends, are awkward about showing appreciation to others who deserve it. "Oh, I like your hair!" may get an unstated reaction like, "What was wrong with it yesterday?" or "What a phony. I know from your tone of voice and the look on your face that you hate my hair."

Visual Recognition

Can the employer handle the delicate matter of praise so that it has a positive effect and doesn't backfire? The employer can indeed. The world-class approach to recognition and celebration has the following attributes:

1. It is visible and public (or semipublic).
2. It has a strong next- and final-customer bias.

Trade Secrets

A year after I had provided advice and a seminar at a company, I received some feedback. It was a copy of a company newsletter. At the bottom of page 1 is a boxed note: "Because this newsletter may contain competition-sensitive information, distribution should be limited to _____ employees and should be treated as _____ proprietary."

Why the ominous warning? My main contact at the company explained: "Recently a copy of the newsletter got in the hands of a customer who promptly demanded a price reduction because of documented yield improvements on his program."

The good news is that the company continues to publicize its people's continuing and impressive improvements. Feedback and recognition are too important to abandon simply because some of the information might leak.

---

3. It focuses on teams first (from small ones all the way up to the team that is the whole company), individuals second.
4. It includes results, on-going activities, and praise.
5. It is active and frequent.
6. It ensures consistency: Self-recognition and external forms of recognition are for the same things.

There *is* an approach that can meet all six attributes. For lack of a better term, we'll call it *visual recognition,* the close partner of visual control signboards (featured in Chapter 5). It evolved in Japan but now is in partial use by good companies around the globe.

Milliken—Standout Example

Milliken, the textile manufacturer headquartered in Spartanburg, South Carolina, stands out above other Western companies in its uses of visual recognition. The photos in Figure 9–1 are from Milliken plants and offices.

The first, Figure 9–1A, shows what I call an "alcove of excellence."

A. Alcove of Excellence

B. Wall of Fame

Figure 9–1. Visual Management at Milliken

C. Cost Accounting Contributors

Every area, office or plant, has one of these display zones. This large one is chock full of charts proclaiming recent improvements, giving the status of on-going projects, and naming the teams and persons involved.

If you were to get a plant tour, you would have several tour guides, each an operator from one of the plant's sectors (e.g., slitting and brushing). Each guide would show you detailed charts in the work area and probably take you to the alcove to see graphs showing overall team accomplishments: processes brought under control; steady improvements in scrap, lead time, inventories, flow distances, setup times; and other "vital signs."

Figure 9–1B shows part of a corridor called a "wall of fame." It is plastered with plaques, photos, copies of letters of merit, and the like; Margaret Thatcher is even pictured—in connection with an award to Milliken Industries Ltd. in the U.K. Every area has its own wall of fame.

Wall photos aren't recognition enough, so Milliken's company news magazine, called *The Torch: Pursuit of Excellence,* is filled with more of the same. The May 1988 issue contains thirty-nine group photos and forty-three individual photos, all with a short story about their achievements. Other photos show people at recognition/celebration events.

The third photo, Figure 9–1C, shows cost accounting's "pursuit of excellence." It tells us that 100 percent of the department's associates submitted at least one OFI (opportunity for improvement) idea. Also on display are photos and brief summaries of accomplishments of "corrective action teams." (Increasingly, companies are putting Polaroid cameras in the work areas, to be used for capturing employee recognition events, as well as recording before and after conditions.)

Milliken hands out many types of awards: warp operator of the month, the quarter, the year; preventive maintenance associate of the month/quarter/year; style changer . . . , fixer . . . , super associate of the month/quarter/year. Awards go, as well, to outsiders: of seventy freight carriers Milliken deals with, twelve have received awards.

The Milliken approach clearly is visual; directed at what's important to next and final customer; both team- and individual-focused; active and frequent; and concerned with results, activities, and recognition. The photos do not directly tell us if the sixth requisite, consistency, is met. Nevertheless, we can bet that it is, as evidenced by the following:

- Mr. Milliken himself, as well as other senior executives, are in many of the photos. As much time as they spend recognizing improvements, they must feel the improvements are consistent with company goals.
- Human recognition does not stand alone but is backed up by a full range of signboards that track process improvements. Both types of displays are all over the company's plants and offices. (What do managers manage? They manage activities and results, many of which are on display. How do supervisors supervise? Good ones do it more with praise than with abuse, and praise is all over Milliken's signboards, walls, and newsletters.)
- The displays are sources of personal and team pride, particularly since employees plot their own improvements on the displays and sometimes have the chance to lead tours in which they explain the improvements to visitors.

PERFORMANCE RATING

The full and complete visual system packs a wallop: It replaces most of the vast array of reports and forms (including the paperless kind on video screens) that managers and supervisors have had to put up with. One that remains is the performance-rating report for every employee.

I realize there is a school of thought that says performance rating is bad or unnecessary. Rating may seem even less necessary for a company using visual recognition/visual control, which motivates continual improvement. With improvement taken care of, why rate people? Also, since supervisors dislike it and do it awkwardly, and since subordinates get uptight about it, why rate people?

The quick answer is *meritocracy*: Pay and promote based on merit, a concept that many of us believe is fundamental. In a meritocracy, merit must be judged.

The judge does not necessarily have to be a supervisor. Another way is for the team to rate each member's performance. Regardless of who does it, there are four main performance factors to be judged in the world-class company:

1. Work output—quantity and quality
2. Innovation
3. Communication
4. Leadership

These four have always been central in rating professionals and managers. In the improvement-driven company they are dominant for *all* employees.

In any group of employees there are likely to be one or two who greatly outperform the rest—in output and quality. Someone else is innovative, always thinking of good ideas, solutions to pressing problems. Another perhaps is neither speedy nor a fount of good ideas but is a communicator: able to clarify things others have trouble saying, draw sketches, make flip charts, deal with experts and people in another group. Finally, someone in the group is a leader—one who inspires others to buckle down, to innovate, to communicate.

Only one of these talents is tapped and rated in the old-style organization: output. A system so limited is very unfair! It bottles up talent and keeps the whole group from looking good, not to mention most of the individuals in it.

Of course, other, nonwork factors are always included in employee rating systems. They need not be discussed here, just recognized: coming to work on time, neatness and cleanliness, getting along with others, and so forth.

SUGGESTIONS

The traditional system does allow one type of employee contribution to improvement: suggestions. While performance rating is reactive ("How did I do?"), suggestions are action-oriented.

The woeful suggestion rates of Western companies were mentioned in earlier chapters. (Milliken is one of the few, if not the only one with world-class numbers: an average of about eight suggestions—opportunities for improvement—per employee per year.) As EI, visual recognition and control, and related concepts take root, the numbers should incline sharply.

Cash, Prizes, and Suggestion Lotteries

Suggestion systems commonly pay for ideas based on a percentage of estimated savings, and, often, a small minimum sum for any suggestion. A growing number of firms are ending cash payments—at least for small suggestions. Instead of money, the suggestions committee (or "czar") awards a premier parking space, tickets to a sports event, or a nice dinner. Vaughn Beals, CEO at Harley-Davidson, explains his company's policy:

> We have never added up and we never will the cost savings that come out of [employee involvement]—on the simple basis that if that becomes the focus, some dumb cluck is going to decide that more is better, and then everybody's focus is, "gee, look at all the

---

Words and Meanings

Milliken has had excellent results using error cause removal (ECR) forms. But some people are sensitive to words like "error," which somebody might take too personally. Now, at Milliken they have changed the form's name. Instead of ECR, it's OFI—"opportunity for improvement."

Japanese industry went through a similar name change a few years ago. The Japanese word *bakayoke* roughly translates as fool-proof, as in "fool-proof your process." Now the preferred word is *pokayoke*, which has a meaning akin to the English term "fail-safe."

money I'm saving—I ought to get a piece." The thing we do . . . is give em a belt buckle, . . . a picnic once a year, . . . all the beer they can drink (that's Harley beer, by the way—it really is), and we just say thanks. Their satisfaction is they made the product better, they had fun doing it, and they have some control over their environment—which is what it's all about.[6]

A payment method destined to become very popular is the suggestion lottery. A version of it has been adopted by Electrolux Cookers (kitchen ranges) in Spennymoor, England, as an element of the plant's "total involvement system (TIS)." Divisional manager Alex Sutherland kicked off TIS with a personal message inside a slick, multicolor folder, which explained the goals and described phase 1, "elimination of waste." All employees received entry forms on which they record waste-eliminating ideas.

The suggester gets an automatic small prize (e.g., a Parker pen), then discusses the idea with his or her supervisor. If the supervisor approves and implements it, the entry form goes into the lottery pool. Once a month, one form is drawn for a prize worth fifty pounds at a local retailer. Twice yearly there is another drawing for the company's top-of-the line cooker, worth eight hundred pounds. The more entries, the more chances to win.

Another example: At a U.S. firm, each suggestion pays $1, and the name of the suggester goes into a hat. Once a month one name is drawn. The reward: a paid day off—with the person's boss filling in!

Call it tapping people's gambling instincts. But there's more to it than that. Lottery awards are consistent with perhaps the best-accepted (or most-tested) principle of motivation: infrequent, random reinforcement. The same body of research also reveals what does *not* work: rewards so regular or frequent that they come to be expected.

Some might feel it is miserly not to pay well for suggestions. On the other hand, there are other ways to offer financial rewards—such as merit raises, bonuses, and profit sharing, each of which grows as more good suggestions are submitted. Also, many of us are convinced that nonmonetary rewards for suggestions are about as effective as cash.

Numbers Game?

Aside from the issue of pay and reward, there is the question of whether or not to count suggestions. When we hear numbers like 50 or 150 suggestions per employee per year, we know how it works: Every good idea, no matter how small, gets written up and goes through the approval and implementation sequence. If response is simple and quick, the cost of running the suggestion effort may be modest. (Milliken achieves twenty-four-hour, yea-or-nay response from supervisor back to OFI submitter; it requires some paperwork but little fuss.) Still, isn't the best system the one in which improvement is everyone's job? Sure it is. Then, we might ask, why make a fuss over every improvement?

Companies that are nonchalant about suggestions tend to fit this profile: They now have some employee involvement (notably, operators holding problem-solving meetings) and are in businesses with low labor content and products with whopping profit margins: medical products, instruments, specialty electronics, and professional service firms (financial, consulting, law, etc.), for example. With their margins, they are lax about suggestions. Their EI emphasis (relying little on suggestions) is narrowly focused—mostly on cutting delays between departments and improving quality and customer service.

A different approach, followed in some companies, is to write up just the big suggestions. Strive for lots of incremental improvements with everyone involved, but let problem-solving teams and supervisors process the ideas. Limit the formal suggestion system to whopper ideas, with big potential cash awards as the carrot. That conforms to the way R&D-driven companies and universities handle scientific breakthroughs: Those who dream up and perfect the innovations are rewarded handsomely.

Measure and Tally

Those who favor de-emphasizing suggestion counting must confront this counterargument: Performance that isn't measured isn't performed. There are enough grains of truth in that maxim to convince me that the laid-back approach is weak and wrong.

The typical company suggestion program—today as in the past—yields zero suggestions per year from most employees.

Suggestions that do trickle in don't arouse much excitement, because reviewing them is a hassle. The solution is to streamline the suggestion system. Here are some possibilities:

- Every suggestion includes a self-assessment check sheet. It is short and simple, something like this:

Suggestion's Effect on Each of the Following (check one):

	Less	Neutral	More*
Throughput time	___	___	___
Space	___	___	___
Defects	___	___	___
Staff support	___	___	___
Safety risks	___	___	___
Job difficulty	___	___	___

* If any checks are in the "more" column, your suggestion needs more study before submission.

If "more" is checked even once, it is not yet a suggestion. If all checks are in the "less" and "neutral" categories, approval—by the supervisor—is almost automatic.

- Suggestions exceeding the department's monetary authority go through an extra step: an approval committee with rotating membership. (At Imprimis's large disk plant, every employee, line or staff, serves a short term on the suggestions committee.) Since quick action is all-important, each office or plant sector might have its own rotating committee, which could meet half an hour daily to study and sign off on suggestions.

- Certain kinds of suggestions can be processed publicly, on display boards. In one Japanese electronics plant, supervisors walk through their assigned areas several times a day with instant cameras. They snap pictures of things needing improvement—a large pile of parts, a long reach or walk distance, a safety hazard. On the spot, the supervisor and the work team write a page suggesting how to fix the problem; sometimes it is as simple as moving a table. The write-up and photo are tacked to a wall. A division manager walks by several times a day and writes "okay" if the idea is accepted.

This approach is briefly described in a book recently translated into English from Japanese.[7] An accompanying photograph shows thirty-nine photo-suggestions completely covering the company's "wall of suggestions."

While this system is limited to things easily shown in a picture, that can cover a lot of territory. Further, the visual suggestion approach can be reduced to a daily routine: getting a new set of photo-suggestions up on the wall and keeping the wall filled.

- A final point: If the suggestion system is streamlined and fair, it will produce a continuing flood of ideas. With plenty pouring forth, the best overall measure of results is just number of suggestions per employee per year, tracked on trend charts. Make the charts large and visible and in prominent places in each area, with a summary chart for the whole company on a main wall at company headquarters. The charts serve as one of the company's proud evidences of good management of people and problems.

PAY FOR SUCCESS

Suggestions, along with recognition and pay for knowledge, help rev up the improvement effort. As a result, savings pile up, and extra profits roll in (or losses are stemmed).

On the other hand, the traditional enterprise (the one without things like suggestions and EI) considers money-saving and revenue-increasing ideas to be managerial in nature. So managers feel it only fair that they receive some of the savings or profits—on top of regular pay. The rest of the work force is left out.

The world-class enterprise cannot operate that way. It must spread the fruits of the improvements, because so many deserve it. There are plenty of ways: profit sharing, bonuses, gain sharing, stock distribution, group or individual incentive pay, and incentive gifts.

Incentive Gifts

The last one, incentive gifts (trip to the Caribbean, jewelry, pink Cadillac), has been common only in sales. Today, with so many more deserving people, companies are seeking new ways of sharing success. An advantage of incentive gifts is that they can have a memory effect: Employees on a company-paid trip to Acapulco come back loaded with photos, some of which go up on company bulletin boards—a little personalized "wall of fame."

Output Incentives

While incentive gifts are for special reasons and special occasions, incentive pay for output can be earned every day. Common examples are sales commissions, farm piecework, and output incentives in manufacturing.

Costs of output incentives. While most manufacturers do not pay output incentives, a substantial minority, in most parts of the world, do. For several good reasons, though, output incentives are falling off in use. Paying people for quantity simply doesn't sit well with the goal of ever-better service to the customer. Here are a few reasons:

- The customer wants quality first. Output incentives can and do drive people to leave out steps, make errors, and skip machine maintenance, which degrades quality further.
- The customer wants quick, flexible response, which conflicts with pushing for speed on a single task.
- The customer wants low cost, but output incentives even fail there. Often (or usually) more costs go up (costs of administering the incentives, extra storage, handling, scrap, accounting, and so on) than the one, direct labor, that goes down. Sometimes direct labor does not even go down, because of the extra labor required to rework the rejects, caused by haste.
- People on incentives don't have time for training, employee involvement, SPC, group projects, or process ownership.

Multifactor incentives. Some incentive systems try to correct for a few of the weaknesses. In another book I described the three-factor incentive plan at Land and Sky Waterbed Company. Operators were on piece rates. In addition, they got a 5 percent wage increase for every job they mastered; and a quality bonus of 25 percent, which declined for each quality defect. Also, operators lost 65 cents for every defect discovered by end-of-line inspectors, but lost only 25 cents if they discovered and marked the defect themselves.[8] That was quite a good system when it was first implemented in 1982. Today, we would favor the jobs-mastered incentive but not the other two.

Nucor Steel, on everybody's excellence list, employs a hybrid system that seems to work well. It combines profit sharing, group incentives based on tons of good-quality steel produced, and employee involvement. Nucor employees receive more in extra pay than in base wages.[9]

Sales commissions. The retail sales commission is bucking the toss-out-incentives trend—for a special reason: Retail clerks on commission don't stand around. They try to be helpful. They smile. They help steer the customer to the right goods. They treat hurried shoppers with quick response and casual ones with tender, loving care.

Sometimes, it is true, customers dislike shopping in a commission store, but usually the reason is something else: untrained sales clerks or company-imposed nefarious sales tactics, like bait-and-switch. On the whole, retail commissions pay off in *better, faster service to the customer.*

In wholesaling and industrial selling, the same thing is true: Commissions keep the sales force busy calling on customers, smiles and good grace fully in evidence. Commissions are *not* the cause of spikey sales patterns—huge surges in sales at the end of each month, each quarter, each year, which cause high costs and service havoc to product makers. The cause is periodic quotas and profit targets.

Bailing Out of Output Incentives

It's not always easy to drop an incentive system. The data-entry clerk paid by lines typed or the packer paid by the carton gets accustomed to the extra pay. And managers fear losses of productivity. To smooth the transition, some companies do it in two steps:

1. Switch from individual to group incentive. This is quite painless when people are at the same time being reorganized into cells or flow lines—for example, when a piece-rate-paid packer becomes a member of a cell that does final testing, packing, and labeling. Usually there is no room in a cell for one person to produce faster than the whole team. In office cells, where it's easy to pile documents high, rules to limit the size of each stack (kanban rules) need to be imposed.
2. Phase out group incentives and phase in some other pay system— one that does not rob people of their accustomed extra pay.

One trend is to convert from wages to salaries, which offers employees better year-around job and pay protection. This option eases the transition from incentives, as well being an all-around step toward more equal treatment of people and a better climate for employee involvement. American Steel and Wire Corp. switched all hourly employees to salaries several years ago. [10]

Some of Square D Corporation's household circuit-breaker plants have adopted a hybrid approach. [11] After seventeen years on individual incentives, they reorganized into "focused factories" and put each one on its own group gain-sharing plan. I recall visiting Square D's Lincoln, Nebraska, plant years ago. Final assemblers were glowingly called the "flying fingers." Their fingers flew in order to earn up to

115 percent pay based on formal time standards (the company capped incentive pay at the 115 percent level).

Under the new plan, base pay was reset at the recent historical average pay with incentives. Gains or losses above or below that are shared 50–50 between the work group and the company. The old plan was based just on number of units made, which usually meant made and dumped into a stockroom. The new plan's basis is the group's number of *good* units "packed out"—no reward for making for the stockroom. Industrial engineers don't set time standards any more; they work on improved methods, equipment, and quality (a wrenching change for some of them).

This was not a Square D corporate program. The company's mandate was simply to cut costs, which didn't happen at first: Labor productivity plunged and costs went up. The teams were responsible for quality but had no experience or training in dealing with the causes of bad quality. To treat the deficiency, plant managers provided multifaceted quality training for all employees. In the Lincoln plant, productivity recovered after about six months, and it has steadily risen since—to about 20 percent higher than the individual plan yielded.

Main areas of improvement are in reduced breaker rejects and rework. Now assemblers will halt production if, say, welds are straying toward the low side of the tolerance range; they will alert welding and get the problem resolved. Before, assemblers hated to stop.

The plants' gain-sharing plans probably will evolve in the future, perhaps to include pay for knowledge and such measures of improvement as lead-time reduction. Right now employees have their hands full getting accustomed to their new roles as quality improvers and problem solvers.

Long-Term Incentives

While piece incentives are being phased out, other, longer-term kinds of incentive are roaring in. The incomers include bonuses, gain sharing, profit sharing, and stock ownership. These share the wealth and foster a sense of community and permanence.

In 1989 PepsiCo Inc. inaugurated "SharePower," which provides stock options for all 100,000 of its "permanent" employees (those who work at least 30 hours a week).[14]

Bonus. The U.S. Bureau of Labor Statistics reports that 70 percent of all bonus plans have been implemented in the last five years.[15]

Left Out

Incentives, even for managers, are still uncommon in certain industries: In hotels, only 45 percent of site managers receive stock options and bonuses, versus 92 percent for all companies. [12] And, according to one report, only 3 percent of supervisory nurses receive any form of incentive pay. [13]

Bonuses are not just for senior managers. The Hay Group reports that 43 percent of companies offering bonuses to executives also offer them to lower managers, and a third of the bonus plans cover key technical and professional employees. [16]

Closely held Charles Machine Company, producer of Ditch Witch equipment, makes all employees stockholders—and also pays all employees bonuses based strictly on company sales.

It is more difficult to implement sweeping plans in large corporations, but Du Pont Company has done it. The company's new bonus plan, being phased in over five years, is for all 20,000 employees in its fibers business unit. Everyone takes a 6 percent pay cut, with the money going into an "at-risk pool." Employees get it back as bonuses, based on how well the division does in meeting its 4 percent (after inflation) target earnings growth. If the target is just met, employees get their 6 percent back. If they beat the target by 25 percent, people get another 6 percent. On the downside, at 80 percent of target earnings, employees get just a 3 percent bonus—and no bonus at all below 80 percent. [17] (One of the division's five plants is excluded from the plans, inasmuch as the plant's unionized employees rejected it.)

The growing popularity of bonuses may be partly a copycat phenomenon: the West copying Japan's entrenched bonus system. Japanese firms usually pay bonuses semiannually to employees. They are sizable when times are good and shrink when profits drop.

If there were no reports on Japan's use of the bonus, it still might be in a growth spurt. Three virtues of the bonus make it right for the times: First, the many firms that have their work forces involved in rapid improvement welcome more ways to reward performance. Second, being a one-time payment, it is more affordable to the company than a pay increase. Third, a bonus can be associated with recent success, whereas a wage increase carries on, continued success or not.

Gain sharing. Gain-sharing plans have grown even more sharply. According to the U.S. Bureau of Labor Statistics, 75 percent of plant gain-sharing plans are no more than five years old. Gain sharing at Square D (described earlier) is typical: emphasis is on group productivity (output) with good quality.

Hold it! While the idea of gain for all is unassailable, a plan based on output and quality is at odds with a world-class viewpoint: Recognize and reward the activities (employee involvement in continuous learning and improvement), and things like output, quality, and profit will take care of themselves. Many companies, however, have a long journey on their hands, and point A, where the journey starts, is *zero employee involvement.* Gain sharing based on productivity and quality may smooth the transition to total employee involvement.

Profit sharing. The new wave of enthusiasm for profit sharing includes large companies like Alcoa and Ford, which apply it to all employees. At Ford in 1987 profit sharing yielded an average of $3,700 extra pay for its 156,000 eligible wage-earning and salaried employees. The Alcoa plan fires up when operating profit exceeds 6 percent of the company's U.S. assets (which is a high return for the industry). About one-fifth of profits in excess of that 6 percent go into a profit-sharing pool, which is then disbursed.[18]

Honeywell's Industrial Automation Systems Division has come up with a novel approach. The division gives a portion of its profits back to the plants, not for employees' pay envelopes but for their use in funding factory improvements and buying equipment. The incentive is the chance for teams to do what they think is best with some of the wealth they have helped generate.[19]

Some companies have had strong long-term incentives for years. Hewlett-Packard's plan includes all full- or part-time employees who have been there for six months or more. Profit shares are passed out twice a year, and everyone gets the same percentage of the profit-sharing pool.

Stock ownership. Sometimes profit sharing can take the form of stock distribution.

At Herman Miller, the top-ranked furniture manufacturer on *Fortune*'s list of most-admired companies, every full-time employee receives company stock quarterly, based on company profits. In addition, the company pays out cash bonuses monthly, and it limits the CEO's pay to

---

Pay Attention!

At Hewlett-Packard they tell about what used to happen when President John Young announced company profits in a company auditorium (with simultaneous transmission to all H-P sites). Young gave the profit figures first, then continued reviewing total company performance. People didn't listen to the rest of the message; they were busy with calculators figuring their profit shares.

Today, Young saves the profit announcement until last, and says, cheerfully, "Now you can get out your calculators."

---

no more than twenty times the average plant employee's total compensation.[20]

Special incentives. Conventional incentives are based on output, profit, or cash savings. In the world-class company, output and money are no longer the control mechanisms (see Chapter 8). Accordingly, a few companies have keyed their incentive payments to other things. For example, one company has experimented with executive bonuses for lead-time reduction, and also for "linearity," which is a measure of how close a team comes to meeting its daily production rate.

With benefits costs soaring, it was only a matter of time before companies tied *benefits* to achievements. CRS Sirrine, Inc., a Houston-based architecture and engineering firm, passes out health benefits based on individual job evaluations. A new hire pays the full premium for the firm's group health plan. After six months, the employee's performance is rated; highly rated people become "core" employees with health benefits fully paid by the company. New hires have up to eighteen months to achieve a high rating; during that time they continue to pay the full premium.[21]

At Motorola's cellular phone plant near Chicago (a showcase of excellence) incentive bonuses are paid for such things as reducing design-to-production time for new products.[22]

Do these trends sound the death knell for profit- and savings-based incentive plans? Not at all. The purposes of tying incentives to profit and savings are legitimate: One is to share the wealth when there's wealth to share, which is a fine idea that helps the firm stay on an even keel financially. Another is to encourage a sense of community or family, which improves coordination and also helps cut personnel turnover.

The purpose should *not* be to simply motivate or to control costs and cut wastes. It won't work. Immediate feedback motivates; delayed feedback does not—or does so only weakly. More important, profits and cost savings are the result of thousands of controls and a steady stream of improvements. In other words, control and improve, and profits take care of themselves. Then, as profits rise, the company's task is just to divvy up the wealth—including to all stakeholders, not just to stockholders and to senior managers.

10

❧

World-Class Product Development

WHICH COMES FIRST, the product or the customer? The answer is, it's a bad question. Separating product development from customer relations means trouble: Designers pursue their own fancies, leaving operations and sales in a panic over how to provide and sell it.

The earthquake in design and product development puts an end to that way of mismanaging products, customers, and suppliers. It brings design out of isolation and into the thick of the action: rubbing elbows with customers, finding out what operations can and can't do, tapping the design expertise of suppliers, and getting to know other parts of the business via cross-career reassignments.

The thrusts of the design shakeup are in five main directions: design partnership, design for operations, design for cost, structured product development (including quality function deployment), competitive analysis, and time to market. The five concepts have become well known in big industry in a short time. Design partnership deals with how to get organized, so we take up that topic first.

DESIGN PARTNERSHIP

Not long ago the major automakers had huge car design staffs. They saw their job as developing complete specs for every part, made or bought. The companies' own manufacturing engineers and the supplier companies' product and process design people stayed out of it until later. The penalties for late involvement were (are) severe. Specs often did not match production capabilities; they sometimes didn't meet market requirements either. Design cycles stretched out in the confusion of trying to fix the specs.

Today's approach has car designers working *with* the others. Some manufacturers, such as Boeing, call this the *design-build team*; to others, it is *simultaneous engineering*. One effect is a slimming down of the major companies' product design staffs, and growth of suppliers' engineering groups. These shifts in design resources should continue until suppliers' design capability about matches that of their customers, which would be about the right mix.

Another trend is to break up some of the corporate design "campuses" and disburse designers to the operating sites. Specialty steelmaker, Allegheny Ludlum, for example, has 275 of its 400 R&D people located at its factories, where they work with process engineers and marketing development teams.[1]

Extended Design-Build Team

The effect of these trends is that they push people together to form an extended design team—the more extended, the better. If the product designer teams up with a process designer, that's nice. Join with product and process designers from supplier and customer firms—even better. In full bloom, the design partnership pulls in a raft of others as well.

Polaroid, for example, sets up a program office across the hall from product design. The program office is a fixed group of ten to twelve people, who come from purchasing, quality assurance, test engineering, and manufacturing engineering, plus a production supervisor and operators. They work with the product design team and later set up a miniline for trial production. The group stays intact through full production so that it can deal with major redesigns. Polaroid set this up in the late 1970s and has used it for several major product offerings.

Xerox plans new products in its 5028 series of copiers in somewhat the same way. Assemblers join the extended design team at the start of the second prototype, which gets them involved in planning the pilot plant, staging, and processes. One assembler said, "I feel like I died and went to heaven. I'm part of the design team."[2]

Skunk Works

The team approach to design is not all that new; it's the team's composition that breaks new ground. The giants of product development in recent history include off-in-the-corner teams; Lockheed's fabled skunk works quickly come to mind, as does Xerox's PARC (Palo Alto Research Center). The sad part about PARC is that it lined plenty of other people's pockets, while delighting many a consumer. That is, the product ideas ended up elsewhere—as the basis for companies like Apple and Atari; or, as with Ethernet, a computer network of "smart" cabling, a brilliant but slow-to-get-anywhere Xerox product.

Today's "new, improved" skunk works are organized for turning good ideas into products and services, sales and profits. An example is Motorola's "Project Bandit," which contributed to Motorola's winning of one of the first Malcolm Baldrige national quality awards. The Bandit team had people from enough different functions to develop an integrated product design, process design, and support system. In just eighteen months the team had a new, highly successful line of pagers (beep devices) in the marketplace, produced on a mixed-model, zero-setup, lot-size-of-one, automated production line.

Other banditlike project teams have been springing up in other companies around the world.

The *team* approach to product development, bandit or conventional, is necessary and vital; it provides structure for deliberate development projects. But does every innovation have to be deliberate—a *project* on a timetable? A resounding *NO!*

Many, if not most, important innovations come about in less structured ways—out of the heads of dreamers and inventors on the one hand and opportunistic entrepreneurs on the other. The trick is to create an environment for product development of the more random kind, while also having a strong project-team structure. One company stands out in the world as past master and old hand at doing it well: McDonald's Corporation.

Innovations Welcome

McDonald's is known the world over for delivering uniformly high-quality fast foods in spick-and-span restaurants. We should know it as well for its string of successful new products: French fries and hamburgers made from frozen stock, Quarter Pounder, Big Mac, fish sandwich, eat-with-your-hands pie, Egg McMuffin, Chicken McNuggets, McDLT. All were innovative in one way or another at their time of introduction, and all met McDonald's requirements for quality, speed, efficiency, production in a squeezed space, customer popularity, and profit. Moreover, only one, the Quarter Pounder, was developed by

McDonald's itself. The rest came from restaurant owners (franchisees—the customers of McDonald's Corporation) and innovative, hard-charging suppliers.[3]

One example is the fish sandwich. It emerged from the persistent efforts of Cincinnati franchisee Lou Groen and Bud Sweeney of Gorton Corporation.[4] Groen, in a Roman Catholic area, was losing his Friday customers to a local fish restaurant. He developed a fish sandwich and pitched the idea, with slides and a cooking demonstration, at McDonald's headquarters. Groen got the green light to try it. His sales soared on Friday—and hamburger sales the rest of the week rose, too.

But Groen's messy, complex production methods wouldn't work for the whole chain. Enter Bud Sweeney, account executive at Gorton's, the only fish supplier bothering to respond to a McDonald's call for help in developing a frozen, ready-to-fry fish product. Sweeney tried out many options over three months, spending most days cooking them himself in a McDonald's store (he flipped burgers, too). A clam-strip product made it all the way to a five-store test, but then bombed, eliciting this comment from McDonald's president Harry Sonneborn: "You'll never see a seafood product in a McDonald's."

Sweeney didn't quit. In 1962, a year after he started, Sweeney had it, a fish product approved for chainwide adoption. Still, he had more to do: help find local fish suppliers, freezer equipment, and a fish fryer—and trot around the land convincing store operators the fish sandwiches belonged on their menus. Gorton, Sweeney's employer, got a windfall of business.

By the time Chicken McNuggets was launched in 1980, McDonald's had a full-sized product development staff. It took ten years of testing chicken before the staff came up with the basic nuggets idea. But the nuggets had to be developed: Bud Sweeney again to the rescue.

Sweeney was lent by Gorton's to lead a chicken SWAT team, which got help from several sources: The unique tempura coating came from Gorton's. McDonald's product development and quality assurance people handled product specs and test marketing. A chef brought in from a Chicago hotel developed four dips. Keystone Foods, a major supplier of frozen beef patties, developed production lines to debone chicken and new equipment to cut it into chunks in such a way as to appear hand-cut.

The SWAT team brought McNuggets to market in five months, record time for such a product. Keystone completed a $13 million chicken plant in just one hundred days; it did so with no guarantees, written or oral, from McDonald's. Said Herb Lotman of Keystone: "McDonald's would never hurt a supplier. If . . . it didn't work out, they would find something else for us to do with the plant."[5]

Keystone ended up getting 55 percent of McDonald's chicken business and thus became a major chicken producer. Keystone couldn't keep up with demand for the whole chain, so another supplier, Tyson Foods, stepped in. Following McDonald's long-standing policy—that suppliers could not corner a technology developed for the company— Keystone gave Tyson its process specs. Tyson, already a major chicken producer, took things further—developing a new breed of chicken. Called Mr. McDonald, the new breed was almost twice the weight of a typical fryer, which made deboning easier.

Broad Networks of Aggressive, Competitive Suppliers

McDonald's product development partnership includes more than just food suppliers. Providers of paper products, equipment, construction materials, cleaning supplies, and transportation also get a piece of McDonald's action—if they are good and aggressive. For example, a whole new class of heater/air conditioner emerged from the joint efforts of Jim Schindler, McDonald's chief equipment and construction man, and Mammoth Furnace Company. It was a rooftop model with industrial capacity, but two-thirds the size and cost of commercial units available at the time.

McDonald's suppliers constantly jostle with each other. Any hint that the company or any of its powerful regional operator co-ops is dissatisfied with a supplier's performance quickly spreads. Another supplier pounces and takes away business—until the deficient supplier shapes up.

For example, Golden State Foods, which started out supplying frozen patties, became a major provider of syrup, then tartar and Big Mac sauces. Golden State thought it could develop a syrup of better quality, "the only factor that would encourage McDonald's to change."[6] Its syrup was a success, so Golden State built a syrup-making facility and finally convinced West Coast operators to buy its syrup. Later the company leaped into sauces when it heard reports of too many bad-quality recalls from McDonald's main sauce supplier. Golden State built a sauce plant in Atlanta and pushed the other company permanently out as a McDonald's supplier.

The landscape is littered with suppliers, including many big-name food makers, who weren't keen enough for McDonald's business. Failings of the majors include not modifying a recipe or a size (cheddar cheese, muffins) to meet a McDonald's need; and not extending credit, not sticking with agreed prices, and not taking care of McDonald's during a shortage (hamburger, root beer, ketchup, and pickles).[7]

Using *All* Design Resources

We see, from the McDonald's discussion, how a company can attract extensive resources, in both structured and random fashion, to bring a steady procession of new products to market. The McDonald's system should be familiar to manufacturing people who have studied the partnership approaches to product development favored by leading Japanese producers. Main features, clearly evident in the McDonald's system, are:

- *Quality first.*
- *Balanced contributions.* Encourage contributions from company designers, customers (franchisees), and all kinds of suppliers. A company that tries to do all development "in house" gets out of touch with customers' needs and suppliers' capabilities.
- *Balanced emphasis.* Place emphasis on processes as well as products. Strong new products coupled with innovative processes have a much better chance of freezing out competitors than good products alone.
- *Diverse approaches to product development.* Have some projects led by internal company teams, others by aggressive outside parties.
- *Share the wealth, don't hog it.* Strive for *strong* suppliers and customers who can continue to invest in new products.
- *Repay performance with loyalty.* Be quick to award business to new and existing providers with good ideas so that they will take reasonable risks to keep developing new products.
- *Keep the door open to new contributors with a better idea.* Specifically, make product and process specs available to designated new players who are eager and capable.

DESIGN FOR OPERATIONS

Design partnership, which gets the right people together, itself has a close partner. It is design for operations (DFO), which provides an improved set of design methods. The goal is a product or service design that is easy to make or provide.

A good example of DFO comes from the grocery industry and dates back over one hundred years. The founder of the A&P supermarket chain in the U.S. was John Hartford, a stickler for uniformity. All stores were laid out and stocked alike. "The boss boasted he could walk into any A&P store blindfolded and 'lay [his] hands right on the pork and beans.' "[8] Not only did this design of the product (displayed food items) make shelf-stocking easy, it met a customer need!

Design for Manufacturability

In recent years, most of the DFO action has been in manufacturing, where it's called design for manufacturability (DFM). DFM is well defined and in wide use among major manufacturers, even though few companies knew about it until about 1985 when published articles on it began to appear.

Geoffrey Boothroyd, professor at the University of Rhode Island, fathered the movement with publication of his report, "Design for Assembly," in 1980.[9] He and his colleague, Peter Dewhurst (both originally from England), have perfected the concepts, run seminars for practicing engineers, and developed computer software to handle some of the steps.

Others have developed similar methods, including Hitachi's Production Engineering Research Laboratory, which had sent some of its people from Japan to a Boothroyd seminar. Later General Electric licensed the Hitachi method, improved it, and developed training materials in English.

Now DFM is in a new phase: spin-offs, or special applications. An example is design for finish quality, which has to do with choosing materials and designing shapes that can be painted effectively.[10] Another is design for printed circuit board assembly.[11] There are also software spin-offs: Boothroyd and Dewhurst's first software package applied to machined metal parts, but more software packages—for injection molding, forging, and other methods—are following. One industry, appliances, even has its own trade magazine devoted to DFM: *Appliance Manufacturer*, subtitled, "The Magazine of Design for Manufacturing Solutions."

I mention these few details of history to make the point, again, that the outpouring of DFO activity in the 1980s truly was like an earthquake. And it is still picking up steam. And it is including all the business functions. And it is spewing forth all around the globe. And, while it has recently been centered in manufacturing, DFO applies well and naturally to the service sector, which should be caught up in its own strong DFO movement before long.

DFO Guidelines

As the word spreads about DFO and the uses of it multiply, various authors propose design guidelines. Stoll has compiled a list, in DFM terminology, of some of the guidelines most commonly mentioned. I have adapted that list and extended it to other kinds of business; see Table 10–1. First and second columns in the table are stated in the jargon of the piece-goods and process industries, respectively. The third column is in language for the services sector—actually generalized terms for any industry.

In most situations, the first guideline is by far the most important. Minimize the variety of what goes into the product or service, and almost everything improves: fewer steps, less chance of mistakes, easier to fix mistakes and do repairs, easier to zero in on doing a few things well, easier to customize tools and equipment, less labor, easier to

---

What Makes B&D Go?

Black & Decker, in danger of rolling over and slowly perishing when Far Eastern tool makers (like Makita) started invading its markets in the late 1970s, is big and tough again. How did they do it? Lots of ways. Here's one:[12]

It used to be that every B&D market—British, German, U.S., etc.—did its own designs. At one point the company made one hundred different motors worldwide for its power tools. Now it's down below twenty and aiming at five.

The name of the game is fewer variations, fewer parts, fewer suppliers, fewer contracts, fewer production technologies, and so on—and at the same time, more and more product offerings brought to market in less and less time. In power tools, B&D launched sixty new or rejiggered products in two years, mostly the fast-growing cordless type. All are designed around a motor. So just plunk the new product's components down beside the right motor line, set up for assembly and pack, and off it goes to market.

Table 10–1. *Design-for-Operations Guidelines*

Piece-Goods Industry*	Process Industry	Services (or General)
1. Design to minimize parts variations	Design for a minimum number of ingredients/materials	Design for a minimum number of operations
2. Design for a minimum number of parts		
3. Design for modularity: ease of joining, separating, rejoining	Design for modularity: ease of mixing, separating, or remixing	Design for modularity: ease of coupling/uncoupling services
4. Design parts that can perform multiple functions	Design ingredients/materials that can perform multiple functions	Design service elements that can perform multiple functions
5. Design parts that can serve multiple uses	Design ingredients/materials that can serve multiple uses	Design service elements that can have multiple uses
6. Design parts for ease of fabrication	Design ingredients/materials for ease of mixing or processing	Design service elements for ease of combining into a complete service; avoid off-line or "misfit" elements
7. Avoid separate fasteners and connectors	Avoid separate connectors, splicers, and combining agents	
8. Minimize assembly directions: design for top-down layered assembly	Design to minimize backtracking, reversing, multiple trips through the same process	Design to minimize backtracking, reversing, multiple trips through same service elements
9. Maximize compliance: design for ease of assembly	Maximize compliance: design for ease of processing	Design for ease in following specifications
10. Minimize handling; design for ease of handling and presentation	Minimize handling; design for ease of handling and presentation	Minimize handling; design for ease of handling and presentation
11. Evaluate assembly methods	Evaluate processing methods	Evaluate methods of combining service elements
12. Eliminate or simplify adjustments during assembly	Eliminate or simplify adjustments during processing	Eliminate or simplify adjustments during service
13. Avoid physically flexible components	Avoid physically changeable ingredients/materials	Avoid service elements that tempt nonstandard performance

* This column is adapted from Henry D. Stoll, "Design for Manufacture," *Manufacturing Engineering*, January 1988, pp. 67–73.

train, fewer manuals and specs, easier to automate, fewer suppliers, fewer stock locations and records, fewer transactions, less management and administration, and more.

DFO Guidelines in Combination

Some of the guidelines are closely related—especially 1, 2, and 7. In assembly work those three (minimizing variations, parts, and fasteners) are especially important. For example, if a subassembly now consists of two members and a fastener, the design team might ask three questions:[13]

- Does either member have to move?
- Does each have to be made from a different material?
- Does either have to be removed for servicing?

If it gets three "No" answers, the team says, Okay, why not design it as a one-piece subassembly?

Sometimes the cost reductions can be startling. *Business Week* demonstrated this with an eye-catching photo, shown below.[14] The photo's caption refers to a product with so few parts "that an engineer can assemble it blindfolded." Actually, Bill Sprague, the engineer in the photo, does it in two minutes. The product, a new NCR electronic cash register, has only 15 purchased parts, down from 110 in the previous model. It's push-and-snap assembly, because the cash register has been designed with zero screws and fasteners (guideline 7). (Sprague, by the way, has joined a new NCR multifunctional "bandit" design team.)

Most of the other DFO guidelines were followed to some extent. The design team used Boothroyd-Dewhurst software to analyze assembly methods (guideline 11). They designed and adopted multiuse parts (guideline 5); for example, access doors for different purposes on both sides of the cabinet are identical, and they borrowed a speaker and a cathode-ray tube (CRT) from other products. Assembly is easy to do with little handling (guidelines 9 and 10); in fact, assembly time was reduced about 80 percent.

The team had trouble with guideline 8, design for bottom-up layered assembly. The cash registers go to a wide variety of customers, from Burger King to hardware stores. A common requirement in installation is that emerging wires and cables not be visible. So wires and cable go through a hole in the bottom cover. Not the best design for layered assembly, but the customer's requirements come first.

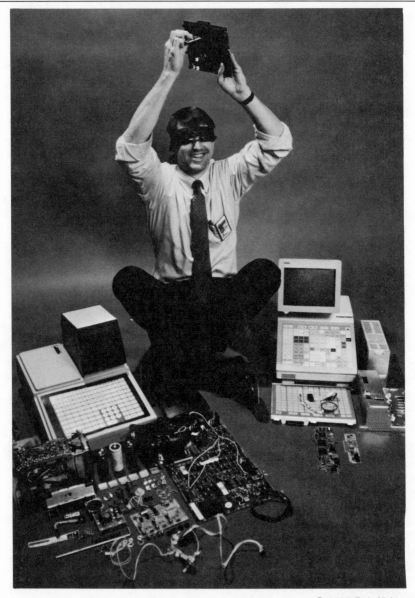

"NCR's New Cash Register Has So Few Parts That an Engineer Can Assemble It Blindfolded"

A tale from the field illustrates guideline 3, design for ease of joining, separating, rejoining. A cash register at a fast-food restaurant in Colorado was in need of an updated printed circuit board. The NCR service man planned to switch boards during off hours, but there weren't any; it's a twenty-four-hour-a-day business. The service man waited for the right moment. It came in mid-afternoon when no patrons were in the restaurant nor at the drive-through window. He took off the cover, opened the snap-off sheet metal box top, swapped the circuit boards, and snapped it all together. Total time: less than one minute.

DFO Guidelines—Further Examples

Remaining guidelines warrant a few additional remarks, especially as to uses in the process and services industries.

Consider guideline 4, multiple functions. I am at my personal computer and gazing squarely at an example of a multiple-function part: a toggle switch that locks in a floppy disk and also activates the disk drive. For the process industry, a multiple-function ingredient would be one that, say, controls evaporation as well as thickens. In services, an example of a multiple-function element is a change-of-address procedure that updates several of the service provider's records and sends me the name and phone number of my new service rep.

Examples of guideline 5, multiple uses, are: in processes, an ink that works on paper, plastic, or metal; in services, an airline that moves passengers, mail, and freight on the same planes.

In services, guidelines 6 and 7 blend together as: ease of combining into a complete service; no off-line or "misfit" elements. As an example, avoid the need for leaving the client to fetch a file folder or get an opinion.

Service industry examples of minimizing backtracking, guideline 8, come to mind easily. Or I should say, too much backtracking is what sticks in the mind. Who hasn't had to stand in a line for one service element, then in another line for the next element, and later go back to the first line? We call it bureaucracy, red tape, and worse.

A design that maximizes compliance, guideline 9, may rely on color-coding, templates, clear marking and labeling, and so forth; make it hard for something to be put in the wrong place. Boeing's 1988 problem with misconnected aircraft warning devices was resolved by designing connectors that will go together only in a certain way; for example, different plugs for each engine's warning devices. As an example in services, a keyboard may be designed with a clear plastic overlay, which "hardens" the keys so the data-entry person can't drip coffee into the mechanism.

Guideline 10 calls for designing for ease in handling and presentation. Examples are avoiding turning a part over, reversing a roll, or handing over a client to another server.

Guideline 11, evaluate methods, simply means use the many diagnostics available for checking out a design. These range from flow charting to value analysis to test marketing to use of some of the new design-for-operations computer software.

Eliminating or simplifying adjustments is guideline 12. One example is designing chemical stability into a process. As a services example, wouldn't it be nice if self-service copiers were designed to automatically detect and adjust for what is put on the glass plate: long or short sheet, inserted crosswise or lengthwise?

A service example of guideline 13, avoid service elements that tempt nonstandard performance, is a rule common in supermarkets: Cashiers may not keep purses or other personal containers at the cash register. This is a design for prevention of theft (which is nonstandard indeed!).

The Well-Designed Service

Design for operations has been formalized for goods, but not services. Thus, the DFO guidelines for services are preliminary. No doubt they can be improved and refined. That does not mean the services sector is backward in its design approaches. In fact, the world's highly successful service providers, such as Service Master and McDonald's, seem to be adept users of a number of the guidelines.

It's not just big-name service providers. Manor Care Inc. has employed a number of the design guidelines for its new Sleep Inn motel chain. Specially designed laundry washers sit behind the desk clerk. Instead of staring at the TV between customers, the clerk launders. It's easy. The washer has different buttons that trigger automatic cycle adjustments and mete out correct amounts of soap and bleach for washing sheets, towels, and other items. In motel rooms, shower stalls are round so housekeepers don't have to fuss with dirt-collecting corners. Those and other innovations in design result in a need for only twelve full-time motel employees, 13 percent less than the average for no-frills motels. [15]

Genius Quotient

While the DFO guidelines may seem like "just common sense," they certainly have not been commonly practiced. Designers have developed products and services not for operations but for "functionality"—which in the current jargon means providing the required functions. Never mind about whether it is easy or hard, cheap or costly to build or provide; the company made that somebody else's job. The frequent result was hard-to-build, pricey products and services that functioned poorly.

A decade of product failures in Xerox's copier division is typical. (This was in the 1970s, and since then Xerox has dealt decisively with the situation.) A consultant called in to assess the problem noted that Xerox was loaded with brilliant design engineers who focused on developing copiers with

> . . . incredibly complex technology. . . . Everything inside a Xerox machine was special. You could not go out and use a normal nut. It had to be a specially designed nut. The concept of using as many standard parts as possible was not even thought of.[16]

Lacking any guidelines, our product designers did what interested them. Xerox's engineers were *not* interested in doing things the same way as last time—in using a standard nut or a dimension from the preceding copier. Perhaps the feeling was, We aren't earning our salary if we don't at least make a small change—to every part and every dimension.

Now, with new design guidelines, the company is telling the design engineer *not* to make small changes—unless they are significant eliminations, reductions, and simplifications. Can we expect our designers to eagerly accept such a reversal in common practice?

Why not? Tinkerers and technicians have always admired the simple kite experiment of Benjamin Franklin and the lady who can work minor miracles with a hairpin. It is not hard to accept simple elegance as the hallmark of genius.

No-Change Designs

If the DFO guidelines are complete—and if the design team follows them—the design will be "right the first time": few or no design changes. A study at Tektronix reveals the cost of its design (engineering) changes.

Each one triggered nineteen other actions: design approval, supplier selection, bill of materials change, revised schematic drawings, and so on. While the changes were often aimed at improving efficiency (read, *labor* efficiency), repeated design "improvements" resulted in growth of overhead costs that more than offset the "efficiency" improvements.[17]

Not long ago it was impossible to conceive of a product that did not have to incur a few design changes. Now the idea of *zero design changes* is on the goals list along with zero defects, zero inventories, zero delays, and zero breakdowns.

DESIGN FOR COST

The DFO guidelines seem to make sense, the executive might say, but can they make a difference to the bottom line? Indeed they can. Independently, both Ford and General Motors have found out the same thing about design and cost: Design is only 5 percent of the cost of a car, but it determines about 70 percent of manufacturing costs.

That's a lot of leverage. It seems to require not just guidelines but also a direct, explicit attack on cost—by the product development team. That means we don't just ask for a design that works and is producible. We don't wait for a preliminary sketch or mock-up to get a cost estimate. We provide the team with a target cost at the outset.

Dan Challgren, director of product industrialization at Allen-Bradley, says, "We request target cost information from marketing very early in the stages of product development. . . . We estimate the manufacturing costs, and if they're way off base, . . . marketing can modify its specifications; cancel the project, or re-evaluate target costs and see what they do to the [profit] margins."[18]

Designing for Loss Minimization

It's a novel viewpoint, but one that makes sense: Designers should bear responsibility for losses—even social losses. We credit a Japanese, Dr. Genichi Taguchi, for convincingly making the point. He also provides a method for predicting average loss for a given design. The "Taguchi loss function" combines estimates of monetary losses with data on frequency of losses.

According to the American Management Association, eight out of ten new products is a failure.[19] Designing to a target cost, based on the price the market will bear to make the product a hit, improves the odds of success; equally important, it cuts off the cash early for projects that don't have a chance.

STRUCTURED PRODUCT DEVELOPMENT

Design for operations is a worthy goal. But how about designing for quality? for the customer? to best the competition? These goals must be provided for as well. Two new "structured" approaches, quality function deployment and product development mapping, help meet the need.

Quality Function Deployment

Quality function deployment (QFD) is a funny term for a nice, structured tool of product development. QFD's aim is to translate "the voice of the customer" into detailed technical requirements, all prioritized with the aid of competitive data. Its structure comes from matrices. The main "what-how" matrix lists customer wants (what), technical requirements (how), and an us-versus-them competitive assessment. When the matrix is filled with all that data, the chart takes the shape of a house—the *house of quality*.

Figure 10–1 is a QFD matrix for a dry cleaning business. It could be used for improving an existing business or for planning a new one. Branching off the central what-how matrix is data useful for planning the dry-cleaning service or service improvement:

- Symbols show relationships between the whats and hows. Double circle, worth 9 in importance, appears six times. For example, "completely clean" garments strongly depend on clear solvent and clean filters in the dry-cleaning (D.C.) equipment. That accounts for two of the double circles.
- "Importance weighting" is simply a total of the ratings, keyed to symbols, in the columns. "Good equipment maintenance" scores highest: 9 points each for its affect on quality of the cleaning and pressing, plus 1 point for how maintenance helps keep service turnaround time short.

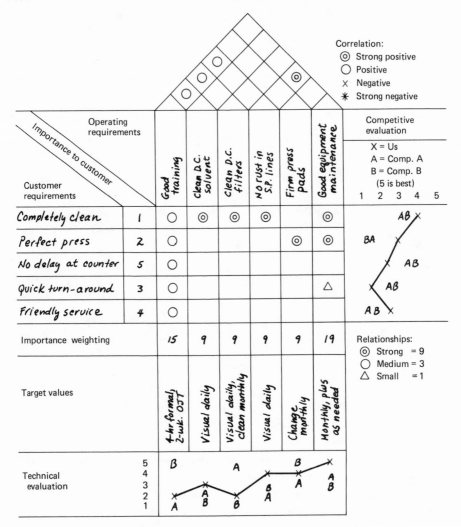

Figure 10–1. QFD in Dry Cleaning

- Voice of the customer enters again via the diagonal, "importance to customer." "Completely clean" garments is the customer's first concern, ranking number 1; "no delay at counter" gets a 5.
- The house's roof shows correlations among the hows. One intersection is double circled. Its interpretation is that "good equipment maintenance" has a strong positive correlation with "no rust in steam-press lines" (since steam in the equipment generates rust, replace steam-press components regularly).

- "Target values" makes the hows specific—often a numeric target: Change press pads *monthly* to keep them firm.
- Comparisons with competitors A and B go to the right and at the bottom. "Us" is better than either A or B on cleaning and pressing, worse than either on counter delays. How did we become number 1 on pressing and cleaning? For one thing, we do a better job of equipment maintenance, which is high in importance.

The data in the house of quality come from surveys, studies, checks, comparisons, reverse engineering, calculations, and reckoning. QFD obliges the company to do these things; it helps ensure that the design team deals with *all* the critical factors—that none slips through the cracks. Structured thoroughness is the strength of QFD.

Is that all there is to it? It could be. But, full-blown QFD offers a selection of other data matrices for further planning. Figure 10–1 is used in the *product planning* stage, in which the voice of the customer is loud and clear. We'll not go through the three remaining steps— *product design, process planning,* and *process control planning*—in which company language replaces customer terms. In other words, QFD planning can help link product development to operations and process control.

Product Development Mapping

While QFD has achieved renown in a short time, it is not the only structural aid to product development. Wheelwright and Sasser offer an intriguing approach they call product development mapping.[20] While QFD directs itself to a product or service, mapping looks at a whole product line over a life cycle. It helps pinpoint gaps (open marketing channels) and suggests a path of product extensions that capitalize on investments already made.

Figure 10–2 is a skeletal example of a product development map. Time extends to the right and functions (features), value, and price climb vertically. Product development, signified by dots, results in a prototype product or service, box 1. If it survives pilot testing and trial marketing, it is refined into a core product, box 2.

The cash invested in the core product provides leverage for next-generation products. They include an enhanced, higher markup version, box 3, and a stripped-down "cheapo," box 4. The enhanced product is nice but too uniform for certain up-scale market segments, so third-

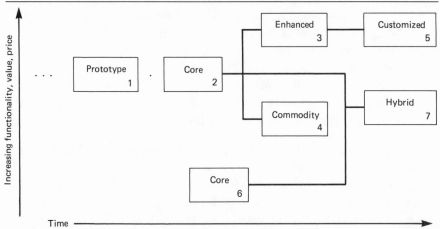

Figure 10–2. Skeletal Product Development Map. Adapted, and reprinted by permission of *Harvard Business Review*, from "The New Product Development Map," by Steven C. Wheelwright and W. Earl Sasser, Jr. (May-June 1989). Copyright © 1989 by the President and Fellows of Harvard College; all rights reserved.

generation products include a wide variety of customized versions, box 5. Useful overlays on the map would include statements about resources needed and market channels served. For example, it may make sense to cluster resources into cells, each for a different family of customized products.

Another development team sees a tie-in between the core product in box 2 and another, box 6; the result: a hybrid of the two, box 7.

A local news story recently offered an apt example. Seattle is about to award a contract to haul its garbage to a remote site. Three of the bidders are waste management firms that have transportation and remote sites locked up. The fourth bidder is a recycler; it just wants part of the contract—to join with one of the three others in a hybrid deal. The recycler would have first crack at the garbage, cycling out the good stuff, and the other company would haul and bury the remainder. The proposed hybrid service enhances the bids of each company.

It is easy to think of a possible product development map for a waste management company: Core business is residential garbage. An enhanced service is handling dumpsters for commercial accounts. Customized services splinter off in several directions: landfill real estate, recycling, medical waste, chemical waste, and gaseous emissions, for example.

Putting it all down in map form can clarify trends and highlight opportunities (perhaps a stripped-down trash disposal service?).

While QFD is product-specific and mapping is broad-brush, competitive analysis includes both perspectives.

COMPETITIVE ANALYSIS

Where does one go for competitive information? There seem to be five main sources: Sample (buy and try) the competitor's product or service, check with your competitor's customers, be active in trade associations and specialty groups, trade data with competitors, and hire knowledgeable people from outside your own firm.

All of these nudge the firm toward a broader outlook on competitive analysis: benchmarking the world's best, regardless of industry. David Kearns, CEO at Xerox Corporation, talks about starting with competitors, but that driving competitive analysis outside "was the key." He mentions going to the auto companies, IBM, Florida Power & Light, Westinghouse, and similar top enterprises. In addition, Kearns makes this critical point (with syntax reminiscent of Satchel Paige): Don't be content with benchmarking the other firm's present performance; worry instead about their *rate of improvement*, "because by the time you understand something, if you're behind to start with, you're not gaining."[21]

In most companies that I visit, there is no clear visual evidence of competitive analysis. Nor do those showing me around and discussing their plans often bring up the subject. When I ask about it, the usual answer is, Oh, sure; engineering (or product development) does that.

I am not impressed unless the evidence of competitive analysis is easy to spot. World-class competitive analysis requires that everybody in the firm be aware of how they compare. The data ought to be in plain view: on wall charts, in the lunchrooms, in the halls. Operators should have a hand in tearing down competitors' products or checking with competitors' customers.

The purpose is not just to assist the design and development team. It is to guide and drive everybody to change, improve, and excel.

Employee-centered competitive analysis is impressive at Du Pont's film manufacturing plant in Brevard, North Carolina. Operators in finishing regularly tear down competitor's products. Comparative samples are on display for all to see. Also, each month marketing makes data on competitors' quality and probable costs available to plant people.

Competitive data of a different sort is on display at a Siecor plant in Texas. (Siecor Corporation, a joint venture of Siemens and Corning

Competitive Data on Display at Siecor

Glass, produces fiber optic cables and communications connectors.) The chart shown in the accompanying photo is up on a main bulletin board. It displays average number of suggestions per employee per year in the U.S., 0.14; number at the Siecor plant (early 1989), 2.8; average in Japan (may represent only top companies), 24; and number at Matsushita, a Siecor competitor, 79.8. Employees can take pride in the plant's suggestion totals, which are twenty times higher than U.S. averages and have steadily risen month after month. On the other hand, comparison with a competitor strikingly shows the need to press on.

Membership in trade associations is a vital source of competitive data. I spoke at the 1988 convention of the Independent Battery Manufacturers Association, in which great gobs of invaluable information were shared among company representatives. Suppliers of equipment and raw materials pitched their wares, global leaders in the industry gave state-of-the-art reports, and gossip centered around what the dominant companies were doing and with what results. Any independent battery manufacturer that skips all this is at risk.

But trade association magazines and conventions are not enough. Their tendency is toward in-breeding. The battery makers, for example, all seemed to be five years behind the times in quality, employee involvement, and design for manufacturability, and they appeared to be thoroughly misinformed about just-in-time—and how widely it applies *inside their plants* (they see it mostly as a purchasing concept).

A wealth of new ideas for getting a leg up on the competition is "out there," readily available. The professional societies collect and serve up the latest lore within their fields (the American Society for Quality Control and worldwide sister organizations are especially good), and they draw in people from all types of business and the nonprofit sector.

The manufacturing sector has access to a wealth of special information from a unique organization, the Association for Manufacturing Excellence (AME). Founded in 1984 and headquartered in Wheeling, Illinois, the AME is dedicated to nothing less than spreading the news about the new elevated standards of performance and how to get on the path of continual, rapid improvement.

AME sponsors workshops nearly every month at a member company's site. These are plants that have an impressive story to tell. It is valuable to the visitors, regardless of what business they come from. Plants whose managers are active in AME tend to be far ahead of typical plants in the same industries—ahead in everything from rate of quality improvement to remaking their cost and control systems.

I mention AME because it is a new kind of association, one that promotes a broad view linking all the business functions. AME is a forum for unification of the wide assortment of concepts and techniques associated with the outpouring of new business knowledge. We need more such associations, or to remold existing ones to a broader point of view.

TIME TO MARKET

Extended design teams, DFO guidelines, design for cost, QFD, and competitive analysis provide for design discipline; they drive the herd in a common direction and corral the mavericks. Better designs are just one outcome. Another one, a critical competitive advantage, is quick design-to-market response.

Speed for Infrequent Product Introductions

At Dana Corporation's Warner Electric Division, the design team includes a design engineer, two designer-draftsmen, a manufacturing engineer, a quality-assurance manager, and a buyer. Marketing people and others sit in on a when-needed basis. The team approach worked: Design-to-market time for a new line of advanced clutch was 36 weeks, compared with 36 months for similar products in the past.

Production time plunged as well, partly because the team designed for manufacturability, and also because operations were reorganized into focused cells for the product line: Setup time fell to 3.5 minutes from the prior 1.75 hours, and throughput time dropped to 1 day, compared with 17 weeks previously.[22] Dana/Warner considers itself to be a "production shop." New product designs are infrequent, and once a product is added to the line, production of it carries on for years. What about companies providing design-to-order products or services?

Speed for Custom-Designed Products

Square D's medium-voltage switchgear plant in Smyrna, Tennessee, is that kind of business. Plant manager Gary Abrams says one of their goals is "to become a time-based competitor," but production is only about 20 percent of total lead time; the rest is field drawings, engineering work, customer approvals, postrelease drawings, and ordering components.

Square D's own engineering might take four weeks of the total lead time. That does not mean four weeks of "under-pencil" time. Instead, it's the usual practice: The schedule allows engineering four weeks, so the order sits idle in engineering until four days before it's due; then engineers scurry to finish in four days.

The new approach, just being perfected at Smyrna, doesn't allow jobs to sit around. An engineer gets going on a job right away, finishes it in a few days, and sends it out for customer approval. The intention is to do whatever it takes—different scheduling, more flexible work assignments and work hours, more engineering resources—to keep jobs from sitting in in-baskets.

Actually, quick response in product development doesn't mean more resources—except perhaps to phase in. The same annual number of projects get done; the only difference is disallowing wait time before starting each one. (A kanban—maximum queue—rule, such as no more than three active projects per engineer, is quite feasible in any type of project work, including product development.)

Computer-Aided Design

Regardless of whether or not design jobs loiter in an in-basket, computer-aided design (CAD) is available to help speed up and improve the design work. CAD routines are available for designing anything from menus to medical regimens to bridges to industrial molds and dies to works of music and art. CAD offers designers quick multiview visualizations, design revisions, documentation, and drafting assistance.

A clear competitive and customer-serving benefit of CAD is its contribution to quick response. In companies with lots of designers, sometimes at several sites, CAD has another big plus: It provides all designers access to the file of component designs, which helps restrict the number of design variations (DFO guideline number 1, Table 10–1). That is, the designer may be able to select the standard already-designed item instead of designing a new, scarcely different one. (A minority view is that CAD tends to restrict designers to selecting from standard patterns, which might stifle a certain amount of creativity.)

MONITORING DESIGN PERFORMANCE
(DESIGN FOR RESULTS)

Time to close the loop. As they say, If it's not measured it won't get done. So in design, there must be measures of performance that back up goals, targets, and guidelines.

As a minimum, the performance measures should echo most of the DFO guidelines. For example, the first guideline says cut the ingredients or number of operations. Then, the first measure might be stated:

Number of operations—Should be small for a new service; should decline for a re-designed service.

In addition to general guidelines and echoing measures, how about a few project-specific targets? At CalComp, maker of graphics terminals and plotters, a target for the team designing the new Artisan 1023 plotter was 20–20–20: no more than 20 fasteners bought from no more than 20 suppliers located no more than 20 miles from CalComp's Anaheim plant. The team did not quite hit the targets but came close. For one thing, while the previous model had 175 fasteners (screws, bolts, etc.), the 1023 has just 26.[23]

Project-specific measures might also include cost of design changes and total product cost, which is a check on success in designing to target cost for the project. Cost of returns and field repairs are still other measures that help close the loop.

The latter measures, of course, can be done only after the product or service has been sold, which involves the marketing and sales function. In this chapter, we've nimbly stepped over a number of issues that are not easily split off from product development: the role of marketing. It's a topic big enough to deserve its own chapter, which is next.

11

❧

Marketing for Total Gain

I T IS SAID that marketing and salespeople are a unique breed. Maybe so. But part of it is a defense mechanism: defense against the rest of the company, which forever promotes policies that *restrict sales!*

Keep prices high. Keep number of models low. Cut back on inventories. Smooth out demand. Smooth out sales. Don't interrupt production cycles. These suggestions, coming from the rest of the organization, don't sit well with those judged on how much revenue they bring in.

In contrast to being defensive toward their own company, marketers are, of course, offensive toward their customers. On the other hand, the customer (at any stage in the chain of customers) is defensive, suspicious, and cynical.

Why isn't there a set of policies that will suit everybody? There is: *marketing for total gain,* which means customer-serving policies that make everyone shine.

When the marketing and salespeople prudently kept their distance from the rest of the organization, marketing was said to be the four P's: product, place, promotion, and price. Forces are now in motion that expand the list. The new elements include cooperation, competency, and capacity, plus talent, timing, and teamwork (if you like, the three C's and the three T's). We'll talk about those, and blend in some thoughts about improving the P's as well.

SELLING YOUR COMPANY'S CAPACITY AND COMPETENCY

The world-class company doesn't limit itself to promoting its products. It has a cornucopia of attractions to stir up customer interest, orders, and loyalty; they include continually improving service, production, quality, delivery, capacity, flexibility, and response. Price, too.

In other words, a company once known for one or two distinctive competencies—say, good design and after-sale service—now is blessed with talents of all kinds. The new long list of competencies has been carefully fashioned to be mutually beneficial—good for the customer and for the providing company as well. One of the competencies is unique, new, different: ability to *improve* (not stagnate)—which is the key to gaining customer *allegiance*.

Bragging Rights

The role of marketing, then, is to sing the company's praises, highlight its ability to improve, and educate the customer on the mutuality of benefits. More specifically, marketing generates ads, proposals, and bids that crow about a host of competencies—which may include:

- *Design partnership (simultaneous design).* Our designers work with yours in making the product line ever better
- *Competitive analysis.* If a competitor has something good, we do too—only better
- *Guaranteed quality at the source.* We provide you with our process capability data and samples of our SPC documents; and we do your tests at our end
- *Demonstrations of our rates of improvement.* Snap photos of some of our wall displays, which track all things bearing on good service: quickening changeovers, declining nonconformities, rising equipment reliability, falling rework, improving product and employee safety, nose-diving lead times—and more
- *Demand-tuned resources and schedules.* These result from our quick changeovers, just-in-time response, and flexibility; with flexibility, we respond to current demand and don't have to try futilely to guess demand mix way out in the future
- *High training and employee versatility.* Our employees can adapt to changes in customer demand

- *Planning for a prudent amount of excess equipment capacity.* Also includes the ability to marshal more labor to run the equipment when there are surges in customer demand
- *Error-proof billing and exact counts.* We use customer's standard container, where feasible
- *Simplified ordering and absence of paperwork.* We invoice only monthly for key customers

Even though standard marketing writings say nothing about this slant on promotion, some of it has always been done—and recently its use has been steadily growing. Avis's old "We try harder" slogan is an example of claiming an organizational competency—in contrast to just talking product and price. Ford told us that "Quality is job 1." AT&T said that "We wrote the book on quality," and the cover of the book was featured in TV ads.

Those are minimal examples, and they smack (a bit) of hype. The competencies I'm talking about are specific, measurable, and backed up by proven successes and see-for-yourself data.

Milliken brings its customers to its showrooms, where, proclaimed on huge banners, is "Milliken: The Home of Quick Response." Milliken, in partnership with other elements of the textile and apparel industry, has the quick-response data to back up the claim. Customers also go to examine the "wall of fame" (photos of top Milliken performers—see Figure 9–1B) and probably to see some of the many improvement charts on the walls of offices, labs, and factories. A special customer will even have a look at a single weaving machine (in a sea of others) dedicated to its—and nobody else's—orders, on which is a attached brassy plate inscribed with the customer's company name.

K2, the snow-ski company, plunged into world-class manufacturing in fall 1987. By the following summer, inventory of skis in process all over the plant fell from some 300 carts full (about 50,000 skis) to perhaps 20 carts. K2's worldwide sales agents, who came to the mother plant for an annual conference, had a look at those and other improvements of similar magnitude. They went away wide-eyed—and eager to vigorously represent the K2 line.

Small businesses are wowing customers, too. Oston Company, a Canadian firm with about one hundred employees, makes custom supermarket checkout counters. Oston is a premier just-in-time producer, delivering counters within three days of the order; it maintains no in-process or finished inventories, and can change a paint gun in twenty-five to thirty seconds. (Four paint colors circulate continuously right up to the nozzle of the sprayer; changeover consists of a jet of air, then solvent, then air, which dumps half an ounce of paint residue—and all is ready for the new color.) Marketing phones the customer just before the job is run—say, on Monday—asking for any last-minute changes, such as the color. Last question: "Still want delivery on Wednesday?" "Yes, I guess so." "What time?"

Clearly, the best places to promote a firm's competencies are via proposals, bids, and in-person visits. Advertising is more restrictive. Can't get much of anything into ad copy in view of severe space limitations. Along with short, bold statements about the product or service, there can be room for no more than a brief message about competency of the firm.

High Volume, Low Cost

While everything else is improving, products and prices are, too. Good companies simplify their products and services: fewer parts and fewer operations. Customers may still have variety. One way is via well-designed spin-offs. Another is a few basic items with plenty of "plug-in" modular add-ons. The idea is to market basic products or services that are so well designed, made, and delivered, and at such a low cost, that customers "beat a path to our door." The name of this game is *high volume, low cost.*

The strategy is not new, but it wouldn't work when design and operations were miles apart, prone to making a mess of things, and incapable of holding down costs. With few options for sales growth, marketing turned to proliferation of products and services as the hook. That just made everything more complicated and hard to manage efficiently. The product line grew and costs did, too. Actually, with a profusion of products and services, many in process at the same time, the cost of any one became impossible to find with any confidence. So product and pricing decisions were made in the dark.

In contrast, consider the enlightened company. Its high-volume, low-cost strategy includes setting up a dedicated team with its own resources. Team and resources are arranged into a cell or flow line, such that most product costs are contained and visible. Product and pricing decisions are made in the light of costs known with some confidence.

IBM is an example of a company that has made this strategy its

---

Shoes "R" Us

Toddler University, Inc., a maker of children's shoes, made a marketing coup: Got the shoes account at Kids "R" Us (the children's apparel arm of Toys "R" Us). It was easy—after Toddler's designers came up with a patented innovation: a shoe insert in five sizes that allows shoes to be made in just one width. That cut the number of sizes to be made, carried, and sold from fifty-five to just eleven (the eleven basic children's lengths).[1]

---

centerpiece. Initial planning took place in the early 1980s. By 1983, the abbreviated term HVLC (high volume, low cost) was tossed around the company familiarly. A later example is Caterpillar, whose HVLC product is internally called a "saleable stock tractor." It is a commodity model with a good price and fast delivery.

While HVLC has cost reduction as its goal, it opens the door to price cutting—or improving profit margins.

Market-Based Pricing

It's time to reiterate and expand on a point made earlier: Although most companies cling to cost-based pricing, the best have adopted or lean toward pricing based on the market.

New or redesigned products. Market-based pricing is the job of a product strategy team whose members come from marketing, design, finance, and operations. For new or redesigned products, they establish a target price and hand it over to the product development team, as follows:

1. Set target sales volume. It is the volume needed to pay off the investment in design and development, get good prices on materials, equip a facility, hire and train people, and, overall, make the product a hit. Performance of similar products in the past guide the effort.
2. Do market research to find the probable price that will produce the target sales volume.

Customer-Push Pricing

Retailers usually set prices based on what they have to pay wholesale. Not Charles Lazarus, founder of Toys "R" Us. He would say, "I can sell this product at great volumes at a certain price."[2] That becomes the price, and the cost he pays the wholesaler goes down from there.

---

3. Subtract a target profit margin to get a target cost. That becomes an upper limit for the product development team, which continually estimates costs and rejiggers designs.
4. Kill projects early if the target cost is out of reach.

In brief, set the price in order to find the cost.

Existing products. Costs are known for existing products—those already on the market. That modifies the market-based pricing concept a bit. If the company has a full-blown continual improvement effort going, the way is clear for a continual competitive assault. The product strategy team orchestrates the following:

1. Evaluates periodic samples of and data on competitors' designs, prices, capacity, flexibility, and problems.
2. Periodically audits its own company's costs (see cost-audit discussion in Chapter 8).
3. Does this better than the competition so as to become the price-cutting champion of the industry, with resulting sales and market-share gains and steadily increasing profit margins.
4. Finally, closes the loop, makes sure all its people—who, after all, are the core of the cost-cutting machine—see the results. Trends go up on large wall charts; or, if the information is too sensitive to keep on display, are presented to all employees monthly. Trend data are discussed in regular small-group meetings, and with a different team member leading the competitive meeting each time.

Figure 11–1 is an example of the total effects—for the company whose cost-cutting engine is well tuned. It shows costs going down and prices falling at a lesser rate, which increases profit margins;

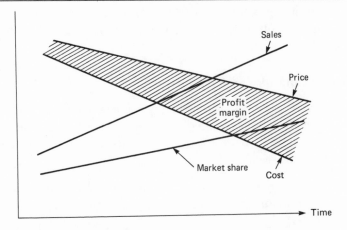

Figure 11–1. Coordinated Attack, Existing Products

and sales rising sharply, with market share increasing as well. Each product or product family should have its own similar chart.

Profit bias. In either case, new/redesigned products or existing ones, profit margins are a result, not a starting point. Too many companies hold rigidly to profit guidelines, which often keep marketing and product development people from going for new business and growth in old product lines.

To be sure, there is plenty of case evidence on the folly of pell-mell growth. In fact, hurtling growth is seldom successful. (For example, in the franchising industry many of the failures stem from overaggressive expansion, while the success stories often are tied to careful growth.)[3] Fast, controlled growth—product by product, rather than aggregated—is the goal. Just focusing on total sales can lead to product-line proliferation, which generally has poor overall results.

Let's look at the issue more closely. Typically, a firm's pricing and "positioning" plans for a given product are biased in favor of a certain profit margin and against growth. This can be the kiss of death, because many of the world-class competencies tend to "kick in" naturally when sales of a given product reach a critical level: Get sales up to the point where a dedicated team with its own resources can handle that one product, product family, or customer group and nothing else (until it's time to regroup around another). In that simple operating mode—team in a cell dedicated to one thing—overhead costs melt. The stage is set for team-driven continual improvement, cost/price reduction, sales growth—and, finally, profits.

So, short-term thinkers, repeat this a hundred times every morning while shaving or putting on your makeup: *Proft is a result. Proft is a result. Proft is a result* . . .

Smoothing Demand/Capacity Patterns

A competency-based marketing strategy thrives not only on sales growth; it depends as well on getting away from typical herky-jerky sales patterns and peak-and-valley operations. A joint attack on the problem has the following features:

- Marketing alters sales bonuses to smooth sales. (Do everything possible to stamp out "channel stuffing"—inflating end-of-period sales totals.)
- For customers who order in surges—typically end-of-period spending—sales and marketing offer this deal: Customers, book your orders at any time—all surges welcome; but take delivery at more regular intervals, closer to real usage.

The Bonus Onus

They changed everything at Physio Control: Formed focused TEAM-BUILT cells, put each cell on daily-rate schedules, abolished work-in-process stockrooms, cut setup times, got rid of most labor reporting, etc. With everything else getting fixed, one problem now stood out like a clear-cut in one of the nearby forests: Sales always took a sharp turn upward at the end of the year.

Everybody thought they knew why: Sales bonuses were paid that way. For no good reason; it's just the way it was.

The company wasn't going to stand for it. In fall 1987, a team of marketing, finance, and manufacturing people began studying how to change the bonus system. They got inputs from probably a hundred people.

The result: failure. Physio's fiscal year ends on the calendar year, as is the case for many of its major accounts in medical and emergency care. Their customers' habit, policy, or necessity of spending end-of-year cash proved to be a greater obstacle than Physio's sales bonus system.

- Operations smooths capacity peaks and valleys, which, along with simple quick-response methods, cuts costs. This allows still more price cutting and improved service to customers.
- Marketing and operations jointly plan competitive promotions (white sales, Mother's Day, etc.) and large orders. Together they hatch a marketing plan that is workable—that does not impossibly strain capacity, wreck delivery performance and salespeople's credibility, or seriously elevate costs.

On this last point, I am able to mention two steps in the right direction. One is Sears Roebuck's sea change in its pricing practices: from an emphasis on price-cutting sales to everyday low prices. Sears launched its new strategy, from a position of weakness, in spring 1989. Within a few months, its major competitors had felt noticeable pain—in the form of lower sales. The second welcome change, in the same year, involved major producers of consumer goods, including Procter & Gamble, Kraft General Foods, and a Philip Morris unit: a shift away from heavy reliance on promotions (coupons, contests, and discounts to retailers) and toward advertising.[4]

We may hope that these strategic marketing changes—away from sales, coupons, games, and the like—are long-lasting and also not just a North American phenomenon. Promotions may seem to make sense from the narrow perspective. But they raise havoc—disruptive, costly up-and-down demand spikes—throughout the long chain of customers.

I am not including auto-industry rebates or frequent-flyer and hotel guest programs. They are costly offerings and reflect basic weaknesses (excess cars, seats, or rooms), but at least they don't cause spikey demand patterns.

We've considered how to promote competency with improved products, lower prices, and smoother sales, deliveries, and operations. These expand the company's arsenal of weapons for attracting good customers, which is marketing's first job. But the marketing task continues. Existing customers are a valuable asset to be nurtured, developed, and *partnered*.

PARTNERSHIP

Good customers are like money in the bank. Should be, anyway. But in conventional practice, the seller pays for the same promotion, selling, and order-processing expenses again and again—and passes the costs on to the customer. What's more, the customer pays for the same purchasing costs over and over again. By developing a healthy partnership, the two parties can bank the wasted cash.

In my 1986 book,[5] I suggested that the job of purchasing is *supplier development*. My view today is more well rounded; it looks in the other direction and says, The job of marketing is *customer development*. Put the two together and we have the nurturing of long-term partnerships, exclusive contracts, and mutual gain. It's what Johnston and Lawrence refer to as a "value-adding partnership," which means a joint attack on all forms of waste, leaving only activities that add value for both parties.[6] Let's consider a few specifics.

Mutual Gain

Assume I am a supplier working toward a real partnership with key customers based on world-class excellence:

1. My company's many competencies mean a superior ability to respond to current demand. That permits a deft shift from negative to positive selling. Negative selling is pushing stockpiled inventories, off-spec goods, or capacity of the wrong kind upon the customer who really wants something else. Positive is relying on my firm's capability to directly and quickly handle each demand, with unquestioned quality. (When we no longer hear about factory outlet stores, "big sales" of overstocks, cut prices for "seconds," and fuss about warranties and returns, business may collectively congratulate itself.)

2. My customer agrees to a long-term exclusive (or semi-exclusive) contract; also to provide a twelve-month rolling demand forecast. With just my company as supplier (instead of multiple suppliers, the usual practice), and with a contract instead of sporadic orders, my customer's administrative costs drop.

3. With much more of the customer's business, we gain scale economies and cut peak capacity, overtime, and inventories. With higher volume, my company may no longer have to process internal orders for that customer; we may be able to smooth the customer's demand pattern and convert from irregular orders to a regular repeating schedule. If the volume of business is large enough, we set up a dedicated operation just for that customer—with costs contained and known. In any case, we cut the price. Or,

One-and-a-Half Suppliers

An exclusive contract is a risk. Right? After all, your source could have an explosion or fire, a strike or a long run of unacceptable quality. Or, if you are high-tech, your exclusive supplier may fail to keep abreast of new technologies. So isn't the old wisdom right? Have several suppliers for every item?

For most items—those widely available—the answer is no. There are plenty of other sources to turn to if your exclusive one fails.

For the critical case, the modern answer is the so-called one-and-a-half supplier concept: One supplier is guaranteed two-thirds of your business for the contract period (usually one to five years); a second is guaranteed one-third. (An alternative is two exclusive suppliers, each guaranteed 50 percent.)

more likely, we hold the price cut in reserve as a bargaining chip, playing it if necessary to cement the partnership.

(An example is GM's 1989 plastic-body minivan. Budd Company is exclusive supplier of driver's-side body panels; GenCorp is exclusive supplier of right-side body panels. Each specializes in, makes the costly tooling for, and gains scale economies on just one part. GM has the security of two suppliers capable of making both parts, and since it is easy for GM to compare their performance, the two suppliers are driven to match each other's improvement rates—and cannot afford to get lax and sloppy.)

4. As close partners, we and our customer cut out the "middleman." We communicate and deal directly. Where goods are involved, for example, we direct-ship to our customer-partner, without the extra costs, damage, and other problems of putting the goods into a distribution warehouse first.

5. Customers visit our place often enough to be like extended family; our people are at customers' sites just as often. Chains of command are rarely used, so that designers in the two companies meet together, operators talk to operators, and others do the same. This leads to resolving problems and aggravations via direct, low-level contact.

6. The customer receives preferential treatment—inside our schedule or backlog. We reserve capacity for that customer, which means less that has to promoted and sold. We wish all our capacity were presold like that, in which case our selling costs would drop nearly to zero. We would become marketers and contractors, not sellers.

7. When our partnership is well developed, our customer has some access to our books and *real* costs; this averts disputes and disharmony over delicate pricing and profit issues. In return, we have on-line access to our customer's inventory or backlog files and forecasts, which averts mistrust stemming from habitual overstatement of needs by the customer.

8. In a few isolated cases, where business is very large and steady, we, the supplier, would consider setting up a small dedicated facility right next to the customer's. (Some suppliers set up shop right on the customer's premises.) The customer gains the benefits but not the risks and headaches of ownership.

As an example of several of these points, Simpson Industries, Inc., an engine parts maker, got the full "snoop" treatment from General Motors. The GM team checked Simpson's books, even including medical plan costs, and privately interviewed line operators to gauge the state of labor relations. Simpson's president and CEO, Robert W. Navarre, calls it an unprecedented partnership. What did his side of the partnership gain? Eighty percent of Simpson's business is now locked into sole-source, long-term contracts; there's not much capacity left that has to be promoted and sold.[7]

While Simpson doesn't have a dedicated plant located near to each customer, Johnson Controls, Inc., does. It operates ten plants making car seats and trim in that manner.[8]

Marketing as Advocate

Of course, the customer is not a passive partner. In fact until recently, customers, not suppliers, were the usual initiators of value-adding partnerships. It was the auto companies telling their suppliers, "You *will* . . ." and the electronics majors bringing their suppliers in for a "quality day" followed by efforts to winnow the number of suppliers to a few who were quality-certified.

That has changed. As a supplier, if you have attended several quality

Partnering or Integrating?

Partnering takes time and energy. The customer puts up with it in order to get better performance. To escape the bother, why not just do it yourself? Vertical (backward) integration, it's called.

Some say that vertical integration is right for some businesses, not for others. Those holding that viewpoint think the auto industry is *not* right for it. They point to General Motors, the most integrated (by far) of the major automakers. They think vertical integration sapped GM's competitive strength (reasons: high wages and prices, complacency, inflexibility of GM-owned suppliers). Indeed, GM is doing its best to retreat from it.

Here's the curious part of the argument: that vertical integration *was* a correct strategy for the auto industry back as far as the 1930s—when Ford was even more famous for it than GM.

It won't wash. Vertical integration is not and never was a good idea (except for special reasons, like seizing essential technologies). It violates the Peters and Waterman principle, stick to your knitting. A company can't be good at very many things. Never mind the so-called synergies. Ford succeeded with vertical integration for several decades because nobody knew any better. We needed the knowledge explosion of the 1980s to set us straight.

days and felt the same heat from umpteen major customers, the handwriting is on the wall: Time to enhance the marketing approach—to promote quality, quick response, flexibility, design partnership, continual cost reduction, and the other things that customers are suddenly interested in.

One of the first companies to fully market these kinds of competencies is Zytec, the specialty power-supply maker. Table 11–1 shows the content of the first two pages of a Zytec promotional document called, "Just-in-Time (JIT) Manufacturing Partnership." The two pages summarize the rest of the booklet. Topics include such things as number of pieces sampled for process capability studies, schedule-change and order-cancellation policies, and a fifteen-item, question-and-answer sheet.

Table 11–1. *Zytec's "JIT Manufacturing Partnership"*[*]

[Page 1]

WHAT IF YOU COULD . . .

1. REDUCE YOUR COSTS
2. IMPROVE YOUR QUALITY & PRODUCT RELIABILITY
3. REDUCE YOUR INVENTORY
4. ASSURE YOUR DELIVERY

FOR WAYS THAT ZYTEC CAN HELP . . . WE INTRODUCE THE
    ZYTEC . . . "JIT MANUFACTURING PARTNERSHIP"

[Page 2]

THE "JIT MANUFACTURING PARTNERSHIP"
ON-TIME DELIVERY AND QUALITY

Zytec is committed to being the best at what we do. To that end, we constantly measure and manage for more effective processes and top quality at every stage.

We have learned that measuring results and improving our processes can be accomplished most effectively using techniques such as:

• Process capability studies
• Statistical process control
• A total quality commitment
• Extensive training in skills
• Extensive training in methods and processes
• Improving employee support from management
• Feedback on results and problems
• Just-in-time methods of production

These techniques are even more effective when customers and suppliers work together as a team.

This booklet provides information about our "JIT Manufacturing Partnership" with our customers and/or suppliers as we work together to achieve excellence that you can depend on.

[*] Used with permission of Zytec Corporation.

For example, here are Q&A items 2 and 13:

   2. Customer's Question. Do I need to implement JIT in my production to benefit?

   Zytec's Answer. *No!* Assured on-time delivery eliminates expediting and eliminates need for safety stock, regardless of your methodology.

13. Q. What else can we do to eliminate costs?
    A. Eliminate packaging. Delivery to your factory instead of a warehouse can be made using returnable, rolling racks instead of individual boxes. This eliminates pack/unpack cost and handling.

A different twist on marketing advocacy is what Northern Telecom calls "power marketing." Telecom has organized a Technical Advisory Council of twenty-two of its key customers, plus the Bell companies. The council's purpose is get embroiled in *Northern Telecom*'s product development. Members get their engineers involved in design reviews, product approvals, and enhancements before the design is locked in. They participate in testing, come to know all about Telecom's facilities and capabilities, and can link their computers to Telecom's design data base. Company president Roy Merills says, "We believe the upside benefits [of open access] far outweigh the negatives, and so do our customers."[9]

Of course, a company can't get away with marketing (or revealing) what it can't deliver. So, wised-up marketing people may become vocal advocates of a full set of world-class competencies inside their own firms.

The shift toward a marketing-driven partnership has been reflected in the kinds of speaking events that I get involved in: In the "old" days, the sponsor sometimes was a buying company and the event was a "supplier day." Now it's symposia arranged by marketing people for key *customers*. I speak about building chains of customers and world-class performance trends and techniques. Other speakers follow with specifics on the sponsoring company's new strengths: quality, quick response, involved employees, and so forth.

At one symposium, attendees were from computer software companies. One cosponsor was a service company specializing in copying, packaging, and shipping software for software houses; the other cosponsor was a manufacturer of computer memory diskettes. Both companies are leaders in their fields in the use of techniques such as statistical process control and just-in-time—and anxious to tell about it.

Sourcing and Certification

The customer reps at symposia such as the one I have described should take a lot of notes. Part of their job must be to size up suppliers.

With a long-term partnership in mind, the supplier's current price is *not* the deciding factor. It is all too easy for a supplier to quote a low price. What counts for the long haul is the supplier's ability to improve.

Supplier selection. I have not yet seen what I consider to be an excellent set of criteria for sizing up and selecting suppliers.

Leading firms now have quality high on the list, sometimes equal with price. Delivery performance and certain other measures of service are in there, too. Many more supplier competencies belong on the list; these are some prominent examples:

- Quality at the source
- Process capability
- Declining defects, errors, and nonconformities
- Declining lead time, work in process, flow distance, space
- Cross-trained operators who collect data, do preventive maintenance, use SPC, and engage in quick changeover and process improvement projects
- Commitment to continual training (significant percent of budget)
- Simultaneous design and competitive analysis
- Volume flexibility—pertaining to both equipment and labor

It is not a coincidence that many of these criteria for supplier selection are what I've mentioned earlier as items for suppliers' marketing people to promote. It is a meeting of the minds. What the supplier wants to provide is what the customer wants.

Certification and recognition. Supplier selection overlaps with certification and awards. The customer's certification team has two tasks: One is to certify *companies*—firms that have a history of good performance; their names go on approved supplier lists. Criteria for supplier certification are about the same (but more quantitative and structured) as the criteria used for supplier selection.

The other task is to quality-certify *items*—specific goods and services. (After much debate, the Customer-Supplier Technical Committee of the American Society for Quality Control has developed a list of supplier certification criteria for the piece-goods and process industries.[10] Certification amounts to evidence that the supplier takes care of quality at the source, so that the buyer may skip receiving inspection. Quality is audited once in a while to show that everything is still okay.

When one or two suppliers are finally under contract and everything is certified, the on-going routine takes over. Except that what's on-going is not so routine anymore.

Organizing for Partnership

On-going activity means a continuing effort by both parties to strengthen the bond—a mutual partnership in profit and success. In the old days, the big companies with clout squeezed and squeezed, sometimes utterly sapping the supplier's strength. No matter, they thought. Plenty of other suppliers to put under contract—and squeeze.

That never made sense. It caused steady deterioration of the supplier base. This went on throughout most of the world. Top Japanese companies called a halt to the practice first.

Today, supplier development and partnership is the replacement for putting suppliers in a vice. Frito-Lay, for example, has a vice president for supplier development.[11] CalComp no longer has just plain buyers. It has supplier development teams—with representation from quality, design, and other areas. Motorola has organized a "Partnership-for-Growth Advisory Board." With representatives from fifteen key supplier companies, the board meets three times a year; it debates Motorola's supplier selection criteria, offers suggestions about specs, and so forth.[12] In a survey of one hundred companies active in just-in-time, 77 percent said they used dedicated sourcing teams whose members come from quality control, design, purchasing, and sometimes a few other functions.[13]

The trend toward partnership continues. But there is a hitch—especially in the big, multisite company. It wants to be able to do world sourcing, to find the best suppliers, and to seek volume discounts based on the sum of requirements from all its sites. In other words, it wants to use its *leverage*. The company also wishes to be fair; it wants all its sites to treat common suppliers consistently. The case for centralized sourcing and buying seems strong.

On the other hand, it is beneficial to have each site develop familylike ties with each supplier site; here the word isn't leverage, it's *partner power*.

Black & Decker's answer is "two-tier buying." Small centralized staffs at U.S. headquarters in Maryland and European headquarters in London purchase the big-ticket items. The rest of the buying, about 50 percent of B&D's total, is decentralized; that includes bulky items like injection moldings.[14]

McKinsey and Company, the consulting firm, offers a surprising slant on the issue of placement of the purchasing group. McKinsey is telling some of its clients that their big price reductions gained by central buying were not worth it, because it "slowed down the purchase cycle so much that they were being disadvantaged in the operations."[15]

THE OTHER PARTNERS

Between the supplier and buyer are two other parties to be "partnered": distribution centers and freight haulers. Still other special kinds of partnering are cropping up to meet special needs for achieving world-class results.

Special Partners

An example of the latter is when two or more suppliers team up to provide and market a joint product. In one case, Budd Company, maker of automobile doors, formed an alliance with ITT's North American Mechanical Systems Group, which produces mechanical and electromechanical devices for autos. Their project is to develop and produce a modular door, to be jointly and separately marketed to any automaker.

Budd and ITT have no formal agreement. They just kick in equal money and rely on team success (avoiding "pride of authorship" problems), and they jointly produce the final product with existing resources.[16]

The auto industry, among others, is encouraging its suppliers to form such alliances, which shrinks the number of items a final assembly plant has to try to manage. When the number of items under any one roof is very large, systems of control become too complex to be effective.

In the automotive and aerospace industries, the sheer size of some parts is another reason for restricting the number of items brought in for assembly; there simply is not enough space to keep thousands of large parts where they belong—at lineside.

Partnered suppliers are stepping in to fill the need for preassembled modules. They specialize in it, perhaps for several companies, which yields design improvements and scale economies, including volume discounts on their own purchased materials.

World-Class Carriers

The world's freight haulers—trucks, planes, trains, ships, and barges—are in a new era. Their customers are requiring delivery on a specified day, sometimes within a given hour and to a certain dock. Munson Transportation, an Illinois trucking company, reports that 65 percent of its customers now measure trucking service levels by arrival times.[17] That is one of the new criteria for *carrier certification*. In the old days, the load left the shipper, and when it might arrive was anybody's guess.

Technology to the rescue: Several firms now offer orbital satellite tracking systems to show just where a truck (or other carrier) is at any time. To some of our "cowboy" drivers, such systems are probably as welcome as road ice and high winds. But necessary. Edward J. Krajca, a transportation manager at Chrysler, says, "We are too involved in the tracking of our shipments. We want that responsibility to move to our carriers."

Satellite systems, in Krajca's mind, solve a lot of problems. For example, the carrier can use the data in the exception mode: Tell Chrysler only when a load will *not* arrive on time, so an alternate mode can move the materials and avoid shutting down one of Chrysler's JIT assembly plants. Better yet, the carrier can use the data to exercise better control over things that go wrong: in other words, provide quality at the source, or, in Krajca's words, "service without any defects."[18]

Partnering with carriers means the same thing as between provider and user: development of familylike relationships. It works well when the same driver or crew for the same carrier moves the same kinds of loads along the same route repeatedly. The driver or crew gets to know the people at both ends, personalizing to the point of sharing birthday cake and maybe invitations to each other's company picnics. To get to this desired state, customers are reducing their number of carriers to just a few, certified "core" carriers. That, at the same time, means fewer customers the carrier must deal with; administrative costs go down for both parties. 3M Company once had some one thousand less-than-truckload and 240 truckload carriers; now thirty-one core haulers move 87 percent of 3M's less-than-load shipments, and just seven handle over 91 percent of its full-load business.[19]

Distance can get in the way. On the other hand, Chrysler has one repetitive "milk run" extending some 1,700 miles. It begins in El Paso with pickups of seat belts and wiring from two component plants, stops in Fort Worth for cruise controls, and gets to the Detroit area fifty-six hours later for unloading at Chrysler's assembly plants.[20] The freight partnership—several source and destination plants plus a carrier—keeps freight costs at full-load rates and still permits frequent small-lot, just-in-time deliveries.

World-Class Distribution Center

Some freight haulers also provide warehousing services. Today's demands for speed and accuracy have produced some new wrinkles on that type of combined service. Federal Express, one of the world's foremost logistics experts, has set up "PartsBank" distribution centers near its air terminals. Among its customers are Jaguar and Volvo-U.K., for which FedEx delivers auto parts to dealers. Another is the Louis Feraud fashion house, which has FedEx move garments from plants in Germany, to an air terminal in Brussels, across the Atlantic to a PartsBank in Memphis, and then by plane and delivery vehicle to fashion retailers around North America as needed.[21] Still another is IBM, which, for all its computing and communications power, is not an expert in logistics; FedEx warehouses IBM computer modules, which must come together as systems, quickly, when salespeople book orders.

Regardless of who operates the distribution center (DC), there seem to be some emerging guidelines. First are the goals. For the world-class DC they are continual reduction of:

- Handling, transactions, and other overhead
- Defects (toward zero-defect handling)
- Throughput time
- Space

Second are operating guidelines, which include:

1. Minimize transactions, first of all for high-use ("star") items. Methods include employing the visual kanban system to and from the supply point as well as with willing customers; invoicing by period, not by order or shipment; and using standard containers, which permit no-count receiving.
2. With producers, seek final-use demand data (e.g., point-of-sale data) as the basis for synchronized scheduling. The idea is for the DC and the supplying production system (could include several production stages) to get on the same schedule, one that is close to actual sales of the final product.
3. Minimize useless handling: Stop rehandling full-case star items going to star customers; go to direct-shipment from the factory. Locate stock using ABC principles; for example, A items highly accessible—near to automated handling and docks, B items traveling farther but still on conveyors, C items having to be fetched by a vehicle. Dedicate some docks—those serving JIT suppliers

or customers—to deliveries by the hour. Finally, shorten conveyor paths within the DC.

One company quickly put much of this guideline to good use. I received a letter with this comment: "Following our discussion with you during a coffee break at your seminar in Denver, we drastically shortened the conveyor path between picking drop-off and packing, making it possible for pickers and packers to operate as a team and avoid the necessity of complex conveyor controls and long queues behind packing. Queues were cut from two hours to 20–30 minutes."

Another company that partially follows this guideline is Wal-Mart, which is well known for efficient deliveries to its retail stores. To further improve service, Wal-Mart's DCs have set forth special handling procedures for over 250 key "basic stock" items.[22]

4. Avoid building mammoth DCs. Size creates management and accountability problems; and it usually requires complex handling and computer systems, which increase picking delays and equipment and information system failures. Moreover, it creates its own pressure to hold stock—to "keep that costly space filled!" In contrast, when DC space is tight, people are forced to consider direct-shipment, bypassing the DC.

5. Where the "super DC" already exists, break it into DCs-within-a-DC, each with its own team, system, and other resources. The team focus in on process improvement and total quality— for itself and each of its partners. For example, one team might run a mini-DC for big-customer/few-item accounts; its system would be simple, and its work-flow-based team might include such people as: dedicated inbound driver, loader, clerk, service reps from both supplier and customer, picker, and outbound driver. They work closely together to remove aggravations and to define and permanently fix problems.

Close the Warehouses

Two major food companies, Campbell Soup and Frito Lay, got the idea at about the same time (around 1985): Direct-ship wherever possible, and close down some of the distribution centers. The best warehouse is no warehouse.

6. For special activities, such as break-bulk and load consolidation, set up special procedures and perhaps a separate area and team; as much as possible, break the load and consolidate at the door, and put away only the overflow.

The partnering that we have been discussing has several objectives, including quick response, the last but certainly not least important topic in this chapter.

SELLING FAST RESPONSE

Not long ago I had a phone call from a manager at a multibillion-dollar company. His job title: manager of time-based strategies.

That may be a first. It is a job title that puts a strategic stamp on what had been thought of mostly as a set of techniques going by names like just-in-time and quick response. When something is called "strategic," I guess that means it has wide-ranging effects. That surely is the case for time-based competition.

Time-Based Competition

The importance of time-based competition has occurred to many besides the person who coined or publicized the term (namely, George Stalk, Jr., vice president of the Boston Consulting Group).[23] As we have seen, it is the basis of primary marketing thrusts by Milliken ("Milliken—Home of Quick Response") and Lucky Market ("Three's a Crowd"). Fred Smith, CEO of Federal Express, made an industry of quick-response mail—and now has added parts delivery. Luciano Benetton carved a sizable niche out of the fashion industry, employing quick response to a degree previously unimagined in the garment trade—ability to deliver mid-season reorders within two or three weeks.[24] Fax, cellular phones, and company electronic mail networks—for faster-response communications—have been taking the world by storm.

While Lucky Market's "Three's a Crowd" campaign is novel, line-length policies are becoming common among major North American supermarkets and other retailers. I did my own informal survey. I asked a checkout clerk at an Ernst store (Ernst is a West Coast hardware and home supply chain), "Do you have line-length policies?" I didn't have to explain what I meant. I got a quick reply: "Yes. Three people."

I asked at several other grocery stores and heard about line-length policies that exist but are not quite so firm. In one store, Larry's Market (a small Seattle chain known for premier service), I was told, "We get in trouble if we don't [open another line when line length gets long]."

Of course, we all know about time-based competition in fast foods. Now it is becoming a factor in up-scale restaurants, at least in North American cities.

In my area, there are six to ten very popular restaurants that have fine food and amenities for a high but not outrageous price. They are full all the time. This area has dozens of other restaurants with food just as good and prices about the same, but they are not well known and not full all the time.

It isn't advertising or location that makes the difference. It is *time*. The good ones all make use of unobtrusive keypad devices (the newer ones are portable) used by the table staff for sending orders to the bar and kitchen and for printing out the bill. The devices link to a clock as well, so that elapsed times for all services are recorded. The system directly speeds up the service and cuts handwriting and other errors. In a less direct but important way, it also helps eliminate big lapses and delays, and that may be the key competitive factor. I am referring to the timing data retrievable from computer memory, which signals a troublesome source of delay (e.g., a bad oven thermostat or an unclear procedure) whenever it crops up.

I suspect that few of these restaurants' hordes of repeat customers could articulate just why they keep returning, but it's the same reason why people flock to successful fast-food restaurants: You know what you are getting *and how long it will take.*

What I'm saying is that time-based competition is *two* things: It is *pure unadulterated the-faster-the-better speed,* where that is wanted, as in fast food, mail, and just-in-time production. It is *predictable or invariable response time,* where that is important, *as it is in almost every kind of service or production anywhere.*

Delay costs money. Variable response time costs as well, because it causes delivery to be earlier or later than expected, which means a resource is going to be idled. In the case of human services, variable response causes idleness of the customer, which adds up to lost business. (While the European dining tradition of spending hours at the table remains strong, European patrons are habitually annoyed by waiters who won't appear when there is a need, for example, when it's time for the check.)

The Effects of Time

When a company turned on to quick response begins to have success, its whole slate of goals and performance measures shifts toward controlling causes—and outcomes important to customers. Boston University's Manufacturing Futures Project,[25] involving a survey of companies in the U.S., Japan, and Europe, offers partial evidence. Surveyed companies reported their top-ten performance measures. It's no surprise that "manufacturing lead times" is in first place among Japanese companies. In the U.S., where just-in-time caught on quickly, "manufacturing lead time" is fourth, and "supplier lead time" is fifth.

In Europe, which got a late start in JIT, lead time isn't on the list at all, nor is inventory. The European top ten are all traditional— what we might have seen anywhere in the world two, three, or four decades ago: outgoing quality, unit manufacturing cost, unit material cost, overhead cost, on-time delivery, incoming quality, direct labor productivity, material yield, unit labor cost, and forecast accuracy.

Why wouldn't items such as on-time delivery and forecast accuracy still be on United States and Japanese lists? Because all the things done to chop lead times make on-time delivery a ho-hum thing and forecast accuracy a nonissue.

The 1988 survey is already becoming dated. Today, most of Europe's top companies are up-to-date. It is safe to say that their top-ten goals and measures now are more like those of Japan and the U.S.

While it is a wonder that the importance of quick response has been overlooked so long, it is out in the open now. There is much to do to redress the years of neglect, wipe out delay-based wastes, and mollify the put-off customers. Part of the catching up has to do with measurement.

Measuring Quick Response

Are there lines in company annual reports that show a firm's quick-response capabilities? Hardly ever. I know of one case of it: at Deluxe Check Printers, Inc., a company oft-acclaimed for its service and all-around performance. (Deluxe is one of the companies singled out in 1984 by *Fortune* for its stellar financial performance. Its 1985 annual report was titled "Partnership," which stresses the company belief that it must be a partner, not just a printer.) Deluxe's 1983 annual report stated that its sixty-odd plants had achieved the company goal of two-day turnaround on check printing 95.6 percent of the time. The report also gave the average quality figure: 99.1 percent accuracy.[26]

Deluxe hasn't stood still. In 1989, its turnaround standard had been cut to *one* day. It's a good thing. Competitors like Interchecks have awakened and now are hot on Deluxe's heels.

While other companies' annual reports don't tell about response time, reports for goods-oriented businesses contain a rough surrogate for it: inventory value, on the balance sheet. Elsewhere in the annual report is annual cost of sales. Simple math will get you days of inventory or annual inventory turnover. If, for example, total inventory averages 120 days, that can mean, roughly, that response time—from receipt of raw material to shipped finished goods—is 120 days. Outrageous but common enough among manufacturers stuck on outdated management concepts. (While service companies cannot use the inventory surrogate, any company can measure and report response ratios, including samples of micro-response ratios from its turned-on focused teams. See discussion in Chapter 5.)

One hundred twenty days of inventory is the same as an annual inventory turnover of three, which has been rather typical of North American industry. Japan is higher. Europe is lower.

I've informally looked through a sample of annual reports from well-known companies. My interest was in the inventory turnover figures—the surrogate for response time. I've isolated some of the better companies; I'll not name them because it's such a biased sample: only large, publicly held companies whose annual reports are easy to get. (The *best* performers are among large and small privately held companies, whose annual reports are not made public.)

I'll just mention one of the average or below-average ones—in order to make a point: American Home Products (AHP). Its inventory turnover actually went downhill from 1984 through 1987 before turning up in 1988 (3.4 to 3.2 to 3.1 to 2.6 to 2.7).

Has AHP been sleeping through the earthquakes of the 1980s? Is it unaware of the competitive advantages of quick response? Not necessarily. On balance, I admire AHP. I base this on its high degree of focus in product development and marketing. Ries and Trout tell about the company's swift response when the U.S. Food and Drug Administration approved the drug ibuprofen. AHP launched a massive marketing campaign for Advil and actually was producing the product before it had all the product approvals from the FDA.

It was a risky tactic, but it worked. Advil is the dominant brand of ibuprofen.[27] AHP has a stable full of such brands, including Woolite, Chef Boyardee, Preparation H, Dristan, and Anacin.

The best brands are dug into the consumer's mind like a branding iron's impression on the hide of a steer. Getting to the market first is part of it. Focused marketing—making sure the consumer doesn't mix up one brand name with another or have too many choices—is the sustaining force. (Ries and Trout cite a long list of products that they think have failed because of fuzzy, cluttered brand identification and unfocused marketing: New Coke, Xerox computers, Ivory Shampoo, and Holiday Inn Crowne Plaza, to name a few.)[28]

For all its strengths as a world-class developer of brand names, AHP's poor inventory turnover shows weaknesses elsewhere (e.g., unfocused plants, people, and equipment; or lack of supplier partnerships). Strongly focused brands, though, make an ideal base to build on; just push focus, quick response, low inventories, and, in general, just-in-time and total-quality methods—all of which are related—backwards all the way to suppliers, brand by brand.

12

❧

Success Formulas for Volume and Flexibility

WE HAVE BEEN TOLD repeatedly by any number of experts that the old days of mass-produced, mass-marketed standardized products are going, going, gone. How does the argument go? Something like this, I guess: World competition has made customers more demanding; what customers demand is variety and change; product life cycles have been squeezing down for years; and new computer-based technologies are coming on strong to make it possible for firms almost to customize a different variation for every customer.

There are a few grains of truth in all that—actually three grains: Indeed life cycles are shortening, *final consumers* are demanding and getting variety, and business is using new schemes to change and react fast. But, no, mass production is not declining. In fact it's boom time for mass production, because of more and better approaches for making it work.

I'll offer my reasoning on this matter, and also on how to make a success of not-so-massive production—the lucrative niches where great flexibility is the key. Mostly, I'll treat the topics as *capacity* issues: having the capacity to operate at low cost with high quality and quick response even as demand and designs change in the short and long runs. An important special issue is how to plan for just the right amount of capacity—and capacity buffers—to meet the ups and downs in both sales and operating performance.

263

MASSIVE MASS MARKETS

I'll state the state of affairs: Long-standing trade barriers are being dismantled (notably "1992" in Europe and the U.S.-Canada trade pact), creating awesome new mass markets. Formerly, international companies like Black & Decker had to run job-shop plants—a little of this and a little of that—in Canada and in each European country; now each of those plants will be rejiggered to produce fewer products in higher volumes. Philips (Netherlands), which had to offer seven versions of personal computer for the chopped-up European market, is standardizing to two models in 1990 and later will go to just one for a unified European market. [1]

North American and Japanese manufacturers, banks, insurance companies, brokerage houses, and franchisers are in a frenzy trying to establish a European beachhead—attracted by the opportunities for mass production and mass marketing. If we can think of rather few massively produced products that come from Europe, Canada, and Australia (versus many that come from Japan and the U.S.), it's because those countries have never enjoyed the bounty of mass markets in the past.

Pile 'Em High and Sell 'Em Cheap

Regardless of the lowering of trade barriers, the trend over several decades has been toward exploding, not shrinking sales for major products. A popular movie, rock concert tour, or world sports event played to hundreds of thousands not long ago. Now it's tens of millions; that includes fans who can't fit into huge new stadiums that dot the landscape and thus must be content with satellite TV broadcasts or seeing it later on video cassette. What's next for lottery tickets, which have been made uniform for whole regions and countries? An international lottery selling a billion tickets a week?

Today's hit product—a certain typewriter, car, boat motor, film, burger, beer, or book (including those books that predict the end of mass production)—sells in the millions, while in the 1970s it was hundreds of thousands and in the 1960s, tens of thousands. (Erich Segal's *Love Story*, the best-selling U.S. novel in 1970, sold 400,000 copies; in 1988, Tom Clancy's *Cardinal of the Kremlin* sold 1.3 million. [2]

Today, Kelloggs sells Cornflakes and Sugar Pops in Japan, Domino's has pizza franchises from London to Tokyo, the Soviet Union is awash in Pepsi, Apple Macintoshes and London Fog macintoshes are everywhere, business people of many nationalities pay restaurant bills with American Express cards, and every set of parents with discretionary income the world over buys its kids Legos from Denmark.

Electrolux of Sweden, bent on becoming the world's foremost large appliance maker, now owns numerous old U.S. and European brand names. Part of its global strategy is to collapse its vast number of varieties of refrigerator, clothes washer, dishwasher, and range (cooker) to just a few *world* models or modular components, each made in enormous quantities.

Every time a firm offers a new product or service, its fervent hope is that it makes a splash. If it does, there is the chance of passing into the magic kingdom of mass production, in which costs fall and performance becomes reliable to the point where customers seek its products instead of the other way around.

One ardent advocate of this business outlook is Londoner Alan Sugar, who grew Amstrad into an electronics giant (mainly audio and microcomputer products). Sugar's marketing philosophy is the title of this subsection, "pile 'em high and sell 'em cheap." Amstrad aims at established technologies, then provides products at prices low enough to turn specialty markets into mass markets. Analysts have begun to call this the "Amstrad effect."[3] It seems odd to think of this strategy as noteworthy. Shouldn't it be commonplace?

Flexible Mass Production

I don't mean that nothing has changed, that it's mass production as usual. Product lives are shortening even as sales volumes are rising. Taken together, these trends call for *flexible mass production,* which is not a contradictory term: No sooner do we get the hot new product going than we must plan its successor.

Where does the consumer's demand for variety fit in? Sometimes not at all: A Gucci is a Gucci the world over—no customizing for different markets. (Yes, even pricey Gucci handbags are mass-made and sold—between fashion seasons. People tend to buy what they see others buying, even in luxury goods, which makes it all the more baffling to hear "futurologists" predict the end of volume production.)

Sometimes variety, from market to market and over time, is trivial— just change the cover or the package. The book industry has found that consumers take more notice of a popular novel if it is displayed in the bookstore window in five different colored covers. Seleco, the Italian TV manufacturer, makes two hundred different models, but mostly the models take the same parts until a late stage of assembly. A Mars Bar in Europe is called a Milky Way in North America; only the wrapper differs. Indeed, most product development activity at Mars is designing new wrappers and displays.

In other words, the customizing comes at the end of the process, but the basic item is mass-produced as always. That, in fact, is the essence of it—of the consumer's growing preference for custom products: add-ons, plug-ins, color choices. Putting it differently, it's mass production of components through many links in the chain of customers, only switching over to high variety for the final customer.

It is often true that to maintain or grow sales volumes for existing products, ever more end-process choices have to be offered. 3M sells Post-its in many colors and sizes. But "everybody" uses Post-its, which means large-volume production *in each size and color.*

The profusion of color choices in home products such as appliances and vitreous china (sinks, toilets, etc.) drove the manufacturers nuts for a while. But industry adapts. In some cases the manufacturer now puts the color on late in the process instead of early. Bar-soap makers mix basic white soap, pelletize it, and then later insert fragrances and color for final mixing, forming, and packaging. In certain other industries companies have devised quick-color-change devices; for example, Gatling-like paint-gun equipment, with each sprayer hooked to a different color paint vat and with solvent recirculating until use. Growing color choices notwithstanding, it may still be mass production.

Craftsmanship and art are the real custom products, and they are in high demand and going higher. But most Yuppie-like buying—the endless quest for something different—really amounts to this: being "first on the block" with the new item, whose popularity will soon explode—or already did in another part of the world.

Who cares whether it is or isn't mass production and mass marketing? I do. I'm a consumer. I want to enjoy the fruits of mass production, which include holding the price down and paving the way for uniform, predictable quality. It would be nice if I could at the same time get features, serviceability, quick response, flexibility, and the other dimensions of quality. All of that couldn't be done using best business practices of earlier decades. In the 1980s, however, we learned how to improve across the board. Time to alter our limited views.

BAD RAP FOR MASS PRODUCTION

No doubt about it, mass production has a bad reputation. The performance of Big Industry in the United States, which has been the world's largest mass market (the *only* mass market), has been miserable. Costs rose out of sight, quality and service sank, and the predictable result came to pass: Plants were shut down and hundreds of thousands were out of a job.

It's not supposed to work that way, but it did. Part of the reason was plain neglect: little equipment maintenance, no process control, undemanding customers, costs merely passed on, weakened apprenticeship programs, and so on. Another part of it is quite different: a widespread misunderstanding of the economy-of-scale concept.

The economy-of-scale "law" is this: Bigger school, bigger store, bigger restaurant, bigger factory, bigger machine yields lower costs per unit. As often as not, the law doesn't hold up. The big school is unmanageable, the big restaurant can't attract enough business to make its break-even point, the big factory is a logistics nightmare, and the big machine is a cumbersome, temperamental, inflexible white elephant.

On paper, size pays; otherwise no firm would invest in a bigger plant or machine. Why, so often, do the economies fail to materialize? I'd like to focus on two reasons that usually escape analysis: Capacity-demand mismatches and capacity-mix mismatches.

The Dreaded Triangle

Here is a history lesson that companies never seem to learn: A firm has a smash product. Sales are on a fast incline; the company is hiring; overtime, extra shifts and weekend work are becoming normal; and delivery lead times are stretching out. Looming on the horizon are lost sales—a definite no-no. The company does what seems safe and sane: Orders an addition onto the building or a new high-volume machine. About the time the new capacity comes on stream, demand collapses.

Figure 12–1 shows the series of events graphically.[4] Note the dashed line labeled "apparent demand." That represents acutal orders but *not acutal demand.*

Customers are like poker players. They raise the stakes for no apparent reason and drop out unexpectedly. In business, when demand

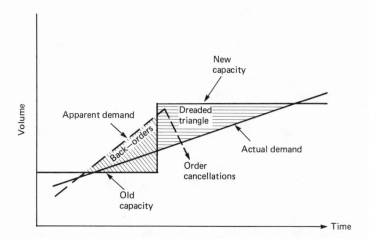

Figure 12–1. "Dreaded Triangle"

begins to push against capacity, customers will hedge-buy, double and triple order, and otherwise inflate demand. Thus, apparent demand is much in excess of real customer needs. Yet sharply rising apparent demand is the basis for adding more capacity.

The truth is the solid line labeled "actual demand." With installation of the new capacity, backlogs and long lead times melt. So does demand: Doubled-up orders are canceled, delivery dates are set back, and customers who built stock in anticipation of shortages live off their hedge stocks.

I am describing the way it happens in manufacturing. Similar things befall service-on-demand businesses, except the false signals triggering expansion are different (services aren't double-ordered or stockpiled). Human customers are sensitive to any change in service, such as a new location, a less homey or friendly delivery, or sudden availability of a competing service.

Thus, there can be a collection of causes of the optimistic projection that leads to the dreaded triangle in a hospital (new hospital beds with no patients to fill them), a bank (a new branch but few new accounts), or a restaurant (lots more tables but mostly roped off and dark).

Clairvoyance is not the recommended cure, because bad projection of demand is only a small part of the problem. Misuse of capacity and big-gulp acquisition of it are the greater problems.

Capacity in Big Gulps—or Small Bites

Sometimes there is no choice: The technology needed comes only in the large "economy" size. More often, capacity can be acquired either that way or in small bites.

Figure 12–2 shows three bad things—zones numbered 1, 2, and 3—that can happen when the large, economy size is chosen. We see sharply rising demand. The company is reluctant to invest in more capacity. Finally, the worsening backorder condition is corrected by adding a new machine. It's a big one. Has enough capacity to meet projected growth for the next three years.

What happens if the forecast is right on the mark? As Figure 12–2 shows, for three years the equipment is underused, probably not paying its way—zone 1. Then, in the fourth year, the company is in the hole again—in the backorder mode. The machine is run day and night without maintenance, which erodes quality and delivery performance and shortens the machine's life—zone 2.

Forecasts are rarely right. Demand may well taper off. If it does (see the line labeled "actual demand (a)") the machine never pays off; it's the dreaded triangle again—zone 3. If demand surges ("actual demand (b)"), that machine and maybe more like it are needed.

Figure 12–2. Alternatives in Acquiring Capacity

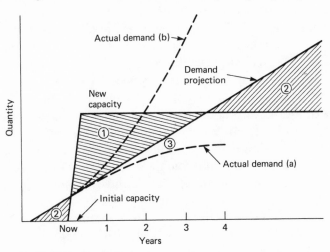

① Underuse
② Overuse: Running equipment day and night without maintenance,
       thereby ruining its performance and shortening its life
③ Dreaded triangle

A different company policy could greatly improve management of both capacity and demand: Add capacity in the form of small machines instead of big ones. It works something like this: Install a machine with enough capacity for just one year's projected demand; order another like it for delivery a year later. Watch sales for a few months. If demand stays the course, take delivery of the second machine on schedule; if it falls off, cancel or postpone delivery; and if it rises, speed up delivery and place an order for still another machine.

Companies rarely do it this way, because all they analyze are the costs of the machine itself and the labor to run it—and do so based on a forecast. The attitude about the forecast is, It isn't accurate, but it's the best we have, so it must be the basis of our plan.

Bad thinking. The rational plan is to choose capacity that will work out reasonably well even when forecasts are way off. Small machine policies fit the need—and often are the best choice even if the forecast is right. Trouble is, the large machine usually leaks capacity—and performance, too.

Leakages

The big machine is so costly it cannot be allowed to sit idle. Cut the price, mount a promotional campaign, design and market more product variations, bring work back from subcontractors—do whatever is necessary to keep the supermachine running!

What happens is the machine spends much of its life in a get-ready mode—changing from one product model to another, and another, and another. The machine is like a spoiled child: When it needs a change, everybody jumps—operators, schedulers, stock pickers, material handlers, accountants (open a new account), inspectors (check first output), sales (why aren't you running *my* customer's job?), and others. During adjustment, the machine produces scrap, rework, delay, and great needs for support. After it is adjusted and running right, it requires little of anybody's attention—until the next change.

Is it any different with smaller machines? It surely is. Consider four small machines instead of one big one—same capacity either way. Each small one is assigned just one-fourth of the total product variations, so each needs to be in a state of change only one-fourth as often as for the big machine. All the leakages just mentioned are reduced by the same amount.

The policy also relaxes some restrictions. It allows options such as locating one of the four in a dedicated production line (no changeover

---

Big Company, Smaller Machines

GM's Inland Division in Livonia, Michigan, had a problem in fabrics: Its single, costly cutting machine churned out storerooms full of cut fabric—but not the right kinds for current orders. In 1987, lack of the right items caused missed schedules 479 times, and $3.5 million in stock was pitched.

The solution: Five small cutting machines. They easily keep up with current orders. In 1988 there were only 85 cases of missed schedules, and just $600,000 in obsolete stock.[5]

---

leakages) making just one star product. Like a four-engine airplane with one engine down, four machines can avert a crash when one is in repair. A multiple-machine policy permits buying one at a time—and watching carefully to see if the next one is really going to be needed. It amounts to treating fixed capacity more like flexible human capacity: Add one when demand rises, move one to another area when demand shifts, take one out of service when demand falls.

While we are using equipment as an example, I'll mention again that these points apply to any type of capacity, such as adding a wing on a building, setting up a branch office, or opening another store.

THE MANY FACES OF MASS PRODUCTION

While it may seem that way, I am not suggesting that the economy-of-scale principle has been rendered invalid. It still applies. But only for high-demand items. And only when the large-scale unit of capacity is focused on a single high-demand item or family of similar items, such that major changes aren't going on all the time.

Few products have enough demand to qualify. What about the masses of moderate and low-demand goods and services? Here we may draw upon some of the new and powerful lessons of the 1980s. The good news is that *we now know how to get scale economies without scale.* That is, some of the blessings of mass production are available when the mass consists of a mix of good products instead of a few superproducts and supermachines and plants.

In other words, mass production has many faces. First we consider its traditional faces—involving large-scale operations, then look at some new angles.

Mainstream Mass Production

James River, now one of the world's largest paper companies and (off and on) a darling of Wall Street, began with one paper mill in 1969. How could it grow so fast and so successfully? Its early strategy was to buy money-losing and closed-down mills and focus them. No longer would the mills just run whatever sales could sell. Each mill was assigned a narrow range of specialty papers.

In papermaking, small-machine possibilities are remote. Instead, it's huge, wide, fast supermachines. But the owner does have choices on how to employ the equipment. One is to fritter away a machine's potential by trying to do many things on it.

Alternatively, do just a few things very well repeatedly, aided by volume buys of only a few raw materials from steady supplier-partners. The latter approach is what traditional mass production—and economy of scale—are all about. Too many companies, especially in the capital-intensive process industry, strayed from that formula.

One that has been trying to use the formula "to the max" is RJR Nabisco, which invested nearly $2 billion in a highly automated Tobaccoville, North Carolina, plant dedicated to cigarettes. Next on the list: a $1 billion plant with a single inflexible production line that just makes Premium Crackers. Nabisco projected that eliminating product-to-product changeovers would give it a 15 percent cost advantage over other makers.[6]

Would Nabisco's competitors be wise in building the same kind of plant? Perhaps not. Nabisco may be the only company in its industry with enough "market presence" to be able to afford to get its economies in this way—with a massive, automated, single-product plant.

Market presence is the key. By dint of great design or marketing clout, some products reach the heights; they become household words to consumers throughout the sales region or world market.

A relatively small number of goods and services worldwide—ten thousand perhaps—fit the description. Those "superproducts" may safely adopt an aggressive mass production strategy whose goal is to get a long-term lock on a piece of the market: Improve product reliability and cut costs enough to ward off new competitors and to keep a step ahead of present ones.

Sometimes the superproduct exists, but the company fails to take advantage of it. I am thinking of a certain candy manufacturer, whose products are well known—call it CandyCo. Its production technology has long been a unique asset, but today a few world competitors are investing in new technologies that are closing the gap. Presently, none of CandyCo's products "own" a dedicated production line, but a few come close: Some of their production lines (making and packaging candy) run only two products all year long, typically switching back and forth about every two weeks. It's been that way for years.

I'm dumbfounded by that practice, and I have said as much to company officials. They are *so* close to real mass production—and the utter simplicity of it from an overhead support perspective. CandyCo had enough plants and production lines that it could shift products around so as to have a few truly dedicated lines—no changeovers at all—for its star products. Furthermore, it has a few attractive options for big sales growth in parts of the world where their type of candy is not familiar; sales growth makes it much easier to dedicate capacity.

Part of the problem in the process industry (liquids, gases, sheets, powders, flakes, pellets—crackers and candy, too) is plant and equipment design. The trend has been toward bigger and fewer pieces of equipment. At the same time, numbers of products and varieties keep increasing, which means more varieties competing for a turn on fewer pieces of equipment. Does that makes sense? It doesn't.

Colgate-Palmolive Company designed a new liquid detergent plant in Ohio that goes counter to the trend. Production lines are largely product focused. Each line even has its own blow-molding equipment for making the plastic bottle at the point of use.

The plant has no warehouses. Finished cases are usually drop-shipped to a customer; otherwise they go right to a distribution center. The idea is to run each line at the product's sales rate. According to one spokesman, "If we don't sell, the line shuts down." Company planners fully expected this new departure in plant design and operation to result in a "breakthrough in cost."

PPG Industries, which does big business in glassmaking for the auto industry, isn't letting supermachine inflexibility stand in its way. PPG has constructed a new mini glass plant with half-scale float glass equipment. It can change types of glass and glass coatings much faster and easier than traditional monster equipment can. A second mini-plant is under construction.[7]

Other industries could profit from their own versions of PPG's half-scale plant; for example, film, soap, fabric, baking, perhaps paper—

and candy. The benefit might be the same as at PPG: a facility that's easier to change. More often the aimed-for benefit would be *no* change; in other words, a half-scale plant or production line dedicated to just one product variety. (The half-scale candy line is another option worth serious consideration for CandyCo.)

(Oh, here is the rest of the story on Nabisco Premium Crackers. The $1 billion plant did not get built. That and plans to spend nearly $1.8 billion more for other new cracker and cookies plants are on hold.[8] A leveraged buyout, by Kohlberg Kravis Rogers, loaded RJR Nabisco with so much debt that significant new investments in plant and equipment are not likely. Nabisco, which hasn't built a new baking plant in over twenty years, won't be building a new one soon.)

Mass Production for Turbulent Demand

It may be rational to set up several dedicated lines for a staple like liquid detergent or a dedicated mini-plant for auto glass, but what about high-tech or high-fashion goods? With such products any capacity strategy seems risky; it's sink or swim.

Or is it? IBM has come up with a keep-afloat approach. Their strategy offers mass production benefits when a product is a hit, and quick conversion to another in case of a miss. IBM has been reequipping factories—Austin and Charlotte were among the first—along the lines of this strategy. The new assembly lines feature small, low-cost, glorified pick-and-place robots (IBM's own) that can assemble about anything within a "work envelope" not much larger than a typewriter.

Robots once were associated with low-volume, high-mix operations. Today's robots are faster, especially the smaller ones used in "bench-level" assembly. They are fast enough, in fact, to be used for high-volume, single-product production—the IBM approach. But why try to force robots into a mass production mode? Why doesn't IBM go to "hard automation"—nonprogrammable devices—instead? The answer is that the robots' programmability becomes a "life jacket" when it's time to drop a slow seller and convert to a winner.

That can be sudden. Say that PS/2 (an IBM personal computer) is up and running in several plants, but poor sales lead to halting production. Meanwhile, PS/3 (a fictitious model) is flying high and needs more capacity. Robots are reprogrammed and assembly lines are stocked with new components to make PS/3. The changes would not be easy—rescues never are—but the strategy fits the turbulent sales environment of computer products.

This is another face of mass production, one that seems well suited to just a few companies, such as IBM. Why just a few? Because not many firms have enough volume for single-model robotic assembly lines; thus, the more common use of assembly robots is for mixed-model assembly—where the separate models are not superproducts but the total for all models seems to justify the cost of the automation.

Note: I am not endorsing the design of any of the plants mentioned. Designing a complex facility always involves compromises among the company's factions. Thus, an outsider can usually find plenty of flaws. I am mentioning these specific firms and plants because they illustrate, in general, different ways of realizing the potential of mass production— for the company blessed with superproducts.

MINI-MASS PRODUCTION

What about all the rest, which includes hundreds of thousands of moderate-selling products? If the owning companies will let them, those products have a chance to be stellar performers—via *mini-mass production.*

The "mini-mass" formula is one of quick-change human and machine flexibility, process control, JIT speed (not process speed) and coordination, and, above all, small focused units of capacity. Insurance companies achieve it when they organize people from different functions into a cross-trained team to serve a narrow group of insurance agents. They are likely to call it personalized service, and it is. It is also mini-mass, assembly-line-like production: large volumes of work efficiently processed, rather than spending days (or weeks) in in-baskets and inspection and error-correction loops. The same goes for loan-granting businesses when they bring narrowly trained experts together as a team to give same-day service on loan applications; here the focus is on a type of product (loans) rather than a group of customers.

Manufacturers achieve mini-mass when they begin buying or designing their own small machines that can be fitted into focused cells or attached to focused production lines. The machine, cell, or line is focused on a narrow family of items so that changes from one to the next are quick and easy. Or it makes just one part and never is in a state of change—until the part is retired or redesigned; at that time the machine is thrown out, or, better, retrofitted in the toolroom for dedicated production of another part.

If it doesn't drive costs down, it's not mini-mass production. Operations have to be efficient for present products and also in converting to new, redesigned, or embellished ones. Thus, one more feature of mini-mass production is *mobility:* buildings with utility outlets everywhere, machines on casters, and all resources—offices, people, desks, service counters, and walls moveable—able to regroup for quick, high-yield ramp-up every time designers, or customers, change the product.

ECONOMY OF MULTIPLES

An underlying concept that makes mini-mass production work is *economy of multiples.* Simply put, it means gaining economies by organizing multiple units of capacity, each focused on something different. The economies are generated in several ways, summarized in Table 12–1.

Number 1 in Table 12–1 is a topic addressed earlier: acquiring small units of capacity as sales grow (and divesting as sales shrink), which keeps capacity usage high. Ironically, people's first reaction to

Table 12–1. *Economy of Multiples—Concepts and Benefits*

Concept	Benefit
1. Capacity acquired, assigned, retired one small unit at a time, as needed	Amount of capacity stays close to amount of demand; high capacity utilization
2. Common units of capacity* dispersed to form cells and flow lines	Little process-to-process delay, storage, and handling; excellent coordination and synchronization
3. Dedicated capacity, operating at rate of sales	Small backlogs or finished goods inventories
4. Multiple units of capacity, offering backup protection against failure	High-schedule attainment and on-time delivery performance
5. Small units of capacity, easy to set up—or *no* setup	Toward one-item lots and instant response to model-mix changes
6. Small, dedicated units of capacity, offering more dependability (fewer breakdowns and failures)	Reduced need for buffers
7. Smaller units of capacity, simplifying operations and maintenance	Reduced need for supervisors and staff experts; paves way for self-managed teams

* Unit of capacity often is a machine; can be an office, cell, production line, building, crew, or team

---

"To the rear . . . march"

W e are a company that is well down the road to world-class manufacturing but marching in the wrong direction (replacing multiple small machines with gigantic machines, automating efficient and flexible manual operations, etc.). Makes our management look schizo for sending me here.

—Written remark on evaluation form for Richard Schonberger seminar, Phoenix, 5/11/89

---

multiple machines is that machine utilization will suffer. It probably would if the multiples were bought all at once instead of one at a time.

Numbers 2 and 3 concern splitting up machine groups or other types of capacity so as to form dedicated cells. Benefits include wiping out delay and most storage and handling, and greatly improving connection and synchronization within the sub-chain of customers and with the following customer. The dedicated capacity unit operates at the customer's rate of use, which eliminates most backlogs and inventories.

The fourth concept is avoidance of "putting all your eggs in one basket." In other words, if your single superline or supermachine is down for repairs, you are *really* down. If one of multiple copies is down, just operate the others more hours and never miss a sale.

The last three, 5, 6, and 7, refer to operating benefits that are likely with smaller units of capacity: They tend to be easier to set up, fail less often, and are simpler to run and maintain. Those advantages permit smaller runs, more frequent changes, less buffering, and less supervision and expert help: Operators may largely manage their own processes.

LOW VOLUMES, HIGH EFFICIENCY

We've found our way to economies for both superproducts and modest-selling items. The sure way is through reorganization and focus. If there are obstacles in the way of focus, then we must (temporarily) rely more on other improvement techniques. These include guidelines for quick setup and overall readiness, which can drive out order-to-order and customer-to-customer changeover delays. There are few machines or processes for which setup times cannot be cut at least fivefold. (Exceptions include already-improved processes that have become known for their responsiveness. I am thinking especially of crack emergency teams and stage crews in top-notch theaters.)

Where applicable, kanban may link a quick-change process with a customer at the next process some distance away. The result is a production design in which work may flow in fits and starts with a good deal of process-to-process handling; but at least it flows, and at least the processes connect—something like the way it is in mass production.

What about very low-volume operations: custom products, design-to-order work, prototypes, models, and, in general, "specialty work." Is it doomed to cost a bundle?

The only clear answer is that we know how to perform some kinds of specialty work for much less. Some predict (or hope) that flexible automation can actually produce economies akin to mass production—what Stanley Davis wants to call "mass customizing."[9] We shall get to the root of that point of view, but first let's revisit the low-tech, low-cost options.

Frugal Flexibility

Where volumes are lowest and variety is highest, performance and cost are poorest. At the same time opportunities for improvement are greatest. The means of improvement are a selection of techniques that provide low-cost flexibility, as follows:

Organization. First on the "frugal flexibility" list are cells and cross-trained teams. Examples:

- Medical emergency teams, SWAT (Special Weapons and Tactics) teams, and service teams sent out (say, by Caterpillar, Boeing, or Electronic Data Systems) to deal with a major equipment or software failure
- Product development teams in a "skunk works" and well-organized software development teams
- Machine cells in specialty manufacturing; for example, in tool-and-die making—each cell/team focused on a small family of dies (this assumes a large operation involving many machines; small

shops naturally behave like cells and do not suffer severe problems of bad coordination and flow)

Operations. Techniques for greatly improving on-going operations include cross-training, process control, employee involvement, quick setup/changeover, and supplier partnership. What about kanban? At first glance, it seems not usable in specialty work, because kanban is for items that are frequently used. Actually, that means looking harder for items for which kanban fits; there are plenty of places to look—in light fabrication and assembly, in purchasing supplies and hardware, and even in project work:

- Many companies producing specialty devices (often electrical and electronic) have the possibility of converting *most* of their operations to kanban. In this type of work the product structure is V-shaped: Hundreds of purchased items are converted through several processes into a few thousand varieties of subassemblies, which finally become hundreds of thousands or millions of combinations of specially ordered end products. At early stages of fabrication and subassembly the number of items is small enough to be kept on the floor in small quantities (often one piece) in kanban spaces; work-in-process stockrooms are dissolved.

    One of the earliest (and best publicized) Western examples of full conversion to this kanban method is Hewlett-Packard's Fort Collins, Colorado, facility producing computer workstations in "six million" variations.[10] More recently, Westinghouse converted to the same kanban method in its automation controls business in Pittsburgh and switchgear plant in St. Louis.

- Daily kanban-driven deliveries are attractive when a single supplier is awarded a contract for a commodity group, such as all office supplies or all hardware (screws, bolts, washers, etc.): Supplier comes every day or once a week to fill shelves or bins, and invoices once a month.

- In project and design-to-order work, kanban can cover only a portion of items. For example, a wood shop may buy 90 percent of its items only after an order is booked. The other 10 percent, consisting of common items such as standard framing materials (e.g., eight-foot 2 × 4's), may be stocked and replenished via a kanban system with lumber suppliers.

    At Westinghouse's medium-voltage switchgear plant in Greenwood, South Carolina, which is strictly engineer-to-order, about

20 percent of its eight thousand parts, accounting for 80 percent of volume, are on kanban.[11] The rest remain on work orders.

Housekeeping. It has been my observation that one of the worst problems in specialty work is disorganization: half-completed jobs strewn about, nothing put away, no clearly designated places for anything, no priority control, no preventive maintenance—a general mess. This is especially common in research and development and prototype labs. The solution is, if not kanban, then kanbanlike discipline: exact planned placement of everything, small work queues, no work started without all resources available or assured, priorities set based on need by the customer.

This type of discipline—everything just so—is also at the heart of quick setup, briefly discussed next.

Quick-Change Flexibility

A few of the more general guidelines for quick setup, changeover, and readiness were presented in Chapter 5. They apply widely: to machines, stage and cleanup crews, caterers, freight loading, banquet halls, fire halls, trauma centers, emergency teams, and all manner of service-on-demand businesses. They apply to high-volume super-products and supermachines and to moderate-volume products and machines.[12] They also are vital in specialty work, which suffers from lack of repetition and volume and *needs help.* Consultant Bill Wheeler even has a good example of quick setup in a surgical operating room.

The first guideline (from Chapter 5), the best setup is no setup, is partly a foil for all the others. Quick setup enthusiasm has grown in industry to the point where people have begun to associate it with flexibility itself. No-setup/no-change seems like the absence of flexibility; yet when quick response is vital, the ideal is capacity that does not require setup—in other words, dedicated capacity.

It is not hard to see spending the money for dedicated resources when volumes are high and repetitive, or for emergency services. Actually, there are many other cases where dedicated no-setup capacity is a good choice, because sometimes it doesn't cost much. I am thinking of a few machines saved from the salvage yard and set up in a corner of the building to do just one thing (e.g., make a spare part) when needed. I am also thinking of a simple, cheap, nonadjustable, small version of a big machine.

Most quick-changeover activity entails little expense; it's things like paint (for color-coding) and practice, trays, rollers, and angle iron. Some of the quick-setup technology—particularly robotics and computer-programmability—does cost a lot. Nevertheless, robots and computer controls is the direction in which we are marching, especially after the easy, cheap improvements have been taken.

Robots and computers are, of course, much more than aids to quick setup. They are central elements of a whole category of capacity: flexible automation. Before investigating that special topic, we need to look at the general problem of making capacity responsive to new business.

CAPTURING NEW BUSINESS: CAPACITY ISSUES

One of the great issues in any business is how to respond quickly and well to a sales opportunity. Actually, readiness for a sales surge calls for the same sorts of preparation as for responding to breakdowns and stoppages: Make everything work well, be able to quickly shift resources, have buffers in place, and synchronize schedules.

Buffer Bungling

Things have hardly worked perfectly and in "synch," nor have many firms been adept at shifting resources. By and large, standard practice in many companies has been to rely on buffers (extra capacity): slightly in the form of equipment, somewhat more in the form of labor, and mostly in the form of inventory (where the item is inventoriable). Buffers have often been inadequate and not well chosen for sales responsiveness:

- Narrowly skilled and no backup labor sources make quick response to sales surges (or problems) difficult. Yet, those labor restrictions are common.
- All too often, companies are stingy on machine capacity. In factories, equipment bottlenecks abound, and machines are often run day and night with little time for maintenance, such that a sales surge means factory gridlock.
- The same firms tend to get into a sustained overtime mode, which allows no labor buffer to meet a sales spurt.
- The fast, complex, hard-to-adjust, hard-to-relocate monumental machines generally preferred by industry are ill-suited to quick, low-cost, high-quality response. Long distances from one process

to the next (unfocused arrangements of resources) worsen the problem.

- In companies providing a service or product to order, new business just goes to the tail end of their order backlogs or waiting lines. When queues get too long, they work overtime or turn away business. Where possible, they hold inventory in less-finished forms in order to cut the time to fill orders. Both overtime and inventories are costly.
- Companies making goods for stock produce too far in advance of sale to be in tune with current demand. Hence, they tend to be out of the popular models and to have plenty of the unpopular ones. Rigidities in administration and production dictate these practices.
- Most firms do an appalling job of synchronizing schedules from one stage to the next in the chain of customers. At any given time, it is likely that most of the earlier stages will be working on items that don't match up and don't relate well to end-product demand. One fabrication center is making parts for widgets, another for doodads, still another for thingamajigs. Final assembly is working on gizmos right now. Shipping is in a panic because a customer wants 500 whatchamacallits, and only 127 are in stock.

Winning Combination

Armed with world-class concepts, can today's firms do any better? Absolutely.

1. Many companies are now on a course of continual reduction of errors, defects, disarray, nonstandard procedures, breakdowns, and other failures. Each improvement adds a bit more capacity (plugs a capacity leak). More important, it makes for *reliable* capacity. If capacity to serve is only a sometime thing, new business looks elsewhere.
2. Whether in goods or services, cross-training provides labor mobility: Go to where the work is piling up. Continual skill-building goes along with cross-training; in effect, the two together add labor capacity and flexibility without adding bodies. Building a cadre of trained temporary employees, some on call, provides still more of a labor buffer.
3. To provide time for continual training, labor must be underscheduled. Furthermore, a rapid rate of improvement requires

all employees to be involved, which is only possible when labor is underscheduled. As a bonus, that extra capacity can easily be shifted out of improvement projects and into production any time there is a spike in demand.

4. As the functions get connected, myriad ways to synchronize become obvious, so that capacity is not wasted by having operations in one area way ahead of those in another. At an aircraft manufacturer, two similar shops feeding final assembly were way out of synch: One shop was running fifteen planes ahead of schedule, the other two planes behind. The foreman of the first shop wanted more racks to store the overproduction, but instead bought someone's suggestion that they quit producing until a rack is returned from final assembly (which they didn't realize is the kanban technique). That forced the first shop to lend people to the second—a commonsense answer that had been resisted.

5. Companies are seeing the benefit of planning excess equipment capacity (in order to stay out of the panic mode) and, where possible, multiple small machines. A multiple-machine policy permits organization of cells, which sharply alters the *way* a machine-intensive business responds: A cell operates two hours a day if there are two hours' demand per day for its product; it goes fourteen hours a day if sales skyrocket to that level. The company adds another cell of the same kind if demand consistently pushes capacity.

6. By dedicating a set of resources to a product or product family, changeover time is eliminated or minimized. Where dedicated resources are not practical, continual efforts to reduce changeover times are necessary. These actions permit quicker response as demand mix flip-flops. They also plug capacity leaks.

7. A cell or flow line automatically synchronizes schedules for all its workstations. If one station is working on say license applications, all are. Next, synchronize from cell to cell, via kanban—at least for star products. At AnaMag, which produces rectangular, coated copper wire, the plant manager, after attending a seminar, decided to locate a rewinding operation right next to coating. That forced rewind to change from one to three shifts in order to be in synch with coating.

Synchronization will work well if there is realistic protection against problems that have a history of recurring. The issue of proper protection, or buffer stock, requires fuller discussion.

Frugal Inventory Buffers

For the goods producer, all the above reduce but don't eliminate the need for inventory buffers. Eliyahu Goldratt and Robert Fox have offered what they call the "theory of constraints," which tells managers that while inventory is generally evil, it has its place. Its place, they note, is to allow production to flow and sales ups and downs to be coped with, even when there is a capacity bottleneck.[13]

That point of view might have seemed obvious a decade ago. But all too many companies, caught up in a just-in-time crusade, have wrongly thought that purging inventories is what it's all about.

Actually, slashing delay—becoming quick to respond to the customer—is what it's about. Inventory reduction (not elimination) is a sure, though often not immediate, by-product.

If a theory of constraints—or, more positively, a *theory of response*—is to be complete, it must heavily favor points 1 through 7 above: making things work, quickly shifting labor and equipment resources, providing labor and equipment buffers, and synchronizing schedules. When it comes to inventory buffers, it is technique, more than theory, that is missing in too many companies—including many of the leaders. The techniques I am thinking of effectively buffer with less inventory and much lower administrative costs.

Kanban. One technique is to keep the buffer inventories in kanban containers or kanban squares. In the Chapter 5 discussion of kanban in the office, a point not made is that the three invoices in the green, yellow, and red trays are *buffer stock.*

They buffer against small cycle-time variations, for example, hard-to-read entries on some of the invoices, broken pencil, trip to refill a coffee cup. Individually, they are trivial, but these kinds of small delays occur many times per day every day. To make sure no one runs out of work because of a small delay, each station is buffered by small amounts of *in-line* extra stock (invoices). Kanban assures that in-line buffers never get larger than the planned maximum, three invoices in the example. More than that isn't a buffer anymore; it's plain waste and delay.

Since invoices are usually processed on a first-come, first-served (more or less) basis, the buffer stock must be in the flow. Not so for jobs in factories.

Off-line buffer stock. Factories, too, need buffering. Since many factory goods need not be tied to a certain customer, a special, highly attractive option is available: off-line buffer stock. By off-line, I mean out of the flow, untouched, in a low-cost, out-of-the-way location. An off-line buffer is not for small cycle-time variations, but for the occasional big break in the cycle: machine down, key people missing, power failure, late truck, and so forth.

The plant manager of an Alcoa plant in Tennessee holds the shipping tags for five hundred thousand pounds of finished aluminum foil, kept on hand as buffer stock. I'm sure he hopes he never has to release it, but it's there in case his manufacturing process or supplier of raw materials fails—and history shows undoubtedly that it will once in a while. Manufacturing is a service, and he aims to serve, even in the face of adversity. (Since foil slowly deteriorates in storage, the stock is rotated quarterly.)

The usual, wrong way to treat the five hundred thousand pounds would be to put it *in the flow*, not off line. When in the flow, stock incurs the costs of constant storage and handling: Truck it to a storeroom, put it away, move it occasionally, run into and damage some of it with a fork truck, count and value it, pick it, move it, and load it into an outbound truck; there's a computer transaction for every event. It also has to be in an accessible, high-cost stock area complete with

---

"Look to the hoop before passing off"

The above may or may not be good advice in basketball (looks like something a "run-and-gun" coach would say). It's great advice in managing inventories—where its meaning is:

1. Send goods directly to the point of use
2. Send only the overflow (excess after the use area's kanban zones are full) to storage.

How many firms do it this way? Not many. Instead they put it away (record it), find it, pull it out (record it), and finally deliver it (record it)—even what is to be used the same day. Sometimes the recording system (computer software) is designed to *require* all the extra steps.

Let's restate the advice:

If you can score (add value), don't store.

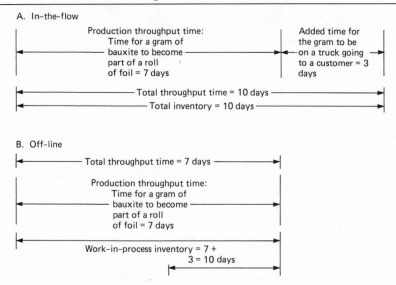

Figure 12–3. Throughput Time for In-the-Flow and Off-Line Buffer Stock

storage and material-handling apparatus. Worst of all, it represents delay—a chunk of time inserted between maker and user.

Say, for example, that five hundred thousand pounds is three days' worth of production. Figure 12–3A shows that, when in the flow, the buffer stock tacks three extra days of delay onto the throughput time: Without the buffer, throughput time is seven days—production time only; with the buffer, it is ten days. *That's three extra days for every order all year long!*

Figure 12–3B shows that keeping the stock off-line adds no throughput time, but still protects against interruption. This way, foil comes out of production and goes right in the truck and on its way to the customer. The customer is closely linked to production, not set off from it by three days.

There is still another advantage of off-line buffer stock. It can (and usually should) be purified: Thoroughly inspect it to make sure all of it is of perfect quality. (In the other approach—buffer stock in-the-flow and handled first-in, first-out—you may never be sure. If you aren't sure of perfect quality, some protection!)

Buffer placement. Sometimes work passes through dozens of processes in going from raw materials to finished goods. Each process could be buffered off-line, in-the-flow, both, or neither. How should the choice be made? By experience and judgment, plus trial and error.

Figure 12–4 is a sketch showing buffer stock choices for each of ten processes in a single product's flow through a hypothetical plant. Kanban squares (lowercase k) authorize production and delivery from one assembly bench to the next; kanban containers (uppercase K) do the same across space (between castings, saw, milling, grinding, finishing, subassembly, and assembly). Two of those spots—between castings and saw and between milling and grinding—are protected both by in-line (see "K"s) and off-line buffers (see 1 and 2). Off-line guards against the *likely* failure of the feeder process (arriving truck and milling machine). No buffer stock, either in-the-flow or off-line, is needed between test and pack, because pack is reliable and keeps the pace.

We have considered an array of simple, commonsense techniques

Figure 12–4. Buffer Stock Choices

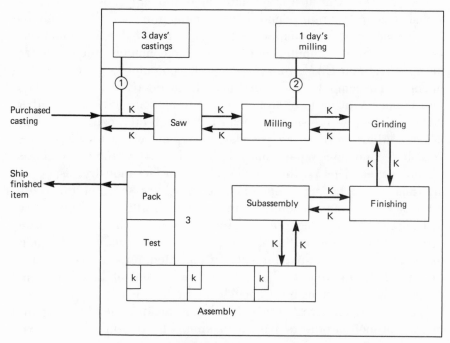

Key: K = One or more kanban containers

⬚k = One kanban square

1 = Off-line stock, because arriving truck is sometimes late (use off-line stock) or early (divert to off-line stockroom); predicted worst case is three days' delay

2 = Off-line stock, because milling machine breaks down on an average of every three weeks; predicted worst case is one day for repair

3 = Zero buffer stock, because packer is reliable and keeps pace with tester

for being responsive to new business. There is a place, as well, for not-so-simple responses to new business, especially the low-volume, high-mix kind.

FLEXIBLE AUTOMATION

In the old days, automation was associated with high volumes. Now a wide and growing assortment of flexible equipment and devices is available for automating specialty work as well. Robots, computers, and programming software are flexible automation's core technologies.

As we have seen, today's robots include fast ones that can be used for volume production as well as the "ordinary" kind that can be programmed to change tools and load work into specialty equipment. Today's programmable controllers (computer processors) have a variety of uses as well. One use is on automated assembly lines. The rest is alphabet soup: running stand-alone computer numerically-controlled (CNC) machines, in machine cells known as flexible manufacturing systems (FMS), in computer-aided design and computer-aided manufacturing (CAD and CAM, and, in general, computer graphics), and as linchpins for computer-integrated manufacturing (CIM).

It is not my place to offer a survey of terms and meanings. Rather, it is to point out where success seems to lie in all this costly technology.

First, where are the big payoffs—today, not off in the future—for flexible technology? What comes to mind first is cutting unusual contoured shapes. This is where CNC shines. In fact industry, especially aerospace, has become dependent on CNC for some of this work, because conventional machines can't do the job with enough precision.

The aerospace and machine-tool industries are hitching up machining centers and CNC to CAD/CAM (computer-aided design/computer-aided manufacturing) with mixed results. In printed reports everything is peachy. The oral reports that I receive often tell of high costs, not keeping the equipment busy enough, and other concerns.

The one area where CAD/CAM/CNC is making clearly successful inroads is tool-and-die and mold making. The reasons, I think, are: (1) makers of "tooling" always seem to have more than enough work, (2) the work is fairly steady (not so spikey), with plenty of die and mold maintenance work to fill in, and (3) the processes and raw materials are well defined and not very diverse (mostly precision cutting of steel).

In a nutshell, the three conditions for success are: enough demand, steady demand, and well-defined, not very diverse processes. Whenever the three are present, costly flexible technology should find a home—sooner rather than later. I intend for this statement to apply to flexible technology in general, including automated information processing, not just CAD/CAM/CNC. I'm also referring to technology that adds value, not the kind that automates the waste. The presence or absence of the three criteria can, I think, explain mixed results in different industries. A few examples will illustrate:

- Automated painting and welding are debugged and paying off in autos and office furniture, because the work is quite steady and well defined. In job shops, because of unsteady and highly changeable work, painting and welding by hand persists—justifiably.
- Computer graphics hardware and software can do about anything in the realm of making patterns, menus, scale models, animation, and presentation materials. Let's consider just the latter: graphics technology for presentation materials. In corporate offices graphics terminals have become indispensable. They chunk out overheads and slides all day and sometimes at night and on weekends. The materials are for all the presenters at all the meetings going on all day in every available conference room. The three conditions for success are present: The work is plentiful and steady, and everyone uses the company's narrowly defined standard formats. (Whether all those meetings and presentations are necessary is not the issue here.)
- A technology that does *not* cut the mustard, because it just automates the waste is the *unit production system* in the apparel industry. It consists of an overhead conveyor system that delivers "Christmas-tree" carriers of cut pieces—say, just enough for one or two garments—to sewers at sewing machines. An operator feeds the system by watching a colored map of it on a computer screen, which shows status at each sewing machine: green for busy with one carrier on deck, yellow for working on the last carrier, and red for out of work.

  Last time I saw a unit production system, in a plant making sportswear, I asked the plant manager, "Are you happy with the system?" "Didn't work for two years," he replied. When I asked if it works well now, he said it does; and it permits finishing a garment in just one day instead of the usual two weeks.

  I asked again if he was satisfied. He paused, finally saying, "I'm not sure." "Why not?" I asked. He explained that his company now has debt to service. If sales are good, no problem. But it's the fashion industry. If orders fall off, the firm could have a hard time paying the bank.

In Chapter 3 we considered a better way to get garments produced in one day: Organize cells, eliminate piecework, train employees in total quality, and wipe out the bundle system.

We are looking for big-payoff opportunities for flexible automation. We should understand that the totality of good applications is small. Theodore Levitt expressed a view that *should be* obvious: "There is no conceivable way in which flexible factory automation dedicated to producing many customized lines of a specific product can achieve the scale economies of an equally modernized plant dedicated to the massive production of narrow standardized lines of that product."[14]

The comment applies to the services sector as well.

We have been looking at capacity mostly from the demand side—products and product volumes. Supply-side ("look at all the new technology!") issues beg our scrutiny as well.

EARNING THE RIGHT TO AUTOMATE

Earlier I noted that mass production has acquired a bad name. Well, the same is true of automation, as two separate studies show. Arthur Anderson & Company polls auto executives every two years, asking the question, What is the key to competitiveness? In five surveys in a row, automation got all the votes. In the next survey, in 1987, automation got only 8 percent of the votes. That was good for twelfth place. The new winner—in first place: management practices.[15]

Every year Ernst & Whinney (now Ernst & Young) does a similar poll of Midwestern manufacturers. Automation held first place for five years in a row from 1983 through 1987. In 1988, it slipped to third, behind employee training and motivation (first) and process simplification—including just-in-time (second).[16]

How could opinion about automation have fallen so low so fast, and why is it especially low in the auto industry? All signs point to *The Great Automation Initiative:* General Motors' $50 billion-plus investment in high technology in the first half of the 1980s. What did it get GM? Loss of market share and shuttered plants. In the space of a decade, GM went from being one of the world's most admired companies to an object of ridicule—for having *squandered* $50 billion. As one GM executive put it, "For that price, we could have bought the entire Japanese auto industry."

Executives in other auto companies and other industries cannot be smug about this. *They would have done the same thing!* GM did what most experts and lay people believed was right, because it had the money and the "bold" leadership.

Bold, action-oriented leadership, much admired these days, *is* a valuable asset—if the agenda for improvement is sound. Today GM's improvement agenda is excellent. High on its list are statistical process control, supplier partnership, cells, leaderless teams, pay for knowledge, simultaneous engineering, house of quality, and most of the other concepts presented in this book. The rest of us can thank GM for using its own cash to run a great research project, whose hypothesis—a popular one at the time—was that automation and high technology offers a shortcut to success. The result: no support for the hypothesis.

Why wasn't the hypothesis supported? What was wrong with the belief that automation was the answer?

The research was not designed to find out. But we can make a good guess. The *reasons* for taking the automation plunge were faulty. The reasoning—at GM and at other companies that did it on a lesser scale—went like this: Management has been nagged for decades by "the labor problem." Machines are unfit, and quality is poor to boot. Past solutions haven't worked. Now a wonderfully promising solution presents itself: Automation. Go for it!

GM and the others *had not earned the right to automate.* Now they are earning it. In the new agenda, labor is not a problem; it is the combustion chamber of the improvement engine. Equipment that was unfit is upgraded and preventively maintained, quality is controlled, and processes are fail-safed. This approach to improvement calls upon automation and high technology when they are needed and for the right reasons: to solve problems not solvable in a simpler, less costly, more direct way with existing resources. It is problem-pull automation, rather than technology-push (or money-push).

Is the automation initiative now repeating itself under a new name: computer integration? It seems so, although companies and their advisers are proceeding more cautiously. Computer integration, called CIM (computer-integrated manufacturing) in the industrial sector, basically calls for computers to talk to other computers, including those of the customer, sales, design, purchasing, scheduling, traffic, and so on. It's quick, it's paperless, it builds chains of customers—it's the future for sure.

Let's see what the pitfalls are—how to earn the right to progress to computer integration. The obvious one is that integration of processes— people and equipment—comes first. For many companies, that is a drastic step, whereas computer integration seems so easy: Just leave people in their geographically separated departments, link them up to terminals, and presto: coordination and speed.

It's a foolish quick fix—which often doesn't fix at all. The safe, sure, frugal way is to move the people into cells, which creates improvement teams and avoids or postpones the investment in information technology.

Let's look at the issue in another way. There is general agreement among adherents of CIM on how to implement it properly. First steps are to define operations in terms of the flow of materials and the flow of data and information.

Wait a minute. If there's anything we know about flows (in the sad state that most of our organizations fell into), it is that they are grossly excessive and prone to error and delay. First step must be a massive improvement effort, which excises the worst of the material-flow wastes and delays.

Data and information flows are rife with waste as well. In operations, most data generated have to do with things going wrong, discrepancies, variability, irregularity, rework, and wasteful transactions (labor, transport, storage, picking, inspecting). As operations gets its act together, data-processing requirements shrink like a snowman in the hot sun.

This reasoning applies partially to customers and suppliers. We welcome data processing that consists of orders. But in forging strong partnerships with customers and suppliers, a sporadic stream of orders is replaced by a long-term contract with regularized schedules and kanban signals or "call-offs."

As data go, so goes information, which is the outcome of data processing. In 1983, in a two-day seminar that I conducted for IBM's Computer Automation Division, I stated that the future of management information systems (MIS) in operations was bleak.

The audience was ready to turn me out the door—until I explained: The future of computers in business operations is bright indeed, but for direct process control, not for creating humanly readable reports from an MIS. The management of operations is shifting toward the source, and so is control and use of data. After-the-fact summary reports going to middle managers and staff experts are late and ineffective. In fact, in some firms the former recipients of some of the reports are gone, the result of eliminating a layer or two of middle management.

As processes are brought under control, largely by operating teams, the need for data shrinks. Of course, data will never be completely eliminated. For data relating to operating problems the ideal is to use them right away in fixing the process: data like energy. For example, plot sample measures on a control chart; if a point falls above the upper control limit, stop, form an on-the-spot team to fix the problem, and erase the control chart.

Of course, sometimes the data ought to be plotted or stored for longer-term studies of trend and cause-effect combinations. Also, the firm cannot always throw the data out, because a customer (e.g., a government agency) may require it. Time to go partners with the customer—to educate the customer if necessary, and to press for the mutual benefits of waste reduction.

In this chapter, we have explored some unconventional wisdom about capacity. The wisdom is profound and ties in neatly to that presented in earlier chapters: creating focused resources that keep costs contained and products flowing "like water," overseen by involved teams whose mission is continual process improvement in the eyes of the customer. Our final task, in Chapter 13, is to see how all this has driven up the performance standards and raised the stakes.

13

⚬⟡⚬

Elevated
Performance Standards

W
HAT DOES it take to become a world-class company? A lot.
Twelve chapters' worth of new thinking—so far. The final task
is to summarize and connect it all. We'll revisit the message of each
of the twelve chapters.

PHASES

Nothing quite like it—the earthquakes of the 1980s—has happened
in the world of work since the twenty-year scientific management period
that began about 1895. The giants of that era—Frederick Taylor, Frank
and Lillian Gilbreth, and Henry Gantt—had dozens of disciples who
wrote prodigiously for the next thirty years. William Leffingwell, for
example, applied every kernel of Tayloristic thought to office work.

It was not just theory, not just books and articles, not just academic
pondering. The ideas of the pioneers of scientific management were
quickly and massively applied, and they are in evidence everywhere
in the business world today.

Plenty of brilliant thought and theory has filled the gap between
then and now, but little of it got much beyond the ink on the page
and the scrawling on the chalkboard. In contrast, continuous improvement in the chain of customers—the theme of the modern upheaval—

is so action-oriented that writers and lecturers like myself can scarcely keep up.

We may think of creating the world class company as progressing through phases: in the 1970s, alarm; and in the 1980s, discovery, learning, and here-and-there flurries of action. Discoveries continue, and the learning never ends, since one of the key discoveries is the power of continuous learning. For the 1990s, therefore, we may predict a phase of more discoveries, learning, and *action on all fronts*.

PRINCIPLES

We're also *un*-discovering and *un*-learning. One thing to unlearn is strategic planning. Rarely have so many highly paid people done so much of anything so earnestly with such poor results. As Stanley Davis notes, with examples from empire-building entrepreneurs, good strategy comes from good actions. When done in reverse, strategy to action, the result is bureaucracy.[1]

The empire builders that Davis cites somehow had an instinct for the right moves—actions that in hindsight look like brilliant strategy. We no longer need to look for leaders with great instincts, a rare commodity. As was noted in Chapter 2, the knowledge explosion of the past decade boils down to basics. It should now be clear, after twelve chapters, that the basics are grounded in customer needs—a consistent mind-set. That consistency suggests that the basics may be reduced further—to *principles*: widely agreed-upon clear directives for action.

Over the past few years, I have made many versions of what I believe to be the emerging principles (a seventeen-item list appears in my 1986 book, *World Class Manufacturing*).[2] The items on the early lists stay there (aside from wording changes), but the list has grown to account for the aftershocks, including the latest ones in accounting and marketing. Now that all four basic business functions (design, marketing, operations, and accounting/finance) have been jolted, the principles may stabilize somewhat. My current list, nineteen items, is shown in Table 13–1.

These *principles of world-class, customer-driven performance* are grouped under eight headings. First are three general principles. Number 1, get to know the customer, is by far the most important. If a firm avidly abides by it, all the rest come to be taken care of, because

Table 13–1. *Principles of World-Class, Customer-Driven Performance*

General

1. Get to know the next and final customer
2. Get to know the competition
3. Dedicate to continual, rapid improvement in quality, cost, response time, and flexibility

Design and Organization

4. Cut the number of components or operations and number of suppliers to a few good ones
5. Cut the number of flow paths (where the work goes next)
6. Organize product- or customer-focused linkages of resources

Operations

7. Cut flow time, flow distance, inventory, and space along the chain of customers.
8. Cut setup, changeover, get-ready, and start-up time
9. Operate at the customer's rate of use (or a smoothed representation of it)

Human Resource Development

10. Develop human resources through cross-training (for mastery), continual education, job switching, and multiyear cross-career reassignments
11. Develop operator/team-owners of products, processes, and outcomes

Quality and Problem-Solving

12. Make it easier to produce or provide the product without error (total quality)
13. Record and retain quality, process, and problem data at the workplace
14. Assure that line people get first crack at problem-solving—before staff experts

Accounting and Control

15. Cut transactions and reporting; control causes not costs

Capacity

16. Maintain and improve present resources and human work before thinking about new equipment and automation
17. Automate incrementally when process variability cannot otherwise be reduced
18. Seek to have plural instead of singular workstations, machines, and cells or flow lines for each product or customer family

Marketing

19. Market and sell your firm's capability and competence

the other eighteen are specifics on how to serve the customer—all through the chain.

Even number 2, get to know the competition, can work off number 1: If you know your final customer well, you also get to know about competitors buzzing around your customer.

The third general principle sets forth the common wants and needs of all customers: continual, rapidly improving quality, cost, response time, and flexibility. (Meeting schedule/delivery commitments could be added but isn't, because it is included in quality, and in any case is a result of the other four.)

The three design and organization principles express today's commitment to *focus:* Cut the distractions in order to do something well. The reductions apply to the input side (components and suppliers) and the output side (where the work goes next)—principles 4 and 5. Focus also cuts across the organization: Get the resources into product/customer-focused groupings (cells and flow lines)—principle 6.

The three operating principles call for still more reductions, plus moderation: number 7, take out wastes and delays along the flow path; number 8, change and be ready, quick; and number 9, operate at the customer's rate, not see how fast you can go.

Human resource development is a group of two: Principle 10 blends what's good for the person with what's good for the company: development of human potential through cross-path training and job switching. Principle 11 connects the human resource to the work in a special way: operator- and team-ownership.

The three principles of quality and problem-solving start with the basic tenet of total quality: Make it easier to do things without mishap (number 12). The effort is data-driven and operator-centered: Record and retain the data at the workplace (number 13) *so that* operator-owners have first use of them (number 14).

Principle 15 states the good news about accounting and control: It cuts out transactions and reporting, and it revolves around direct control of causes, not too-late fretting about cost excesses.

The three principles of capacity, numbers 16, 17, and 18, aim at continual improvement of existing human and physical resources and careful, incremental, focused acquisition of new ones, including automation.

Finally, principle 19 links the totally improving organization with the totally demanding customer; marketing's new role is to clarify mutual advantages and promote them to the skies.

The nineteen principles overlap and interweave. It's about time.

Stand-alone strategies, functions, factions, methods, machines, operators, customers, and suppliers have been the ruin of too many companies.
The antidote is *linkages*.

CUSTOMERS-IN

The linkages are not passive—talk to the customer. They are active—
bring the customer in, form a chain, find a focus. As was pointed
out in Chapter 3, in most situations, this is the most important "big-
bang" step that can be taken on the road to customer-centered, world-
class excellence. But there are pitfalls, and there have been false
starts and frustrations.

Frustration

For an example of frustration, we might turn to McDonnell-Douglas.
Its commercial aircraft division, a money loser despite multiyear order
backlogs, has been undergoing complete reorganization. Everything
was functional; now everything and everybody, from design offices to
the production floor, is becoming focused. One critic, a former senior
engineer at Douglas, says, "They've created chaos. . . . [They] don't
care about design or the wonders of air transport. All they care about
is organization charts." The company concedes that the reorganization
has not paid off so far.[3]

Why not? Well, probably because producing big airliners is one of
the most complex tasks on earth (and McDonnell-Douglas is in the
midst of an expansion to become ten times bigger in the 1990s than
it was early in the 1980s). Getting product/customer-focused is quick,
easy, and can pay big dividends right away in a simpler environment,
say, processing insurance documents. It takes longer and must line
up with many other changes—training, equipment, scheduling, control,
rewards, and so forth—in the complex case.

Pitfall

For pitfalls, we might look closely at the fifth principle in Table
13–1: Cut the number of flow paths (where the work goes next). Taken
to the ultimate, this results in something akin to a freeway—no off-
ramp for miles, so just keep rolling. In contrast, the unfocused organiza-

tion is like city streets with intersections everywhere and travel going every which way—inefficiently.

I've seen a stunning example of a complex factory that *has* been taken to the ultimate—a freeway with *no* off-ramps, not even any in-process stockrooms. It is an ultramodern, high-tech factory that makes a wide variety of pumps. The product line was engineered following modern design-for-manufacturability guidelines, and the plant was planned with extreme thoroughness and care. It might have worked, too, had it not been for certain pieces of advanced equipment that did not perform as the manufacturer claimed they would. With equipment failures and no off-ramps—no other ways to do certain machining steps—the company faced serious delays and angry customers.

Fortunately for them, there was a fallback option. The new long, serpentine, production line was closely linked and did not begin to fill up total plant space. So, reluctantly, the planners had decided to "contaminate" the focused plant by using remaining space for producing service parts for older pump models. Some of the older equipment was retained for that purpose. Then, when the new equipment failed to perform, the old came to the rescue.

The lesson here is a version of "Don't put all your eggs in one basket." We need to connect organizational principles 4, 5, and 6 with capacity principle 18: Seek to have plural instead of singular . . . cells and flow lines for each product or customer family.

Process designers and engineers have always thought the opposite: If there are two lines or two machines, they reckoned, progress is converting to one with twice the capacity. Aside from the hidden costs of capacity leakages (discussed in Chapter 12), the "one-basket" policy leads to occasional failures to respond to a demand or meet a commitment to a customer, and that's not world-class performance.

A related pitfall is the unclear chain of customers. Albrecht and Zemke assert that "The more people the customer must encounter during the delivery of the service, the less likely it is that he or she will be satisfied with the service."[4] The same thing is true of goods production. Cutting the number of providers/suppliers (principle 4), plus getting to know the customer (principle 1) help combat the tendency.

False Start

For an example of a false start, we might consider Rolm, the telephone switchgear manufacturer. Rolm had done the right thing: It set up not one but *three* focused lines, each in competition with the other two. Quality and productivity soared, but overhead did, too, because the three lines had three separate management staffs. Overall, Rolm's costs were uncompetitively high.[5]

We can easily spot the flaw, and it's not in the organization or capacity areas. The existence of three separate high-cost overhead groups points to lack of employee involvement, overplanning, and heavy-handed accounting and controls. The missing ingredients are principles 10 through 15, embracing employee development, process control, problem-solving, and overall ownership, coupled with simplified accounting and direct control.

Competition

The Rolm example raises another issue, a ticklish one: Does internal competition work?

I recall a case where it seemed to. A company making computer memory products had set up two mirror-image cells making exactly the same product, thousands per day. Each cell had the same seventeen machines, plus operators, and the two were separated by a low partition. Each team plotted hourly performance (yield, linearity, rework, downtime, etc.) on charts near the partition. Several times per day, someone from one cell would peer over the partition and read off performance data from the other, which drove the two teams to better and better performance. Competition worked.

But then it turned poison. Good ideas for improvement weren't being shared between the teams, and each team would not let the other use its equipment in cases of machine trouble. In the end management broke up the two-team organization and partially reverted to the old functional grouping of machines and people. (They have since given cells a second chance.)

The flaw? Too much emphasis on internal competition, not enough on external. For help, we may look to principle 2, Get to know the competition—in this case the external competition. The teams on the two sides of the partition might have jointly participated in on-going competitive analysis. To close the loop, they would post their joint performance on charts in comparison against the data on external competitors' performance.

Principle 1, Get to know the customer, would help, too. The customer of the two cells was an assembly group in another part of the same building. One way to forge stronger connections would be to swap a different pair of operator and assembler every two weeks. Each operator would eventually have "stood in the customer's shoes," which has the effect of making operators customer-oriented, thus lessening over-zealous team-against-team competition.

QUALITY—FINDING YOUR WAY

As we've been seeing, it is a mistake to push one principle and overlook another. But at least there are just nineteen principles. On the other hand, there are dozens of new (or unused) techniques of total quality, problem-solving, delay reduction, and waste elimination; they were emphasized in Chapter 4 and are randomly listed in Table 13–2. Must they *all* be active?

Table 13–2. *Improvement Tool Kit*

Fail-safing	Check sheet
Quick setup	Red and yellow trouble lights
Competitive analysis	Undercapacity scheduling of labor
Cross-training	Overplanning of machine capacity
Fishbone chart	Response ratios
Kanban	Direct shipment
Quality function deployment	Maximum line-length policies
Operator-centered preventive main-tenance	Competitive benchmarking
	Lot plot
Off-line buffer stock	Visual control charts
Small machines in multiple copies	Visual recognition
Supplier certification	Robust design
Supplier reduction	Loss function
Supplier development/partnership	Backflush costing
Carrier certification	Costing by audit
Suggestion lotteries	Elimination of labor transactions
Pay for knowledge	Elimination of inventory transactions
Product development mapping	Elimination of utilization reports
Process capability index	Elimination of efficiency reports
Design-build team	Elimination of cost variance reports
Process control chart	Elimination of stockrooms
Design for operations	Elimination of work orders
Multiyear career changes	
Job rotation	
Pareto chart	
Scatter diagram	
Focused organization	
Cells	
Flow lines	

The answer is no. A lot can be done with a few well-chosen tools, especially the data analysis techniques. For example, Simpson Lumber operates a sawmill in which all employees make use of fishbone charts. Every team and every shift works on its own chart, which is posted on a wall near the team's work site, and the plant manager uses a large "multibone" chart as a focal point for his staff meetings. If the sawmill keeps the fishbone efforts going, they should be able to improve nicely for years with little use of the other problem-solving tools.

Other companies have got just as much mileage out of single-minded use of process control charts, and some design-oriented organizations seem to be banking gobs of cash savings through heavy use of quality function deployment.

I suspect it is better to become very skilled using just a few data analysis techniques than to dabble in dozens of them. On the other hand, the improving organization keeps adding to its improvement tool kit in the quest to leave no waste unseen or overlooked.

COWBOYS, KOPS, AND BLUE SUITS

The techniques and tools are weak when used solely by staff people and managers, powerful when in the kits of line employees, and as we saw in Chapter 5, more powerful still when jointly used by product/customer-focused teams of operators and support people.

In other words, people matter.

In my advisory visits, it doesn't take long to form an overall impression of a company's human performance. By how its people operate I mentally stick the company into one of four categories: cowboy company, Keystone Kops company, blue-suit company, or linked-up company. We've been describing the linked-up company—doing the right things to become world-class—throughout the book. Let's look at the others.

In the cowboy company people know what to do and just do it. Most of what it does, it does well. Usually the cowboy company has had benevolent management: treats people well, pays well, cares. Employee turnover is low, employees are experienced and work well together.

The Keystone Kops company looks like a cowboy company on the surface, but things *don't* work well. People are very busy keeping busy, correcting mistakes, taking things out of one box and putting into another, searching for things missing, rescheduling, negative selling, processing returns, making customers mad. Many, or most, companies fall into this category: the average hotel, retail store, manufacturing company, hospital, government agency—you name it.

The blue-suit company . . . well, the name tells the story. Key characteristics:

- Planning: plentiful
- Action: too little and too late
- Linkages: circuitous, indirect, mind-bogglingly complex
- Employee involvement: little or none

Big, old-line companies are blue-suit companies, although most now have a few divisions that are becoming responsive.

One industry, construction, is so fouled up as to be in a class by itself. Delay, lack of coordination, and mishaps (especially return trips from the site to get something forgotten) are normal, everyday events for the average company. Construction crews often cannot even manage to *look* busy enough to fit the Keystone Kops category.

The way up from the depths of inefficiency is clear for the construction industry: diligent recording of every negative event, plus operator-centered data analysis and problem-solving. The rigid foreman system needs to be turned on its ear, because foremen have far too much to do—with every job and every day different—to be able to bear the whole burden of coordination and control. The minds and senses of the crews are the first line of attack on the industry's deep-seated problems.

The path to world-class performance is easiest for the cowboy company. Even so, most such companies are slow to make changes. They glory in their past and present and are slow to see that the future demands a whole lot more. They need, as Tom Peters puts it, "to get outsiders in and get insiders out."[6]

Blue-suit companies often have a dominant strength; good products or good marketing, for example. They also have many talented people—whose abilities are squandered because of ruinous operating waste, system complexity, and overall separation by function. These companies have been the early birds, the first to respond to each earthquake and tremor. Their progress has been uneven, however—and too slow.

How can these "megacompanies" get on the fast track? High-level leadership would help. In most of those companies in which the senior executive group sat through training sessions on quality, the quality improvement effort is in good hands. For the most part, senior executives have a shallow understanding of all the rest. I've found that leaders—at any level—don't lead when they don't understand. Their underlings, carved up into "functions and factions," lead by default. Still, the big companies are making progress. The flood of good ideas is washing the barriers away.

And the Keystone Kops companies? They've never had high aspirations or performance. Now's their chance. The knowledge explosion is spreading like a ripple in a pond, and the lessons on how to get customer-connected are easy to learn and not so hard to apply. Some of these companies are making the right moves, and many will metamorphose into standout performers.

NEGATIVE TO POSITIVE

The organization learns its world-class lessons from a variety of external sources—from books to seminars to community college classes to plant visits. It also engages in self-learning: not trial and error, but trial and learning.

Some behavioral experts say that companies should employ a mix of positive reinforcement, negative reinforcement, and punishment; for example, some advocate ratios like 4 to 1: four positive reinforcements for every one negative or punishment. That may be okay for the average company, but not for the rapidly improving one.

The world-class company transforms negatives into positives. The mishap becomes a challenge to further improvement, another aggravation to remove, one more opportunity to celebrate a success. The cause of the mishap is exhibit A—on display for all to see (e.g., on check sheets, Paretos, fishbone charts). The cause is delved into deeply enough to show that it is not a human mistake but some weakness in the procedures, resources, suppliers, or training. A negative is when you don't have enough information about the real cause.

When an undesired outcome is called an error and treated as one, the *learning is negative:* learning to cover your trail and your tail. One of the messages of Chapter 6 is that the world-class company learns *not* to treat things as mistakes or errors. So turn your negatives to positives and march forward.

A FEW GOOD LINKAGES

In most companies, having a positive view of negative events is hard to imagine. There are *too many* negative events and far too little information about *real causes*. Ironically, in the same companies there is far too much information in total; prominent examples of it are labeled as nonobvious wastes in Chapter 7.

There appears to be a set of root causes of the excesses and wastes: complexity. The word has been used a bit in earlier chapters. It's time to look at it closely.

One way to identify complexity is by number of flow paths. The issue is vital enough to be listed separately as one of the nineteen principles: Cut the number of flow paths (where the work goes next), principle 5.

The other primary way of thinking about (or measuring) complexity is by number of information linkages. Since chains and linkages are this book's theme, it's time to set the record straight: The path to world-class excellence is built on *a small number of strong linkages*; the converse, a large number of weak linkages, equals complexity and poor performance.

Bulling its way into the center of the matter are computers and data communications, with which the business world is *informating* itself, to use a term coined by Shoshana Zuboff. Zuboff maintains that computers not only "produce action" (like automation) but also produce information about the action, which is what she means by informating.[7]

True enough. Informating, via computers, adds a new dimension to the world of work. It's a new dimension, however, only if we compare it to old-style work in which employees were *not involved in data collection*. In the world-class company *all* employees gather data; it's part of their job. That is the key ingredient of employee involvement. It's not merely the chance to submit an opinion or a vote. It is offering informed opinions and votes based on laboratory work. The involved employee is a lab technician who does production work or provides a service and at the same time jots down data about what happens.

Informating is a good term. It expresses what's new. But a computer is not the only, nor the most common, nor the best medium for informating. Best is a chalk board or flip chart paper (including, where appropriate, "chalk boards" done on computer graphics equipment), plus the eyes, ears, and voice of the operator.

COSTS AND CAUSES

As was pointed out in Chapter 8, chalk boards and flip charts in the operating areas also become the cost control system—or, more accurately, the *cause* control system. To restate the central message of

Chapter 8, in accounting and control the important issues have been resolved: Cost and P&L are not the main measures of performance; controls on causes are. In costing, we shall be doing quite well if we just get the signs right: Which activities add and which reduce product costs. Much can be accomplished through cost audits.

As the accounting community tinkers with activity-based costing, it should keep two things in mind: First, profit and loss statements are too gross ever again to be used as the dominant measure of performance and control; no amount of ingenuity in making P&Ls fair and accurate can change that (but by all means, *do* press on and improve the P&Ls). Second, keep it simple and cheap.

One cost matter not taken up in Chapter 8—it had to wait until after discussion of capacity issues in Chapter 12—is cost justification for major capital expenditures. While executives have come part way back down to earth about automation, the business and professional magazines are still sky-high about it. Countless articles grapple with how to justify high technology. Some suggest that we must simply have a certain amount of *faith* in the power of new technology.

Faith instead of hard numbers? The difficulty is that many of the hard numbers, especially on the benefits side, are nonmonetary; these include quicker response, better quality, lower inventories, and new business. Accounting systems have not been able to reduce these so-called intangibles to a common denominator: cost or profit (or return on investment or payback).

While the accounting system can't, a cost audit can—if necessary. When people tell me about their company's rigid proposal review system, I tell them to "fight fire with fire." In other words, do a complete cost study rather than a superficial one that just "dollarizes" the easy factors, such as equipment, direct labor, and energy, topped off by a gross (and inaccurate) overhead figure. (Half-baked, hard-number studies that companies accept in their supposedly rigid proposal systems often just put a veneer of objectivity on one side of a political decision —for example, somebody wants to justify a robot to deliver mail.)

As an example of a *thorough* study, say that the proposal is to regroup into focused cells at a cost of $100,000. The proposal team gets to work:

- It costs out the savings from less scrap and rework, fewer warranty claims, fewer transactions, and so on.
- It estimates revenue growth—derived from better quality, quicker response, greater flexibility, and lower prices.

Funnyware

"**M**r. Farnsworth is here."

"Send him right in." [Bob Farnsworth enters.]

"Bob, I took your proposal home and read it last night. Isn't this the same technology that we funded last year and the year before and I don't know how many years before that? Every year I see one of these, only each time you add another zero. And now you are calling it XYZ. What is this anyway? Can you explain XYZ to me in simple terms?"

"Certainly, sir. You have to understand that the proposals are not for the same thing. It's a series of beneficial enhancements. As the proposal shows, we do a careful cost-benefit on each new feature. It's evolved to the point where today XYZ is really not just technology; it's *thoughtware*."

"What was that word? Would you repeat that?"

"Certainly. We call it thoughtware."

"Farnsworth, I've been in this job for six years. At least 500 proposals have crossed my desk, and I thought I had seen everything. But nobody has ever been brash enough to try to talk me out of megabucks for *thoughtware*. Now get your tail out of here and don't come back until you can tell me what XYZ *really* is. And take your proposal with you."

I made up the names and the dialogue. The rest—the stuff about proposals being generated for thoughtware—is true. Believe it or not.

- It even anticipates such things as a new climate for continual improvement along the chain of customers—and expresses that as a cost reduction stream. The estimates might be based on a pilot project, data gathered from other companies, library research, or a university research study.
- After putting a value on about everything except risk, it reduces the data to the standard company format (any from simple payback to discounted cash flow).

If I were championing the $100,000 proposal to get focused, I would hate to have to conduct such exhaustive research, because I *know* focus is right and that a functional organization is ineffective. It's *not* a matter of faith. Faith has to do with things unknown or unknowable. The earthquakes have given us a knowledge explosion, not a faith explosion. One of the uses of the nineteen principles is in testing out ideas. Any proposal that violates any of the principles has something wrong with it.

I am not suggesting that principles alone—no hard numbers—is the world-class way to process proposals. But principles should play a prominent role somewhere in the screening stages that proposals pass through. Furthermore, data collected in operations—on breakdowns, unstable processes, check marks when the yellow light comes on—can become convincing evidence and justification for funding a proposal to fix the problem.

Another side of the issue is the new emphasis on incremental improvement. Traditional proposal review procedures are big-bang oriented. They aren't designed for handling a steady steam of things like moving desks into a cell, sending people to SPC school, or spending $2,000 to modify a machine for quick setup. In many cases these kinds of improvements cheaply accomplish the same kinds of things hoped for through big-ticket automation.

Companies are so unused to incremental improvement that they try to aggregate small items into a big proposal to send through the proposal mill for somebody's blessing and signature. As an example, a task force might develop an elaborate proposal, complete with computer simulations, to justify implementation of kanban. That's the wrong idea. Kanban is something that can be installed between any successive pair of processes in fifteen minutes, using a few containers and masking tape. Installing kanban one pair at a time is not only *a* way, it's the best way.

REWARD

The spirit of incremental improvement carries over to reward: Close the loop with frequent recognition and celebration—and sometimes payments. None of the nineteen principles deals directly with this matter. It hardly seems necessary, because working in a fully linked company can provide a steady succession of rewards and satisfaction.

The rest of the reward system—bonuses, stock options, suggestion lotteries—is secondary and offers plenty of good options.

Fully linked means plenty of involvement. But casual company attitudes about suggestion systems and suggestion counting, cited in Chapter 9, are all too common. Companies could make money without good suggestion systems in the 1980s when few companies were advanced in employee involvement. The elevated performance standards in the future will not permit such laxity.

PRODUCTS

Part of the satisfaction that springs from being customer-linked comes from problem avoidance. This is true especially for product development people. The product designer may or may not be ready to agree with what Chapter 10 advocates: working closely with the customer's people, including same-company process designers, plus next-company product managers. The designer surely will be gratified by avoiding the usual negatives and criticism: product failures and warranty claims, poor process yields, and round after round of design changes.

As designers and others work more closely with suppliers and customers, old distinctions blur. Instead of a sharp break at the point of sale—"you own it now, buddy; off you go"—provider and customer may link up many times before and after the sale. Thus, the product designer's role extends back and forward in the product's life cycle. Here are a few examples of new and changing provider-customer patterns that are developing:

- Bottlers, canners, and paper companies are in the business of buying empties and discards for recycling. Now there's talk of auto companies committing to buying back and recycling autos.
- Pump-it-yourself gas, assemble- or paint-your-own furniture or toys, and do-it-yourself home improvement kits make the customer part of the product delivery system.
- Most of the computer software companies have help lines offering advice by phone, sometimes twenty-four hours a day. Big consumer products companies print free "800 numbers" (in North America) for customers to call in product questions and complaints. And signs on the back of service vehicles say, "If I'm driving unsafely, call this number:. . . ."

- Today's focused companies are farming out parts of their delivery system to focused service providers, some of which set up shop on the premises; it's not just ancillary services like cafeteria and janitorial, but also computer services, operating a stockroom, or running a specialized value-adding operation on site.

These kinds of examples could fill several pages. The point is that product development is also, in part, supplier development as well as service and after-sale service development. Doors to the design labs have to come off their hinges to meet the need.

ALLEGIANCE

As product development people, and others, link up with final customers, the marketing and selling task is partly taken care of. Putting it differently, marketing does not have to shoulder the burden by itself; the whole organization helps in the customer development effort. The objectives are to gain customer allegiance and to avoid forcing the company (not just the sales reps) into negative selling.

We examined a variety of allegiance-building, positive-selling ideas in Chapter 11, including promoting the firm's capabilities. Trouble is, it's hard to escape from negative selling when the company continues to perform poorly. While there are many success stories, the financial news tells us nearly every day about another company whose stock has been devalued because of "bad guesses about customer demand." Either the company has warehouses full of unsold inventory, or it's out and losing sales.

Enter technology. The bright light of technologies in the present era may be the linkage of point-of-sale (POS) terminals backwards through the chain of suppliers. It's not very high technology. POS data has been available in several business sectors for years, but has scarcely been used.

The first industry to fix upon the great POS potential is textiles/apparel, which is buffeted by both season and fashion changes. The industry, through its many stages of production and service, has been so prone to error as to what styles and sizes are selling well that negative selling has been the dominant activity.

A Kurt Salmon Associates study reveals that the average cycle from fiber to finished garment is sixty-six weeks,[8] which means the early stages are beginning to produce *over a year before they know what styles are selling well.* (Cutting and sewing accounts for just fifteen minutes of that time.) Each stage in the long chain produces partly to forecasts, which are very wrong, and partly to actual orders from the next stage in the chain—which are also very wrong! (One hundred percent on-time completions of orders going to the next stage in the chain sounds good, except that the orders are wrong in the first place. In the cloth industry, or any other, the final customer can be very poorly served by 100 percent on-time internal and stage-to-stage completions.) The greatest potential profit, that arising from reselling popular items in the same season, has been denied the industry because of wrong and slow information about sales patterns.

Since POS data can be sent anywhere easily, it is possible for every stage in the chain to receive up-to-the-minute sales data. Extrapolations of POS data from just a few major sellers can become the basis for buying and producing; ultimately, makers at all stages could be operating on about the same fairly accurate schedule.

The push to adopt this approach is coming from several directions:

- The Limited, a standout women's clothing retailer, gathers its stores' POS data daily. It sends orders, with facsimile illustrations, to makers around the world. About four times a week a chartered 747 from Hong Kong brings clothing to The Limited's Ohio distribution center from which it is sent out to its stores.[9]
- Levi Strauss, the apparel company, has set up LeviLink, which sends POS data by size, color, and style from stores directly to Levi. The company uses the data in its own production and purchasing. According to a company spokesman, stores using LeviLink have seen sales increases averaging nearly 30 percent.[10]
- Major textile companies, such as Burlington and Milliken, have joined forces with prominent retailers, including Sears Roebuck and Wal-Mart, and big apparel houses, such as Haggar Slacks. Their meetings have led to standardized universal product codes (two major retailers had to abandon their former UPCs) and a plan to transform the entire chain of customers. Their three-stage plan is to compress the cycle from fiber to store to just three weeks, which is quick enough to permit reorders of popular styles several times in the same season!

  A variety of just-in-time techniques (e.g., small lot sizes and quick setup) are included, along with POS, as the means of achieving the three-week target. Some of the companies have developed computer software to be used in receiving and processing the

POS data; the software is for sale to any of the hundreds of
large and small apparel houses.

Firms involved generally call what they are doing "quick response"
or "time-based competition." They could just as well call it customer-
based competition, because it is not just speedy; it gets the *right*
goods into the stores.

It is natural that fashion-oriented apparel would be first to mine
POS data in order to synchronize and connect the stages in the chain.
More industries are sure to follow: toys, foods, electronics, appliances,
lumber, hospitals—many others.

Computer memories are chock full of other kinds of valuable information waiting to be mined. For example, Richard Sharp, CEO of the
fast-growing Circuit City chain of home electronics and appliance stores,
has this vision (or plan): A customer calls the company's service department about a problem with a TV set. A video screen calls up the
customer's sales data, credit record, warranty information, TV serial
number, and so forth, and a service technician is dispatched with
the *right parts* in the truck. The system flags best customers and
gives them priority service, as well as getting them on best-customer
mailing lists.[11]

These kinds of leaps forward in customer service do not require
new technology; many companies already have most of the hardware
and even most of the data in their files. The missing ingredient is
the commitment to connect—instead of keeping each stage in the
chain sharply separated from the next.

While data communications technology pays big dividends at the
interfaces (company-to-company and to final customers), the payoff
can be illusory elsewhere.

THE VERY YOUNG AGE OF AUTOMATION

Capacity comes in many forms. Choose wrong, and you may be "inca-
pacitated" for a long time. One of the messages of Chapter 12 is that
analysis often gets you the wrong kind of capacity; for example:

- When analysis revealed huge production volumes, companies
  bought supermachines—which were adept at processing huge volumes of what was selling well last month or last year, but not
  now.

- When analysis revealed a wide product mix, companies spent on high-tech, high-cost flexible automation instead of moving already owned low-tech equipment into cells, upgrading it to process capability, and modifying for quick changeover.
- In either case, companies analyzed the wastes—gluts, shortages, queues, unsynchronized operations (from stage to stage), downtime and changeover interruptions—and invested in complex hardware/software systems to deal with them, rather than fixing root causes.

More specifically:

- Some industries, particularly defense and aerospace, have been utterly bogged down in high tech. Only recently has that sector discovered the power of total quality, focused cells, and employee involvement. The sector has been slow to discover kanban and synchronized no-work-order scheduling systems for star (regularly used) components.
- Totally paperless, computer-screen-driven operations are beginning to dot the landscape in both the service and industrial sectors. They are shining achievements, and many seem to be paying off. But most are rigidly designed and debugged by staff people with no provisions for continual improvement, not even a chalk board for operators to record frequencies of problems by type.

    Some are made physically rigid—networks of machines, conveyors, walls, and utility hookups that can be changed (improved) only at great expense. The flaw is in planning, systems design, and engineering—in rigidities that do not allow easy tightening, improvement, equipment moves, and employee-driven incremental change. It's the old mentality: Plan it, install it, and go on to the next big-ticket project.
- In many industrial companies computer "informating" systems stand in the way of speeding up, simplifying, and taking out waste. The computer system known as MRPII (generally meaning manufacturing resource planning) includes necessary subroutines, such as computerized master scheduling, product structuring, and inventory record keeping. MRPII systems also can do other more-or-less wasteful things, such as generate work orders, track work through every operation, report labor, and produce inaccurate cost reports. Companies are confused.

    Industry needs a bare-bones computer system for interfacing; in other words, a sales and purchasing system. Much of the baggage that comes with big MRPII systems—and their equivalents

Planning and Executing

People like to say that MRPII plans, and kanban (or JIT) executes. Sounds reasonable, but it's not really accurate.

- MRP (I or II) has subroutines that plan and others that get into nitty-gritty shop-floor execution matters.
- JIT plans in a different way: by synchronization—ideally, all stages working to the same rate-based schedule (at least for star items).
- Kanban is partly a planning tool as well: It plans container quantities, move quantities, maximum line lengths, and lot-size increments. Kanban also helps control execution, but differently from the way MRPII does it: by disciplined flows from operation to operation or plant to plant.
- Taiichi Ohno, former Toyota vice president and father of JIT, puts it like this: "The [JIT] system is the production method, and the kanban system is the way it is managed."[12]
- When MRP first took shape, its two unique features were *netting* and *backscheduling*. Advanced JIT companies don't net (subtract quantity needed from quantity on hand), because kanban keeps inventory quantities fixed; they don't backschedule (subtract lead times), because each stage of production is on the same rate-based synchronized schedule.
- Final point: In the transition to direct linkages, companies should be actively engaged in moving more and more parts off work orders and onto rates and/or kanban. New MRP systems can do rate-based planning and accommodate kanban, but real progress is severing the computer link wherever the visual system will do the trick.

in insurance, banking, medicine, etc.—creates confusion, complexity, waste, and high costs.

Companies can still make fat profits by violating some of the principles, for example by automating things that could easily be simplified out of existence (violation of principles 16 and 17). Business in the nineties will be less forgiving of flaws.

LEADERSHIP

I often hear this from people from leading companies: "We already know what to do. Our problem is how to implement it." Those are the words, but the real meaning is, How can we get people (which might mean senior management, first-line supervisors, staff departments, operators, middle management—or all of these) committed?

I don't believe it when I'm told the problem is implementation, because that is precisely what those companies' managers are experienced in and good at. They know how to write mission statements, organize book study groups (which has proven to be a very effective technique[13]) and task forces, hold coordinative meetings, set up pilot projects, assign duties, write procedures, train, fund, and monitor. Implementation of world-class concepts actually is easier than big implementations they've done before.

Knowledge

No, the real problem is commitment, and that's the purpose of this book and others like it, plus the many other forms of spreading the message. To the people who are frustrated by the slow pace of implementation and the obstructions in their companies, I can only say, The ball's in your court. Do your utmost to educate any in your company who will listen, get little fires lit (small projects started) everywhere, and don't stop for sign-offs at every step. You have the knowledge, so you have the power.

That's not to say you are the only one with knowledge—and power. Chapter 1 noted the factions problem, each faction being a fount of knowledge about too narrow an approach to progress. Your task is to win them over, co-opt them, find a problem that calls for their expertise, whether it be organizing quality circles (which are valuable for training) or designing automated storage systems (which are valuable in distribution centers).

On where to go for help, the rule is simple: Go to the specialists—your own in-company people and the industry backing them up—for knowledge; go to the generalists (who peddle only ideas, not software or hardware) for agenda. You, presumably, are a generalist, as I am.

Who Leads?

I understand that some people like myself (purveyors of a message to business and industry) prefer, or insist on, active involvement of the most senior managers. The viewpoint, which we've heard in connection with every single management concept ever proposed, is that the most important success factor is top management commitment.

That may be true, but it doesn't concern me much. While I have my chances to speak to senior people, I actually prefer to capture the interest of those who are up-and-coming—young minds (not always the same as young people), new blood, the next crop of leaders. This is not a short-term exercise. We are in it for the long haul. If the current crop of executives stands pat, too bad. My confidence is in ideas: that the powerful new ones—and mandate for continual improvement—will push out the old ineffective ways and beliefs.

Furthermore, I believe the future is in the hands of the doers—operators, assemblers, clerks, stock handlers, drivers, servers. When I first went out on the public seminar circuit, no company sent operators or union representatives. My private "on-site" seminars were different. Some of the host companies did include operators and labor reps. Today, most do (which I encourage through lower rates for "hourlies"). In several cases, *all* employees were sent—made possible by shutting down operations for a day, by sending half the plant one day and the other half the next, or by arranging a special Saturday program. Now companies send operators to the public seminars as well.

The message—how to become a world-class organization—certainly does *not* go over anyone's head, and operators *are* very much interested—and appreciative. Clearly, I am not alone in putting faith in operator-power. It is central to the way good companies now think about labor resources—not so much as a cost and a problem but as a component of management. (Scott Myers has persistently proclaimed that point of view for a decade or more—in published articles and a book, *Every Employee A Manager.*)[14]

It won't be a disaster if CEOs and presidents don't read books such as mine; their lieutenants and lower-level managers, and even some of their operators, do, and they will run the show *right* half a generation from now—if not much sooner with or without the blessings of their high-level bosses.

CONVERGENCE

While I can look to another generation, some companies can't afford to. The elevated standards of international competition, plus lightning-fast global diffusion of products, services, and information—what C. Jackson Grayson and Carla O'Dell call *economic tectonics*[15]—can wipe out a laggard performer.

The best security is knowledge of how to improve, and that commodity is plentiful. While the lone voice in the wilderness isn't heard, the decibel level is hard to ignore when other voices join into a chorus. What I have been saying in these pages *is* part of a chorus:

- The same themes—serve the customer and involve the employees—sing out in most of the recent path-setting works, including Tom Peters's *Thriving on Chaos*, Stanley Davis's *Future Perfect*, and Grayson and O'Dell's *American Business: A Two-Minute Warning*.
- Loud and persistent voices championing the new belief in controlling *causes* of costs and focusing on the *customer's* primary wants—quality, throughput time, flexibility, and cost—are a large, diverse lot. It includes leading accountants (such as Thomas Johnson, Robert Kaplan, and Robin Cooper); manufacturing experts (Robert Hall, Ed Hay, Robert Hayes, Steven Wheelwright, Kim Clark, David Garvin, Kio Suzaki, Mehran Seperhi, Horst Wildemann, Michel Greif, Christopher Voss, Shigeo Shingo, and a host of others); a very long list of subject-matter experts, especially in quality (a list headed by W. Edwards Deming, Joseph Juran, Kaoru Ishikawa, Armand Feigenbaum, and Philip Crosby). Also, I could list most of the leading management consulting firms among those buying into the new thinking.

We are all in general agreement. The time for chain-building is now.

Appendix: Quick (JIT) Response

W E TOUCHED ON quick-response (just-in-time) techniques in several chapters. It remains here to see how they fit together and to detail the results and benefits.

Results and Benefits

- *First-order results.* First of all, consider what happens when a firm beats the competition; that is, when it is able to market and provide (including produce, where applicable) the product faster than the others. The most important effects are sales growth and taking market share away from the competition. These first-order results are just a milestone. They warrant just a quick cheer. Then, time to press on.
- *Second-order results.* Why press on? To drive laggard competitors into "desperate acts," to force them to rely heavily on negative selling: making sales promises that can't be met, chopping prices below costs, offering rebates, and otherwise swimming against the tide. Where the product is storable, negative selling includes building inventory—a costly, ineffective alternative to being able to operate close to actual demand.
- *Third-order results.* Finally, for every reduction in response time, quality and other performances improve and internal costs drop.

318

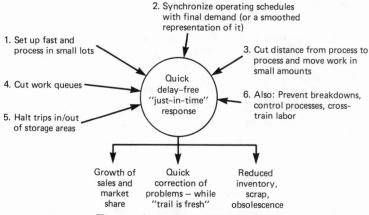

Figure A–1. How JIT Works

Ingredients of Quick Response

The quick-response techniques aim for delay-free processing and delivery through every process all the way to the final customer. They respond to a glaring weakness in plants and offices: Most products take weeks to produce but only hours or minutes of actual work. In human services, same thing: Most clients spend most of their time waiting, precious little of it getting served.

Techniques. As Figure A–1 shows, the techniques most closely associated with JIT are:

1. Set up quickly and process in small lots—ideally a lot size of one: one piece, one person, one document. Large-lot processing is bad, because it forces items in the lot to wait for their turn to be processed, fills stockrooms far in advance of need and

---

Long Lot Size

People in Kodak film processing were asking themselves, "What is a lot size of one—for us?" In several stages of processing it looked like "a roll five miles long and eight feet wide." But in order to *think like the customer*, a lot size of one had to be the little yellow box with a roll of film inside.

often with the wrong products, and "un-synchronizes" the process from others in the chain.

2. Synchronize operating schedules with final demand—or a smoothed representation of it. Primary ways of doing this include:

- Holding schedule coordination meetings
- In manufacturing, converting to rate-based schedules (e.g., a rate of one every twenty minutes, or three per hour, or one every three days) across several stages in the chain of customers
- In services, converting to maximum line-length or flow-time policies. For example, process all of this morning's orders this afternoon; process all received this afternoon tomorrow morning. Use overtime, plus shorter lunch and break times, to meet the policy even on peak-demand days.
- Linking pairs of processes by kanban signals such as lights, gongs, standard containers, designated squares, and abacus boards with green and red beads. A conveyor is also kanban-like, since it synchronizes the rates of every person or process along it.

3. Cut process-to-process flow distances and move the work (documents, materials, clients) often in small amounts; don't wait days, hours, or even minutes to accumulate an "economic load." (It's usually false economics, as it includes only the costs of labor to move the loads. Left out are the costs of huge bulk-handling apparatus, space taken up by that and by the loads in waiting, and, worst of all, the delays in completing service taken up by load accumulation time.)

4. Cut queues of pieces, jobs, or clients, so that the average item does not have to spend most of its life waiting for processing.

5. Halt trips in and out of storage areas; this applies to materials, supplies, spares, reference documents, fixtures, servers, tools—anything. Off-line storage is okay for rarely used items and for buffer stocks kept on hand only for infrequent failures. In the case of direct materials, numbers 1 through 4 keep work queues small enough to allow holding them right at the workplace or at lineside (close down the storerooms).

6. Quick response also requires fixing causes of random stops and slowdowns: Preventively maintain the process so it doesn't break down (includes equipment—and anything else, such as a "human

Inventory: An Asset?

What costs are related to the amount of inventory? Putting it another way, what costs go away when inventory is wiped out? There are three categories:

1. *Obvious*—what the textbooks have always cited:

    - Stockroom costs (space, shelving, insurance, wages for stockkeepers, etc.)
    - Capital (or opportunity) cost, i.e., cost of earnings (interest) lost because capital is tied up in inventory.

2. *Semi-obvious*—sometimes cited in textbooks, often not recognized in industry:

    - Obsolescence—the portion of stock that becomes outdated while in storage
    - Direct inventory administration—inventory record keeping, counting, planning, and management.

3. *Hidden*—not in the textbooks, not recognized in industry, all very significant:

    - Rework and scrap—high inventories invite wholesale rework and scrap disasters
    - Inspection and sorting—lot inspection and sorting is practiced only when inventories are received or made in large lots
    - Indirect inventory administration—the portion of sales, general, and administrative expenses that relates to inventory matters
    - Plant space and apparatus whose sole purpose is to move or hold stock—accounting systems always categorize these *incorrectly* as production costs, not inventory costs; can't be production costs, because they do not add value
    - Data-processing support—that portion of equipment, programming, analysis, operations, data base, and data entry in the plant that goes for inventory tracking and accounting
    - Technical support (engineering and maintenance) for non-value-adding storage, handling, and data-processing equipment.

breakdown," that could stop the process); strictly control processes to prevent scrap losses and rework delays; and cross-train labor for quick movement to where the next demand is.

Benefits. The main benefits of quick response are growth of sales and market share—beating the competition to a sale.

Next most important is exposing and fixing problems quickly while evidence of causes is still fresh, uncontaminated with hundreds of other possible causes. It is the "naturalistic approach" to quality, process control, and process improvement.

The third category of benefits is elimination of costly wastes. One is inventory, which is listed on the books as an asset. Its value as an asset, however, deteriorates. Inventory is a store of obvious, semi-obvious, and hidden costs—which grow over time.

Finally and most important, all the benefits of quick response go both ways: to strengthen the providing company and to meet the wants and needs of the customer.

Notes

Chapter 1
The Great Awakening: Earthquakes in the Business Functions

1. William W. Davis, Dale P. Esse, and Donald L. Teringo, "Successfully Communicating Can Pay High Dividends," *Quality Progress*, July 1987, pp. 36–39.

2. Bill Ginnado, "Teaching an Old Plant New Tricks," *Commitment Plus*, newsletter published by Bill Ginnado, July 1987, pp. 2–4.

3. Carolyn Burstein and Kathleen Sedlak, "The Federal Quality and Productivity Improvement Effort," *Quality Progress*, October 1988, pp. 38–41.

4. Ruth Simon, "Efficiency Is Not Enough," *Forbes*, November 28, 1988, p. 41.

5. See, for example, Mike Parker and Jane Slaughter, "Management by Stress," *Technology Review*, October 1988, pp. 37–44.

6. These numbers come from a study by the U.S. National Association of Suggestion Systems dated 1986.

7. John M. Martin, "The Final Piece to the Puzzle," *Manufacturing Engineering*, special issue on simultaneous engineering, September 1988, pp. 46–51.

8. A. William Wiggenhorn, "Making a Company More Competitive: The Role of Training and Education," unpublished paper presented at Special Meeting on Competitiveness, American Society for Training and Development, Washington, D.C., October 7–9, 1987.

9. P. John Mirtz, "Business Seeks a New Style of Factory Executive," *Industry Week*, October 17, 1988, p. 37.

Chapter 2
Universal Strategy: The Shattering of Strategic Business Thought

1. Al Ries and Jack Trout, *Bottom-Up Marketing* (New York: McGraw-Hill, 1989), pp. 128–29.

2. Stanley M. Davis, *Future Perfect* (Reading, Mass.: Addison-Wesley, 1987), p. 33.

3. Alan L. Frohman, "Putting Technology into Strategic Planning," *California Management Review*, Winter 1985, pp. 48–59.

4. Thomas J. Peters and Robert H. Waterman, Jr., *In Search of Excellence: Lessons from America's Best-Run Companies*, (New York: Harper & Row, 1982), Chapter 10, "Stick to the Knitting."

5. Ronald Henkoff, "This Cat Is Acting Like a Tiger," *Fortune*, December 19, 1988, pp. 70–76.

6. Steve Kaufman, "Quest for Quality," *Business Month*, May 1989, pp. 61–65.

7. David Altany, "After the Bell Is Over," *Industry Week*, February 20, 1989, pp. 15–18.

8. Daniel Deltz, "World Class Manufacturing," *Computers in Mechanical Engineering*, July–August 1988, pp. 18–24.

9. Richard J. Schonberger, *World Class Manufacturing Casebook: Implementing JIT and TQC* (New York: The Free Press, 1987), Chapter 11, "Just-in-Time Production at Hewlett-Packard, Personal Office Computer Division," p. 73.

10. Gary Hamel and C. K. Prahalad, "Strategic Intent," *Harvard Business Review*, May–June 1989, pp. 63–76.

11. Tom Peters, "Confusing the Strategic with the Tactical," syndicated column, *Seattle Post-Intelligencer*, October 20, 1987.

Chapter 3
The "Customer-In" Organization

1. Allyn Southerland, "AEtna's BOAST—Branch Office Agency Service Teams," *Target*, Spring 1988, pp. 18–19.

2. John H. Sheridan, "Sizing Up Corporate Staffs," *Industry Week*, November 21, 1988, pp. 46–52.

3. Wickam Skinner, "The Focused Factory," *Harvard Business Review*, May–June 1974, pp. 113–21.

4. Based on joint research by M. Scott Myers, Jr., and Richard J. Schonberger.

5. Personal communication.

6. Personal correspondence with G. A. B. Edwards.

7. Jim Knapton, "Exploding the Traditions of an Old-Fashioned Industry," *Target*, Summer 1989, pp. 24–28.

8. Duncan C. McDougall, "Learning the Ropes: How to Tell When You've Found an Effective Performance Measurement System for Manufacturing," *Operations Management Review*, Fall 1987 & Winter 1988, pp. 38–48.

9. F. Bianchi, V. Failla, and F. Turco, "Appunti Viaggio in Giappone (5–12 Marzo 1988)," Report of a study mission to Japan (in Italian), Milan: Istituto per la Ricerca e l'Intervento nella Direzione Aziendale.

10. Pierre Pean, "How to Get Rich off Perestroika," *Fortune*, May 8, 1989, pp. 145–46.

11. Regina E. Herzlinger, "The Failed Revolution in Health Care—The Role of Management," *Harvard Business Review*, March–April 1989, pp. 95–103.

12. Shoshana Zuboff, *In the Age of the Smart Machine: The Future of Work and Power* (New York: Basic Books, 1988), p. 125.

13. John Hoerr, "Work Teams Can Rev Up Paper-Pushers, Too," *Business Week*, November 28, 1988, pp. 64–72.

14. On-site visit and personal communication.

Chapter 4
Total Quality: Toward Delighting the Customer

1. *Statistical Quality Control Handbook* (Indianapolis, Ind.: Western Electric Co., Inc., 1956), p. 217.

2. John H. Sheridan, "An 'Edict' For Excellence," *Industry Week*, August 21, 1989, pp. 35–36.

3. Battey does not claim to be the originator of "big Q" and "little q" (a few other firms also use the terms).

4. Gail Snyder, "Kodak Develops Quality Management," *Performance Management Magazine*, Winter–Spring 1988, pp. 10–21.

5. The basic source is Genichi Taguchi and Yu-in Wu, *Introduction to Off-Line Quality Control Systems* (Tokyo: Central Japan Quality Control Association, 1980); available from the American Supplier Institute, Dearborn, Mich.

6. See, for example, Sidney Schoeffler, Robert D. Buzzell, and Donald F. Heany, "Impact of Strategic Planning on Profit Performance." *Harvard Business Review*, March–April 1974, pp. 137–45.

7. Karen Blumenthal and Robert Tomsho, "Compaq, Long an Exploiter of Big Blue's Bloopers, Now Seeks to Be Leader," *Wall Street Journal*, April 21, 1989.

8. Apparently George Buering, a consultant to Kodak, came up with this use of the term *random mishaps*.

9. Vaughn Beals speech to Boeing executives, August 1988.

10. Kaoru Ishikawa, "The Quality Control Audit," *Quality Progress*, January 1987, pp. 39–41.

11. Brooks Tigner, "Crusading for Quality," *International Management*, July–August 1989, pp. 34–36.

12. Brad Stratton, "The Low Cost of Quality Lodging," *Quality Progress*, June 1988, pp. 49–53.

13. See *Quality Progress*, special auditing issue, January 1987; the presidential audit is discussed in two articles in the issue: Kaoru Ishikawa, "The Quality Control Audit," pp. 39–41; and Kaoru Shimoyamada, "The President's Audit: QC Audits at Komatsu," pp. 44–45.

14. David A. Garvin, *Managing Quality: The Strategic and Competitive Edge* (New York: The Free Press, 1988), pp. 49–60. See, also, ten dimensions of *service* quality in Carol A. King, "A Framework for a Service Quality Assurance System," *Quality Progress*, September 1987, pp. 27–32.

15. Spencer Hutches, Jr., "What Customers Want: Results of ASQC/Gallup Survey," *Quality Progress*, February 1989, pp. 33–35.

16. Russell Johnston and Paul R. Lawrence, "Beyond Vertical Integration—the Rise of the Value-Adding Partnership," *Harvard Business Review*, July–August 1988, pp. 94–101.

17. See, for example, Bob King, *Better Designs in Half the Time* (Methuen, Mass.: Goal/QPC, 1987).

Chapter 5
Work Force on the Attack

1. Thomas A. Stewart, "Westinghouse Gets Respect at Last," *Fortune*, July 3, 1989, pp. 92–98.

2. Rensis Likert, *New Patterns of Management* (New York: McGraw-Hill, 1961), pp. 249–263.

3. John Simmons, "Total Employee Participation Equals Quality," *Total Quality Management*, a U.K. magazine, November 1988, pp. 21–22.

4. See Chapter 11, "Just-in-Time Production at Hewlett-Packard, Personal Office Computer Division," in Richard J. Schonberger, *World Class Manufacturing Casebook: Implementing JIT and TQC* (New York: The Free Press, 1987).

5. Gail Snyder, "Kodak Develops Quality Management," *Performance Management Magazine*, Winter–Spring 1988, pp. 10–21.

6. Howard Deutsch and Neil J. Metviner, "Quality Improvement at National Westminster Bank USA," in *When America Does It Right*, ed. Jay W. Spechler (Norcross, Ga.: Industrial Engineering and Management Press, 1988), pp. 84–96.

7. Cynthia Butler and G. Rex Bryce, "Implementing SPC with Signetics Production Personnel," *Quality Progress*, April 1986, pp. 42–50.

8. Ibid.

9. Adapted from Ross Johnson and William O. Winchell, "Production and Quality: What is Quality?" booklet provided to textbook authors by the American Society for Quality Control (1989), pp. 10–12.

Chapter 6
The Learning Organization

1. Henry Ford, *My Life and Work* (Garden City, N.Y.: Garden City Publishing, 1922), p. 83.

2. Donald B. Thompson, "Escaping 'No-Man's Land,' " *Industry Week*, October 17, 1988, pp. 41–42.

3. A suggestion of Robert Hayes, as reported by Brian Dumaine, in "What the Leaders of Tomorrow See," *Fortune*, July 3, 1989, pp. 48–60.

4. Norm Alster, "What Flexible Workers Can Do," *Fortune*, February 13, 1989, pp. 62–66.

5. Bro Uttal, "Companies That Serve You Best," *Fortune*, December 7, 1987, pp. 98–111.

6. Marj Charlier, "At an Arizona Mine Workers Were Wooed Away from the Union," *Wall Street Journal*, August 8, 1989.

7. Therese R. Welter, "Rallying Support," *Industry Week*, February 20, 1989, p. 13.

8. Louis Kraar, "Japan's Gung-Ho U.S. Car Plants," *Fortune*, January 30, 1989, pp. 98–104.

9. Robert Weisman, "Can't Afford a Consultant? Join the Club," *Wall Street Journal*, July 11, 1988.

10. Nunzio Lupo, "Budd May Invest $43 Million in Plant," *Detroit Free Press*, March 18, 1988.

11. Peter F. Drucker, "Low Wages No Longer Give Competitive Edge," *Wall Street Journal*, March 16, 1988.

12. Michel Greif, "Factories Get a New Look," unpublished English translation of *L'Usine s'affiche: communication visuelle et management* (Paris: Les Editions d'Organisation, 1989), p. 31.

13. Brad Stratton, "Learning the Language Is Not Enough," *Quality Progress*, January 1989, pp. 16–22.

14. Bill Ginnodo, "Teaching an Old Plant New Tricks," *Commitment Plus*, July 1987, pp. 2–4.

15. Kenneth E. Leach, "The Evolution of Quality at Globe Metallurgical," *Actionline*, January 1989, pp. 23–24.

16. Karen Bemowski, "People: The Only Thing That Will Make Quality Work," *Quality Progress*, September 1988, pp. 63–67.

Chapter 7
Attack on Nonobvious Wastes

1. Spencer Hutches, Jr., "What Customers Want: Results of ASQC/Gallup Survey," *Quality Progress*, February 1989, pp. 33–35.

2. "Tektronix: Portable Instruments Division (B)," Case study N9–188–143, Harvard Business School, 1988, p. 2; and Peter B. B. Turney and Bruce Anderson, "Accounting for Continuous Improvement," *Sloan Management Review*, Winter 1989, pp. 37–47.

3. Rick Hunt, Linda Garrett, and C. Mike Merz, "Direct Labor Cost Not Always Relevant at H-P," *Management Accounting*, February 1985, pp. 58–62.

4. Thomas E. Vollmann, William L. Berry, and D. Clay Whybark, *Manufacturing Planning and Control Systems*, 2d ed. (Homewood, Ill.: Richard D. Irwin, 1988), p. 276.

5. "Losing Faith: Many Americans Fear U.S. Living Standards Have Stopped Rising," *Wall Street Journal*, May 1, 1989.

6. Thomas E. Vollmann, "Changing Manufacturing Performance Measures," unpublished paper, 1989 Management Accounting Seminar: Performance Excellence in Manufacturing and Service, American Accounting Association, San Diego, March 9–11, 1989.

7. Mary Emrich, "Burning Its Brand on Quality, Texas Style," *Manufacturing Systems*, August 1989, pp. 46–54.

8. See A. V. Feigenbaum, *Total Quality Control* (New York: McGraw-Hill, 1961), pp. 85–106.

9. John M. Groocock, *The Chain of Quality* (New York: John Wiley, 1986), p. 55.

Chapter 8
Minimal Accounting and Noncost Cost Control

1. H. Thomas Johnson and Robert S. Kaplan (Boston: Harvard Business School Press, 1987).

2. Ibid, pp. 7–14.

3. H. Thomas Johnson, "A Blueprint for World-Class Management Accounting," *Management Accounting*, June 1988, pp. 23–30.

4. Peter B. B. Turney and Bruce Anderson, "Accounting for Continuous Improvement," *Sloan Management Review*, Winter 1989, pp. 37–47.

5. Robin Cooper and Robert S. Kaplan, "How Cost Accounting Systemati-

cally Distorts Product Costs," unpublished paper for the 1986 Annual Conference of the Association for Manufacturing Excellence, Chicago, p. 27.

6. Regina E. Herzlinger, "The Failed Revolutions in Health Care—The Role of Management," *Harvard Business Review*, March–April 1989, pp. 95–103.

7. Thanks go to David Taylor, materials manager at Zytec, for providing this information and examples.

8. Remarks and quotations about the Roseville case are taken from Robin Cooper and Peter B. B. Turney, "Hewlett-Packard: Roseville Networks Division," Harvard Business School, 1989.

9. Robin Cooper and Robert S. Kaplan, "Measure Costs Right: Make the Right Decisions," *Harvard Business Review*, September–October 1988, pp. 96–103.

10. H. Thomas Johnson, "Managing Costs: An Outmoded Philosophy," *Manufacturing Engineering*, May 1989, pp. 42–46.

11. Cooper and Kaplan, "Measure Costs Right."

12. Robert S. Forbes, Douglas F. Jones, and Steven T. Marty, "Managerial Accounting and Vendor Relations for JIT: A Case Study," *Production and Inventory Management Journal*, First Quarter 1989, pp. 76–81.

13. Tom Peters, "Workers Perform Best When They Make Decisions," syndicated column, *Seattle Post-Intelligencer*, February 21, 1989.

14. Other voices expressing the same viewpoint include H. Thomas Johnson, who advocates putting "activity-based *information*" [as opposed to cost] to work (see "Managing Costs"); and Thomas E. Vollmann, who refers to "cutting the Gordian knot"— meaning cutting management's dependence on cost information (see "Changing Manufacturing Performance Measurements," paper presented at Performance Excellence in Manufacturing and Service Organizations Symposium, AAA Management Accounting Section and National Association of Accountants, San Diego, March 9–11, 1989).

Chapter 9
Pay, Recognition, Celebration

1. See "Non-specialized Career Paths," in William G. Ouchi, *Theory Z: How American Business Can Meet the Japanese Challenge* (Reading, Mass.: Addison-Wesley, 1981), pp. 29–37, 121–23; and "Combating Specialization," in Richard J. Schonberger, *Japanese Manufacturing Techniques: Nine Hidden Lessons in Simplicity* (New York: The Free Press, 1982), pp. 194–97.

2. "IE Federal Beat," *Industrial Engineering*, June 1989, p. 12.

3. See pros and cons in Richard J. Schonberger and Harry W. Hennessey, Jr., "Is Equal Pay for Comparable Work Fair?" *Personnel Journal*, December 1981, pp. 964–68. It is personally pleasing to find a way to get on the pro side of comparable worth, inasmuch as I have long championed women's economic rights—in print starting with my master's thesis: "Labor Market Survey: The Relationship between Part-Day Employment and the Role of the Woman in the Home" (The University of Iowa, June 1968); also, "Ten Million U.S. Housewives Want to Work," *Labor Law Journal*, June 1970, pp. 374–79; and "Inflexible Working Conditions Keep Women 'Unliberated'," *Personnel Journal*, November 1971, pp. 834–38.

4. John M. Martin, "A Team Approach to Success," *Manufacturing Engineering*, August 1989, pp. 77–79.

5. "Workshop Report: Motorola/Prestolite, Arcade, NY—Common Vision, Uncommon Spirit," *Target*, Winter 1988, pp. 21–24.

6. Vaughn Beals speech to Boeing executives, August 1988.

7. Hiroyuki Hirano, editor-in-chief, *JIT Factory Revolution: A Pictorial Guide to Factory Design of the Future*, J. T. Black, English ed. (Cambridge, Mass.: Productivity Press, 1989), p. 180.

8. Richard J. Schonberger, *World Class Manufacturing Casebook: Implementing JIT and TQC* (New York: The Free Press, 1987), pp. 178–79.

9. Nancy J. Perry, "Here Come Richer Riskier Pay Plans," *Fortune*, December 19, 1988, pp. 50–58.

10. Jolie Solomon, "Managers Focus on Low-Wage Workers," *Wall Street Journal*, May 9, 1989.

11. Personal interviews with managers at corporate headquarters and at plant sites, Spring 1989.

12. Jolie Solomon, "Hotels Eschew Better Benefit Packages, Despite Turnover," *Wall Street Journal*, August 9, 1988.

13. Regina Herzlinger, "The Failed Health Care Revolution," *Fortune*, December 19, 1988, p. 186.

14. Jolie Solomon, "Pepsi Offers Stock Options to All, Not Just Honchos," *Wall Street Journal*, June 28, 1989.

15. Jude T. Rich, "Reincenting America," *Industry Week*, November 21, 1988, pp. 53–56.

16. *Wall Street Journal*, November 29, 1988.

17. Laurie Hays, "All Eyes on Du Pont's Incentive-Pay Plan. *Wall Street Journal*, December 5, 1988.

18. Michael Schroeder, "Watching the Bottom Line Instead of the Clock," *Business Week*, November 7, 1988, pp. 134–35.

19. Ted Rees, Randy Harris, and Harry Lit, "Work Teams That Work," *Manufacturing Systems*, March 1989, pp. 42–45.

20. George Melloan, "Herman Miller's Secrets of Corporate Creativity," *Wall Street Journal*, May 3, 1988.

21. Glenn Ruffenach, "The Boss Says: Earn Your Keep, Keep More," *Wall Street Journal*, August 22, 1989.

22. Lois Therrien, "Motorola Sends Its Work Force Back to School," *Business Week*, June 6, 1988, pp. 80–81.

Chapter 10
World-Class Product Development

1. Gregory L. Miles, "Specialty Metals That Are Special Indeed," *Business Week*, June 16, 1989, p. 129.

2. John M. Martin, "The Final Piece to the Puzzle," *Manufacturing Engineering*, September 1988, pp. 46–51.

3. This and later references to McDonald's are based mainly on information drawn from John F. Love, *McDonald's: Behind the Arches* (Toronto: Bantam Books, 1986).

4. Ibid., pp. 228–31.

5. Ibid., p. 344.

6. Ibid., p. 351.

7. Ibid., pp. 324–25.

8. "A&P's John Hartford Built a Retail Colossus," *Wall Street Journal*, April 18, 1989.

9. For a more accessible reference, in handbook form, see Geoffrey Boothroyd and Peter Dewhurst, *Product Design for Assembly* (Wakefield, R. I.: Boothroyd-Dewhurst, Inc., 1987).

10. J. L. Stauffer, "Product Design for Finish Quality," *Manufacturing Engineering*, September 1988, pp. 75–78.

11. Jeffrey L. Funk, "Design for Assembly of Electrical Products," *Manufacturing Review*, March 1989, pp. 53–59.

12. John Huey, "The New Power in Black & Decker," *Fortune*, January 2, 1989, pp. 89–94.

13. C. F. Vogt, Jr., "Beyond CAD and CAM: Design for Manufacturability," *Design News*, March 7, 1988, pp. 18–19.

14. "The Best-Engineered Part Is No Part at All," *Business Week*, May 8, 1989, p. 150. Further information comes from personal communication with Bill Sprague of NCR.

15. "Working Smart," *Wall Street Journal*, June 1, 1989.

16. Gary Jacobson and John Hillkirk, *Xerox: American Samurai* (New York: Macmillan, 1986), pp. 178–79.

17. Peter B. B. Turney and Bruce Anderson, "Accounting for Continuous Improvement," *Sloan Management Review*, Winter 1989, pp. 37–47.

18. Martin, "The Final Piece to the Puzzle."

19. Therese R. Welter, "Design Inspiration," *Industry Week*, February 20, 1989, pp. 54–57.

20. Steven C. Wheelwright and W. Earl Sasser, Jr., "The New Product Development Map," *Harvard Business Review*, May–June 1989, pp. 112–25.

21. "Payment in Kind," *Quality Progress*, April 1989, pp. 16–20.

22. John H. Sheridan, "A 'Simultaneous' Success Story," *Industry Week*, August 1, 1988, pp. 73–74.

23. Daniel Deltz, "World Class Manufacturing," *Computers in Mechanical Engineering*, July–August 1988, pp. 18–61; and David L. Schlotterbeck, "Spotlight: Improving Low Productivity," *Computer Graphics Today*, May 1988, p. 12.

Chapter 11
Marketing for Total Gain

1. James R. Norman, "At Toddler University, the Chairman Is Getting A's," *Business Week*, January 16, 1989, p. 61.

2. Hank Gilman, "Retail Genius: Founder Lazarus Is a Reason Toys 'R' Us Dominates Its Industry," *Wall Street Journal*, November 21, 1985.

3. Selwyn Feinstein, "In Franchising, Slow Start Tends to Lead to Big Finish," *Wall Street Journal*, June 27, 1989.

4. Joanne Lipman, "Procter & Gamble Promotions May Be Demoted in Favor of Ads," *Wall Street Journal*, July 17, 1989.

5. Richard J. Schonberger, *World Class Manufacturing: The Lessons of Simplicity Applied* (New York: The Free Press, 1986), pp. x, 156–62.

6. Russell Johnston and Paul R. Lawrence, "Beyond Vertical Integration—the Rise of the Value-Adding Partnership," *Harvard Business Review*, July–August 1988, pp. 94–101.

7. James B. Treece, "U.S. Parts Makers Just Won't Say 'Uncle,' " *Business Week*, August 10, 1987, pp. 76–78.

8. Ibid.

9. Neal E. Boudette, "Is Short-Term Really the American Way?" *Business Week*, June 5, 1989, pp. 12–18.

10. Richard A. Maass, "Supplier Certification—A Positive Response to Just-in-Time," *Quality Progress*, September 1988, pp. 75–80.

11. Bruce Paton, "Managing Your IE Career: IE Careers in Non-Traditional Areas at Frito-Lay," *Industrial Engineering*, May 1988, pp. 10–25.

12. John H. Sheridan, "Purchasing's New Clout," *Industry Week*, November 7, 1989, pp. 49–65.

13. Larry C. Giunipero, "AME Research Report: A Survey of JIT Purchasing in American Industry," *Target*, Winter 1989, pp. 25–27.

14. Ibid.

15. John H. Sheridan, "Sizing Up Corporate Staffs," *Industry Week*, November 21, 1988, pp. 46–52.

16. Ralph E. Reins, "Strategic Alliances: A Competitive Solution for the 90s," *Actionline*, October 1988, pp. 16–17.

17. Perry A. Trunick, "Service Drives Trucking Industry," *Industry Week*, April 3, 1989, pp. T1–T20.

18. Ibid., p. T-20.

19. Brian S. Moskal, "Enough Premium Carriers in the '90s? Don't Bet on It," *Industry Week*, August 21, 1989, pp. 31–34.

20. Bryan H. Berry, "JIT Manufacturing: Much More than Reducing Inventories," *Actionline*, September 1987, pp. 18–20.

21. "Mr. Smith Goes Global," *Business Week*, February 13, 1989, pp. 66–72; and " 'Just in Time' in Action," *Federal Express International Newsletter*, March 1989, pp. 1–3.

22. *Wal-Mart Annual Report for 1988*, p. 2.

23. George Stalk, Jr., "Time—The Next Source of Competitive Advantage," *Harvard Business Review*, July–August 1988, pp. 41–51.

24. Curtis Bill Pepper, "Fast Forward," *Business Month*, February 1989, pp. 25–30.

25. Jeffrey G. Miller et al., *Closing the Competitive Gap—The International Report of the Manufacturing Futures Project* (Boston: Boston University Manufacturing Round Table, 1988.)

26. Karl Albrecht and Ron Zemke, *Service America! Doing Business in the New Economy* (Homewood, Ill.: Dow Jones-Irwin, 1985), pp. 147, 149–50.

27. Al Ries and Jack Trout, *Bottom-Up Marketing* (New York: McGraw-Hill, 1989, p. 209.

28. Ibid., Chapter 4, "Narrowing Your Focus," and pp. 113–14.

Chapter 12
Success Formulas for Volume and Flexibility

1. Shawn Tully, "Europe Gets Ready for 1992," *Fortune*, February 1, 1988, pp. 81–84.

2. Jane Mayer, "Publishers Bemoan Brash Style, Big Bucks of Rushdie's Agent," *Wall Street Journal*, March 23, 1989.

3. Richard I. Kirkland, Jr., "Pile 'Em High and Sell 'Em Cheap," *Fortune*, August 29, 1988, pp. 91–92.

4. I thank Steve Hager and Chuck Walter of Hewlett-Packard, Boise Division, for graphically explaining their version of the dreaded triangle to me.

5. James B. Treece, "GM's Bumpy Ride on the Long Road Back," *Business Week*, February 13, 1989, pp. 74–78.

6. Bill Saporito, "The Tough Cookie at RJR Nabisco," *Fortune*, July 18, 1988, pp. 32–46.

7. Bill Saporito, "PPG: Shiny, Not Dull," *Fortune*, July 17, 1989, p. 107.

8. *Wall Street Journal*, December 2, 1988.

9. Stanley M. Davis, *Future Perfect* (Reading, Mass.: Addison-Wesley, 1987), pp. 138–90.

10. See Richard J. Schonberger, "Implementing Kanban at Hewlett-Packard, Fort Collins (A)," in *World Class Manufacturing Casebook: Implementing JIT and TQC* (New York: The Free Press, 1987), pp. 7–14.

11. Karlene M. Crawford, James F. Cox, and John H. Blackstone, Jr., *Performance Measurement Systems and the JIT Philosophy: Principles and Cases* (Falls Church, Va., American Production and Inventory Control Society, 1988), pp. 83–99.

12. A full treatment of machine setup concepts for manufacturing is available, with examples, in Shigeo Shingo, *A Revolution in Manufacturing: The SMED System* (Cambridge, Mass.: Productivity Press, 1985).

13. Eliyahu M. Goldratt and Robert E. Fox, "The Theory of Constraints," vol. 1, Avraham Y. Goldratt Institute, (New Haven, Conn., 1987).

14. Theodore Levitt, *The Marketing Imagination*, new expanded edition (New York: The Free Press, 1986), p. 46.

15. Paul Ingrassia: "Who Makes Technology Work: Autos," *Wall Street Journal Technology Review*, June 12, 1987, pp. 5D & 42D.

16. "Manufacturing Spending Shifts Toward Training and Motivation," *Wall Street Journal*, November 11, 1989, p. 1.

Chapter 13
Elevated Performance Standards

1. Stanley M. Davis, *Future Perfect* (Reading, Mass.: Addison-Wesley, 1987), p. 27.

2. Richard J. Schonberger, *World Class Manufacturing: The Principles of Simplicity Applied* (New York: The Free Press, 1986), pp. 217–18.

3. Ronald Henkoff, "Bumpy Flight at McDonnell-Douglas," *Fortune*, August 28, 1989, pp. 79–80.

4. Karl Albrecht and Ron Zemke, *Service America! Doing Business in the New Economy* (Homewood, Ill.: Dow Jones-Irwin, 1985), pp. 6–7.

5. "Behind the Scenes at the Fall of Rolm," *Business Week*, July 10, 1989, pp. 82–84.

6. Tom Peters, "Tom's Regimen for Keeping the Company in Shape," syndicated column, *Seattle Post-Intelligencer*, August 8, 1989.

7. Shoshana Zuboff, *In the Age of the Smart Machine: The Future of Work and Power* (New York: Basic Books, 1988).

8. Thomas M. Rohan, "The Latest Fad: Flexibility," *Industry Week*, August 18, 1986, pp. 27–28.

9. Jeremy Main, "The Winning Organization," *Fortune*, September 26, 1988, pp. 50–53.

10. Neal E. Boudette, "Electronic Data Interchange: A Leap of Faith," *Industry Week*, August 7, 1989, pp. 52–55.

11. Brian Dumaine, "What the Leaders of Tomorrow See," *Fortune*, July 3, 1989, pp. 48–62.

12. Taiichi Ohno, *Toyota Production System: Beyond Large-Scale Production* (Cambridge, Mass.: Productivity Press, 1988), Chapter 2.

13. See description of book study groups at Digital Equipment, in *Total Employee Involvement*, a newsletter printed by Productivity, Inc., Cambridge, Mass., April 1989, pp. 1–3.

14. M. Scott Myers, *Every Employee A Manager* (New York: McGraw-Hill, 1981).

15. C. Jackson Grayson, Jr., and Carla O'Dell, *American Business: A Two-Minute Warning* (New York: The Free Press, 1988), pp. 285–92.

Index